William Slater Calverley, W. G. Collingwood

Notes on the Early Sculptured Crosses, Shrines and Monuments

In the Present Diocese of Carlisle.

William Slater Calverley, W. G. Collingwood

Notes on the Early Sculptured Crosses, Shrines and Monuments
In the Present Diocese of Carlisle.

ISBN/EAN: 9783743441767

Manufactured in Europe, USA, Canada, Australia, Japa

Cover: Foto ©ninafisch / pixelio.de

Manufactured and distributed by brebook publishing software (www.brebook.com)

William Slater Calverley, W. G. Collingwood

Notes on the Early Sculptured Crosses, Shrines and Monuments

CUMBERLAND AND WESTMORLAND
ANTIQUARIAN AND ARCHÆOLOGICAL SOCIETY.
EXTRA SERIES: VOLUME XI.

NOTES

ON THE

EARLY SCULPTURED CROSSES,

SHRINES AND MONUMENTS

IN THE PRESENT DIOCESE OF CARLISLE

BY THE LATE

REV. WILLIAM SLATER CALVERLEY,

VICAR OF ASPATRIA ;

*F.S.A., and Local Secretary ; F.R.Hist.S., Member of the Royal
Archæological Institute, and Member of Council of the
Cumberland and Westmorland Antiquarian and
Archæological Society.*

EDITED BY

W. G. COLLINGWOOD, M.A.,

*Local Secretary for Cumberland, Society of Antiquaries, London, etc ,
Author of "The Life and Work of John Ruskin," etc.*

KENDAL:
PRINTED AND PUBLISHED BY T. WILSON.
1899.

EDITOR'S PREFACE.

TO collect and to complete, at the desire of his representatives, these papers of the Rev. W. S. Calverley for the publication so long promised, has been a task at once painful and pleasant. It has been pleasant to raise, as it were, a Cross to his memory; but painful to "rist the runes" upon it, hewing them out letter by letter, with unskilled hands, in much diffidence, and in much regret.

The aim has been to compile some such volume as Mr. Calverley intended—a general work giving account of the Christian relics of our north-west corner of England from the time when the Romans left to the 12th century, when a new order of things came into being.

He did not live to write his own book. His working life was too short for all that might have been, though of the time and talents allotted him he made diligent and faithful use. He would have been the last to wish his biography written, and yet we cannot but say a few words upon his life, by way of preface to his work.

William Slater Calverley was born near Leeds in 1847, and after his school days proceeded to New College, Oxford, which he left to take a private tutorship. During this period he was strongly inclined to the study of art, and worked with much promise at one of the schools in connection with South Kensington. Indeed, it was only by an accident of illness that he failed, on one occasion, to win the gold medal for drawing from the figure. But his training was by no means thrown away. Not only was he able to make such drawings as are given in this volume, illustrating the art of ancient days with directness and emphasis, but he learnt the artist's habit of observing form, and recording it. No one had a keener eye for a fragment of sculpture, lurking in a rubbish-heap, or built into a wall; and he was always ready with his pencil and sketch-book to note the find. Wherever he went, he sketched, accumulating the material from which he could make his comparisons and draw his conclusions. That was, perhaps, the secret of his unusual power of generalization, by which he interpreted the Gosforth Cross, and created—it is not too much to say—a new era in this department of study.

He was not satisfied even with sketching and drawing the monuments he loved. He took rubbings of the whole series, most carefully done, and casts of many; and in the chapter on Aspatria he tells how, for the sake of entering into the spirit of the ancient artists and craftsmen, he went to the great labour of reproducing the great Gosforth Cross in stone—the copy which may be seen and judged in Aspatria churchyard; not a mere cast, be it understood, but a sculptor's work of art, following out the original in every detail, and with fidelity to style and spirit not so much as attempted by others.

In spite of this artistic turn he had always intended himself for the Church, and in 1872 was ordained at Carlisle by Bishop Goodwin, taking a curacy at Eskdale, in South Cumberland. Next year he was ordained priest, and appointed curate at Maryport, moving in 1874 to Dearham, where he served three years as curate and eight years afterwards as vicar of the same church. His life at Dearham was one of the greatest energy. Under him the church was restored, the vicarage and churchyard enlarged and improved, and the district church at Ellenborough was founded. It was in this period that he began the series of studies in local history—of pre-Norman stones, among other things—which made him one of the best known of Cumberland antiquaries.

It is an ill wind, they say, that blows nobody good; and church restoration, though often misdirected, has often brought to light remains of ancient art which were totally unknown and unsuspected. In restoring his church, Mr. Calverley met with several important pre-Norman sculptures; and his interest in them brought him into connection with many authorities on such matters, especially the late Professor George Stephens, of Copenhagen, who struck up a warm friendship with the vicar of Dearham, visited him, corresponded voluminously, and embodied Mr. Calverley's discoveries and descriptions in his great work *Old-Northern Runic Monuments.* If on some points the newer generation may find it necessary to differ now and then from the conclusions at which Stephens arrived, it does not alter the fact of his splendid record as a student and collector in general; and, in especial, what concerns us here, his kindly aid and stimulating enthusiasm for research in our little-noticed corner of the land.

When Mr. Calverley, not without the help of such authorities as Stephens on the one hand, and of such local workers as Dr. Parker, of Gosforth, on the other, was able to announce to the Archæological Institute at Carlisle, in the summer of 1882, his reading of Edda-myths on the Christian cross at Gosforth, there was a distinct sensation. Before this discovery, authorities held that Christian monuments contained nothing but Christian subjects—we need not count the speculators who fancied Buddhism, Druidism, astronomy,

and other esoteric mysteries in every sculpture that seemed strange
to them. But Mr. Calverley first showed the fact of the " Pagan
overlap " in our relics, and while some believed, others doubted. In
a while, proof after proof occurred—notably, the discovery by the
Rev. G. F. Browne, now Bishop of Bristol, of Scandinavian legends
on the cross at Leeds, and at Kirk Andreas, Isle of Man. Year after
year, Mr Calverley added new instances. In February, 1891, he
interpreted the Völsung-myth at Halton in a lecture to the Lancaster
Philosophical Society, and later in the year read a paper to the
Royal Archæological Institute at Edinburgh on the same subject.
By this time the success of his new doctrine was assured, and he
was pressed to collect his studies into a more complete form—to
write a book, an idea which he had before him as early as 1886.

But he aimed high; he wished his book to be complete. There
were some sculptures which still puzzled him; there were many, he
thought, still to be found. With a view to collecting such, Chancellor
Ferguson sent out a circular to all incumbents of churches in the
diocese, begging them to report the existence of all crosses, hogbacks, and fragments with interlacing, bosses, or spiral ornament.
A few finds, and some reported finds, put off the moment of setting
to work on the book as a whole.

Meanwhile, Mr. Calverley found himself less and less able to
accomplish what he had undertaken. In 1885 he had been preferred
by Bishop Goodwin to the vicarage of Aspatria, a parish which
taxed all his energies and capacities for work. Ill health overtook
him, and year by year he became less able to give time and attention
to antiquities. As member of Council of the local society, which he
had joined in 1877, he attended its meetings and enlivened discus-
sions with his bright and original views. As F.S.A.—elected 1885—
and local secretary for Cumberland, he reported new finds, such as
the Gosforth hogbacks. He was also member of the Royal Archæological Institute, and a Fellow of the Royal Historical Society. But
in spite of continued interest in the subject, he had no leisure to
collect the mass of his notes and ideas into a continuous essay. An
excellent memory led him to trust much to it, for he was more of an
artist in temperament than a penman, and had not the habit of
writing amid interruptions. " In any fortnight," he used to say,
" when I get quiet, I can write that book." But the occasion never
came; illness closed down upon him, and on September 21st, 1898,
at East Lodge, Hayborough, near Maryport, he died. Three days
later he was buried in Aspatria Churchyard, under the shadow of
the cross which his own hands had helped to carve.

Of Mr. Calverley's life-work as a clergyman, this is not the place
to speak; as a student of antiquities, a list of his papers will give the

best idea of his industry. Most of them were contributed to the Cumberland and Westmorland Antiquarian and Archæological Society, as following:—

Notes on the Sculptured Stones at Dearham Church. Read at Dearham, June 17th, 1880.

Illustrations of Teutonic Mythology from early Christian Monuments at Brigham and Dearham. Read at Egremont, August 30th, 1881.

Sculptured Runic Grave-block at Dearham, West Cumberland, by Prof. George Stephens, F.S.A., and the Rev. W. S. Calverley; forming a chapter in Prof. Stephens' *Old-Northern Runic Monuments*, and reprinted in the *Transactions* of the Cumberland and Westmorland Antiquarian and Archæological Society, 1883.

The Sculptured Cross at Gosforth, West Cumberland, by the Rev. W. S. Calverley; Drawings, Measurements, and some details by C. A. Parker, M.D. Printed in the *Transactions* of the same Society for 1883.

Early Sculptured Cross Shaft at Dearham Church, Cumberland. Read at Kirkby Lonsdale, June 27th, 1883.

Barbon Cross. Read at Caldbeck, August 22nd, 1883. Not printed in the *Transactions*.

Some Ancient Dials in the Diocese of Carlisle. Communicated at Alston, July 10th, 1884.

Sculptured Stone at Isel Church, Cumberland, bearing the " Svastika," " Triskele," and other symbols. Communicated at Carlisle, July 23rd, 1885.

Cross-fragment at St. Michael's Church, Workington. Read at Kirkby Stephen, July 7th, 1887.

Notes on some coped pre-Norman Tombstones at Aspatria, Lowther, Cross-Canonby, and Plumbland. Read at Ulverston, September 13th, 1887.

Red sandstone Cross-Shaft at Cross-Canonby. Read at Ulverston, September 13th, 1887.

The Giant's Grave, Penrith. Read at Penrith, July 12th, 1888; but not printed in the *Transactions*.

The Parish of Westward. Read at Westward, September 13th, 1888. Not printed in the *Transactions*.

Fragments of a British Cross and many Early English and other grave-covers found in Bromfield Churchyard. Read at Carlisle, September 13th, 1888.

Pre-Norman Cross fragments at Aspatria, Workington, Distington, Bridekirk, Gilcrux, Plumbland, and Isel. Communicated at Penrith, July 4th, and Ambleside, September 6th, 1889.

The Dacre Stone. Printed in the *Transactions*, 1890.

Fragments of pre-Norman Crosses at Workington and Bromfield, and the Standing Cross at Rocliffe. Read at Appleby, July 3rd, 1890.

Bewcastle Cross. Read at Bewcastle, August 21st, 1891.

Tympanum at Bridekirk Church. Communicated at Seascale, September 21st, 1892.

Crosses at Waberthwaite Church and at High Aketon Farm in the Parish of Bromfield. Communicated at Seascale, September 21st, 1892.

The Roman Fort at Hardknott. Printed in the *Transactions* for 1893 and 1895.

Pre-Norman Cross Shaft at Heversham. Read at Heversham, September 25th, 1893.

Shrine-shaped or Coped Tombstones at Gosforth, Cumberland. Communicated at Shap, July 15th, and at Penrith, September 23rd, 1897.

The above were written for the Cumberland and Westmorland Antiquarian and Archæological Society, and with some exceptions noted are printed in their *Transactions*.

Mr. Calverley also wrote for the Archæological Institute two papers on the Sculptured Cross at Gosforth—a preliminary paper read at their meeting at Carlisle, August 3rd, 1882, and a second paper with full-sized drawings laid before the Institute at their meeting, December 2nd, 1882, and printed in the *Archæological Journal*, vol. xl, p. 143.

He also contributed remarks on " The Remains of Pre-Norman Crosses found at Gargrave," in a paper by the Rev. C. H. Parez, M.A., printed in the *Yorkshire Archæological Journal*, vol. xii, p. 87.

He read a paper on " The Pre-Norman Cross at Halton," illustrated with rubbings, before the Lancaster Philosophical Society, February 26th, 1891, and before the Royal Archæological Institute at Edinburgh in the same year. Also, in October, 1892, he read to a clerical meeting at Carlisle a paper on " Early Cumberland Saints."

Mr. Calverley wrote also a number of reports as local secretary for Cumberland to the Society of Antiquaries of London, as well as articles in various newspapers on antiquarian subjects. He was continually collecting information for the work which the present volume must now represent, and had gone farther in his researches into the mythology of the monuments than we can follow him ; for only his own recollection could supply the context to many a sheet of notes and jottings, which now make us feel more deeply the loss we have sustained by his untimely death.

From his published and unpublished papers we have gleaned all

EDITOR'S PREFACE.

that was complete enough for publication, and all that has been so
gleaned is printed in large type, to distinguish it from the Editor's
notes and additions, which are printed smaller, so that there may be
no difficulty in recognizing Mr. Calverley's own opinion and statement, expressed in his own words.

Seventeen lithographic plates are by his own hand, overprints
from original papers, prepared and kept with a view to this work. A
few blocks are from his drawings—Halton, the Waberthwaite fragment, and the Tower stone at Workington.

For nearly all the photographs reproduced we have to thank
Mr. W. L. Fletcher, of Stoneleigh, Workington, for whose generous
help Mr. Calverley has often expressed his obligation.

It was his intention to have dedicated his book to the memory of
Bishop Goodwin, to whose encouragement he felt himself greatly
indebted; and in his original prospectus he made special mention of
the assistance given by Chancellor Ferguson, in suggestion, in
information, and in correction—an acknowledgment which is
very heartily endorsed by

THE EDITOR.

CONTENTS AND ILLUSTRATIONS.

———

(The initials "W.S.C." indicate Mr. Calverley; "W.L.F." Mr. Fletcher; and "W.G.C." the Editor).

———

			Page.
Editor's Preface, with portrait of the Author	.....	.....	v.

THE SITES IN ALPHABETICAL ORDER.

Addingham.

| Spiral Standing Cross | ..... | .... Photo., W. L. F. | 3 |
| Anglian Shaft | .... | .... Sketch, W. G. C. | 4 |

Anthorn.

| The "Broken Cross" | ..... | ..... Sketch, W. G. C. | 7 |

Arthuret.

| Churchyard Cross | .... | .... Sketch, W. G. C. | 8 |

Aspatria.

Standing Cross, three views	.....	..... Litho., W. S. C.	11
Hogback, two views	....	..... Photo., W. L. F.	15
Two Spiral Shafts and			
Later head-fragment	.....	..... Litho., W. S. C.	18
Spiral fragment	....	..... Photo., W. L. F.	20
Svastika fragment	....	..... Sketch, W. G. C.	23

Beckermet, St. Bridget's.

Inscribed Shaft: face	...	..... Photo., W. L. F.	26
Do. ornament	....	.... Sketch, W. G. C.	28
Uninscribed Shaft	....	..... Sketch, W. G. C.	33

Beckermet, St. John's.

White Cross-head	....	.... Sketch, W. G. C.	34
White Spiral Shaft	....	..... Sketch, W. G. C.	35
Socket-stone	....	.... Sketch, W. G. C.	35

Fragment A and B : dragonesque shaft ...... Sketch, W. G. C. 36
    Do.   C :   do.   ...... Sketch, W. G. C. 37
    Do.   D and E : drilled shaft   ...... Sketch, W. G. C. 38
    Do.   F : late interlacing...... ...... Sketch, W. G. C. 38

Bewcastle.

Cross-shaft, west side   .... Photo., W. L. F. 39
    Do.   south side   .... Photo., W. L. F. 40
    Do.   The Christ   .... Sketch, W. G. C. 41
    Do.   with Ruthwell Cross   ...... Photo., W. L. F. 42
    Do.   Floral detail   .... Sketch, W. G. C. 43
    Do.   Cross Runes   .... Tracing, W. G. C. 45
Barnspike and Hazelgill Runes   ...... Tracing, W. G. C. 48
Anglian Dial   .... Sketch, W. G. C. 54

Bolton (Westmorland).

Dial, with 7 others   .... Sketches, W. G. C. 57
The Norman Knights   ...... Sketch, W. G. C. 58

Bongate, Appleby.
Hogback   .... Sketches, W. G. C. 59

Bridekirk.

Spiral Cross-head   .... Litho., W. S. C. 60
Tympanum .... Sketch, W. G. C. 61
Font, Baptism Side .... Sketch, W. G. C. 68
Do., Runes   . ... Tracing, W. G. C. 68
Do., Dragons   .... Sketch, W. G. C. 69
Do., Adam and Eve   .... Sketch, W. G. C. 70
Do., Inscribed side   .... Photo., W. L. F. 71

Brigham.

Dragonesque Socket .... Sketch, W. G. C. 72
Cross-head at Vicarage   .... Sketch, W. G. C. 76
Late White Shaft   .... Sketch, W. G. C. 77
Limestone-head, with
Interlaced Wheel-head, and
Two Interlaced fragments   ...... Sketches, W. G. C. 78
Another Interlaced fragment   78

Bromfield.

White Cross   .... Litho., W. S. C. 80
Interlaced Shaft   .... Litho., W. S. C. 84
Red Cross-head   .. .   . Sketch, W. G. C. 85

Page.

			Page.
Late Cross-head			85
Tympanum			85
Hogback			85
Cross-head at High Aketon	.....	Photo., W. L. F.	86

Burton-in-Kendal.

Wheel Cross-head	...	Sketch, W. G. C.	88
" Resurrection " Shaft	.....	Sketch, W. G. C.	89
Neck fragment	....	Sketch, W. G. C.	90
Zigzag Shaft	....	Sketch, W. G. C.	91

Caldbeck.

Dial (in plate facing *Bolton*)		92

Carlisle.

Dolfin Runes	....	Cop. from Stephens	93
Anglian Cross-head	....	Cut from *Arch. Jr.*	95
Anglian Cross-arms	....	Cop. from *Arch. Jr.*	95

Casterton.

The " Barbon " Cross	....	Sketch, W. G. C.	97

Castle Sowerby.

The two lost " Corpse Crosses "		98

Cliburn.

Dial (in plate facing *Bolton*).		
Socket-stone.....		99

Croglin.

Lost Churchyard Cross		99

Cross-Canonby.

Hogback	.....	Sketch, W. G. C.	103
Dragonesque Shaft, two views	.....	Eng. M. Petersen	107
Do. two views	.....	Sketches, W. G. C.	107
White Cross-head	.....	Litho., W. S. C.	109
" Lawrence " Slab	....	Sketch, W. G. C.	109
" Thunderbolt " Stone	.....	Sketch, W. G. C.	110

Crosthwaite, Keswick.

" Bolster " Stone	.....	Photo., W. L. F.	111
" Adam's Cross "	.....		112

Cumwhitton.

Late Cross-head 112

Dacre.

Shaft of the Two Kings .... Litho., W. S. C. 113
     Do. .... Sketch, W. G. C. 114

Dearham.

The "Adam" Stone .... Eng., M. Petersen 117
   Do.,   Runes .... Tracing, W. G. C. 123
Standing Cross .... Cop. from W. S. C. 124
Kenneth Shaft .... Eng., M. Petersen 127
  Do. Head and Edges .... Sketches, W. G. C. 128
Font .... Sketch, W. G. C. 131
2 Dials 132

Distington.

Two "Triskele" fragments .... Litho., W. S. C. 133
Two White Cross-heads .... Litho., W. S. C. 134

Dovenby.

The "Old Thorn Cross" 135

Gilcrux.

Wheel-head .... Litho., W. S. C. 136

Glassonby.

Key-pattern Shaft .... Sketch, W. G. C. 137

Gosforth.

Standing Cross, west face .... Eng., M. Petersen 139
   Do.   Loki Panel .... Eng., M. Petersen 145
   Do.   Heindal episode ..... Eng., M. Petersen 147
   Do.   Gagged Monster & Hart Eng., M. Petersen 150
   Do.   east face ..... Sketch, W. S. C. 155
   Do.   Crucifixion Panel .... Eng., M. Petersen 157
   Do.   Vidar episode ..... Eng., M. Petersen 158
Fishing Stone .... Photo., W. L. F. 168
Snake fragment 169
Sun-dial Shaft 169
Socket in churchyard wall 169
Three Cross-heads .... Photo., W. L. F.
             and
             Sketch, W. G. C. 170

Hogbacks: " The Warrior's Tomb,"
          three views .... Photo., W. L. F.   172
    Do., " The Saint's Tomb," three
          views   .... Photo., W. L. F.   174

Great Salkeld.

Interlaced Capitals, two   .... Sketches, W. G. C.   178
Dial   178

Haile.

Ring-cross .... Sketch, W. G. C.   180
Six Interlaced fragments   ..... Copied from Canon Knowles   181
Spiral Shaft   .... Sketch, W. G. C.   182

Halton.

The Sigurd Cross   .... three drawings, W. S. C.   183
The " Pope " Cross   183
Late Interlaced fragment   183
Anglian fragment   183

Heversham.

Anglian Shaft: face .... Photo., W. L. F.   198
    Do.,   edge.....   .... Sketch, W. G. C.   198
Fragment   198

Hutton-in-the-Forest.

Sun-dial base   204
Interlaced fragment .... Sketch, W. G. C.   204

Ireby.

Late Crosses at the Chapel   205
Market-cross   205

Irton.

Anglian Cross, three views   .... Sketches, W. G. C.   206

Isel.

Three Dials on window jamb .... Sketch, W. G. C.   208
Dial in porch (in plate facing *Bolton*)   209
Triskele fragment, 3 views   .... Eng., M. Petersen   211
Spiral Shaft fragments   ...   . Sketch, W. G. C.   213

Kirk-Bampton.

Tympanum .... Sketch, W. G. C.   214

Page.

Kirkby-Stephen.

The Bound Devil .... Eng., M. Petersen 217
Semi-cylindrical Shaft .... Sketch, W. G. C. 218
Hogback .... Sketch, W. G. C. 221
Late Cross-head .... Sketch, W. G. C. 221
Interlaced Head .... Sketch, W. G. C. 221
Anglian Cross-head .... Sketch, W. G. C. 223

Kirkland.

Churchyard Cross 224

Kirk-Oswald.

Supposed Dials .... Sketch, W. G. C. 225
Dial .... Sketch, W. G. C. 225
Arm of Cross-head .... Sketch, W. G. C. 225

Lamplugh.

Lost Cross 227

Lanercost.

Churchyard Cross 227

Lazonby.

Late Churchyard Cross 227

Long Marton.

South Tympanum .... Sketch, W. G. C. 229
West Tympanum .... Cop. from J. A. Cory 229

Lowther.

Hogback, two views .... Photo., W. L. F. 231
Two undisturbed Hogbacks 235
Cut-down Cross 235

Melmerby.

Lost Cross 236

Milburn.

Two Dials (in plate facing *Bolton*) 237
Cross-socket 237

Muncaster.

Cross-shaft and Head .... Photo., W. L. F. 238
Socket of another 238

Page.

Newbiggin-on-Eden.

Dial (in plate facing *Bolton*) 239
Socket and Shaft of a Late Cross 239

Newton Arlosh.

Dial 239

Penrith.

The "Giant's Grave," four Hogbacks,
  and 2 Crosses; two views .... Photo., W. L. F. 240
The "Giant's Thumb," .... Photo., Jas. Huff 248
The "Plague-stone" (Cross-socket) 252

Plumbland.

Hogback in two fragments .... Photo., W. L. F. 253
Late Coped Stone 255
Spiral fragment (in plate facing *Gilcrux*) 255

Rheda

Cross Lacon .... Sketch, W. G. C. 256

Rockcliff.

The Standing Cross ... . Litho., W. S. C. 257

St. Bees.

Dragon Lintel .... Sketch, W. G. C. 259
Standing Cross ... . Sketch, W. G. C. 260
"Norse" Cross .... Sketch, W. G. C. 260
Spiral fragment .... Sketch, W. G. C. 263
"Resting Cross" .... Sketch, W. G. C. 263

Stainmoor.

The Reycross .... Photo., W. L. F. 264

Tebay.

The Brandreth Stone 269

Torpenhow.

Dial (in plate facing *Bolton*) 270
Interlaced Font .... Sketch, W. G. C. 271
Early Capitals ..... , ... 271

Waberthwaite.

Anglian Shaft   .... two drawings, W. S. C.   273
Standing Cross   .... two photographs, W. L. F.   273

Warcop.

Cross   276

Workington.

Tower fragment   .... drawing, W. S. C.   277
    Do., ... Litho., W. S. C.   278
Curwen Vault fragment I.   ...   . Litho., W. S. C.   280
    Do.   do.   II.   .... Litho., W. S. C.   281
Fretty fragment, two plates   .... Litho., W. S. C.   282
Late Cross   284

EDITOR'S AFTERWORD.

Review of Early Cumbrian Art   .....
    I. Post-Norman Development of pre-
        Norman Forms   .... Sketches, W. G. C.   287
    II. The Norman Period (Dials, Fonts,
        &c.)   288
    III. The Viking Age (Dragonesque
        Shafts, &c.)   .... Map, W. G. C.   290
    IV. The Spiral School (Cumbrian
        native art imitated from metal
        work)   295
            Brayton fibula   ..... from Pennant   296
            Ormside cup .... Sketch, W. G. C.   297
            Kirkoswald Fibula   ..... from Lysons   298
    V. The Anglo-Classic School   ...   300
            Ormside cup .....   2 Sketches, W. G. C.   300
    VI. The British Period   302
    VII. The Story of Cumbrian Inde-
        pendence .... Map, W. G. C.   304
    Index   311

ERRATA.

Page 195, line 14, for " Dryness," read *Dyrness*.

Page 244, line 21, for " Bayley," read *Brayley*.

Page 290, line 6 from bottom, for "of Yorkshire," read *near Yorkshire*.

Page 302, line 6, for " of the twelfth century," read *of the tenth to the twelfth century*.

Page 304, last line but one, for " Gaelic," read *Gallic*.

EARLY SCULPTURED CROSSES, ETC.

THE SITES, IN ALPHABETICAL ORDER.

———

[NOTE. The first three articles, and all matter printed in this small type (bourgeois) are contributed by the Editor.

Chapters and paragraphs printed large (in this " long primer " type) are Mr. Calverley's original writings, previously published or extracted from his manuscript remains.

It is hoped that the prominence given to this note will make farther explanation unnecessary.]

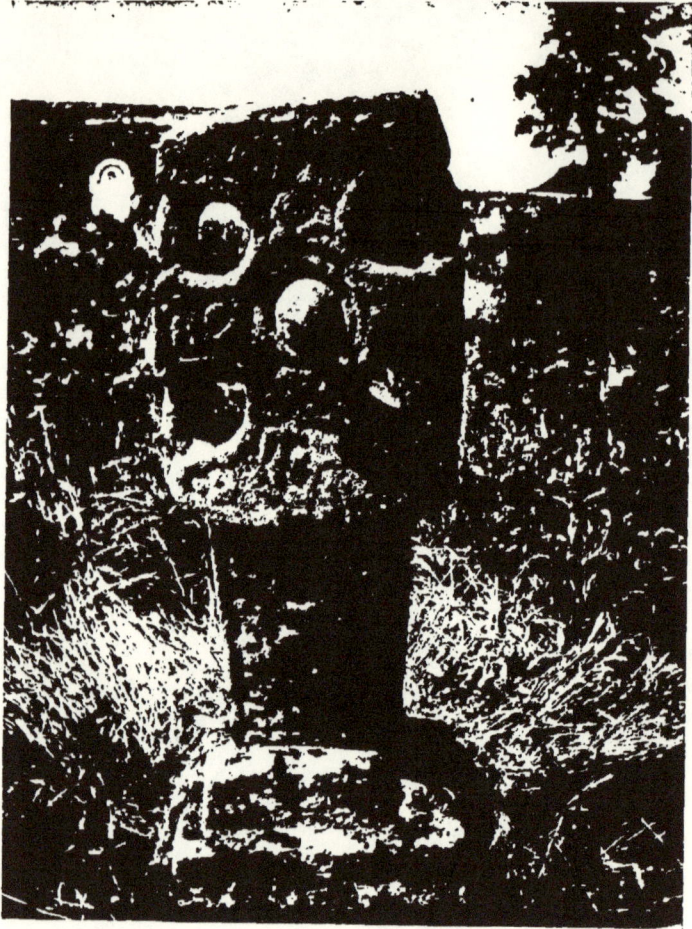

THE STANDING CROSS,

ADDINGHAM.

(TO FACE P. 3.)

ADDINGHAM.

(I.) The Spiral Standing Cross, and
(II.) Fragments of an Anglian Cross.

THE cross now standing in the churchyard, and fragments of another in the porch, are not on their original site, nor very near it. There was once a church on the bank of the river Eden in a hamlet called Addingham which has disappeared; so that there is no village now, but only a parish of that name.

Addingham may have been an Anglo-Saxon settlement of a wide-spread family of Addings, who appear also at Addingham (Yorks) and Addington in Bucks, Kent, Surrey and Northants. Inglewood Forest was well peopled, as place-names show, by the original Cumbrian Welsh, and thickly settled by Angles in the 7th century. An Anglian church may have existed here and possibly a British church before it. The prehistoric standing-stone and circle known as "Long Meg and her Daughters" is two-thirds of a mile south-south-east of this church.

In the only MS. note on Addingham left by Mr. Calverley, he calls attention to the fact that this early church is near a megalithic monument, in the same way as the early church at Crosthwaite (Keswick) is near the "Druid's Circle"; and he goes on to suggest that the "inflected rod" on Long Meg may be a Christian addition to the heathen cup-markings, concentric circles and spirals,—for St. Patrick, according to Tirechan, attempted to purify certain stones at Mag Selce by inscribing Christian symbols upon them; and the mark of a blow from his staff was pointed out on the left side of *Cromm Cruaich*, "the Crooked (fallen) One of the Mound,"—that heathen stone of Cashel which had before been called *Cenn Cruaich*, "the head of the mound." Stone-worship in England, being for-bidden by a canon of King Edgar's time, must have then existed.

So far the unfinished notes. It may be added that from the place-names we should gather that both Welsh and Anglo-Saxons had been driven out of this parish rather more completely than was usual in Cumbria. The names are nearly all of Viking origin; the oldest recorded (Pipe Rolls for 1177) being Gamelesbi (from the Norse *Gamel*, " old," often used as the name of the eldest son) and Glassanebi (from the Irish *Glasan*, as seen in the surname McGlashan) suggesting the preponderance there of Irish Vikings, such as we find elsewhere in the district. The Anglo-Saxon village and church, however, seems to have survived until 1360 when, it is said . (Whellan quotes the story in the *History of Cumberland and Westmorland*) the church was desecrated by bloodshedding, and after a while a new church was built at a distance of more than a mile to the north-east, namely, this church of St. Michael at Glassonby; and to this the crosses were removed, though it is not said at what date. On the old site human bones and other remains have been found: sculptured stones are reported as lying near it in the river; and field-names, as shown by Canon Thornley (*Transactions* C. & W. A. & A. S., 1898) like Kirkbank, Kirkmeadow and Chapelflatt, keep up the tradition of the former church.

(I.) The Standing Cross is of red sandstone, measuring 41 inches high from the pedestal, 20 inches across the arms, and 7 inches thick. The ornament consists of meandering lines, in relief, terminating in rude spirals or volutes. The pattern is rather deeply and smoothly cut, showing some skill on the part of the carver, but the design is not equal to the execution. The arms of the cross are of a peculiar shape, elsewhere seen in this district, with what we might call the Hammer-head. The centre is marked with a boss, in a raised ring.

The back of the cross, not shown in the plate, is in the same style as the front; but on the boss there is an incised Greek cross, with strongly marked but irregularly drawn *serifs*, giving the figure something of the look of a *svastika*.

The cross stands on a red sandstone pedestal cut into three Calvary-steps; the block measuring 27 by 22 inches wide at the bottom, and standing 13 inches high from the ground to the foot of the cross.

(II) The shaft fragments in the porch appear to be remains of a fine red-sandstone cross of the Anglian type. The fragment on the right hand of the porch (going in) and given opposite must belong to a lower part of the shaft. It measures 20½ inches broad by 9 inches thick. Its length is 30½ inches.

The other fragment must have stood higher in the original monument: it is 34 inches long by 15 broad and 8 thick.

One side of each fragment is defaced and the other side considerably worn, but traces remain of fine bold knot-work. The edges of the lowest part of the shaft were decorated with a plait; higher up were leaf-scrolls on both edges.

The design is perfect, and the chiselling deep and smooth, so that it must have been an extremely fine work of art, and of the best period and school.

PART OF AN ANGLIAN CROSS SHAFT;
ADDINGHAM.

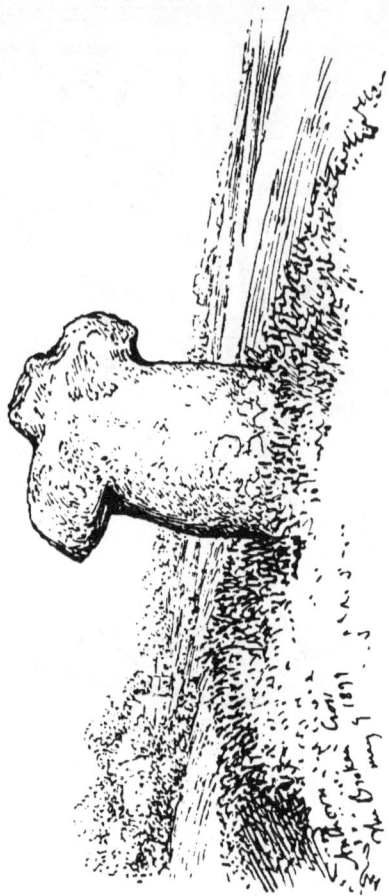

ANTHORN.

THE " BROKEN CROSS."

THE " Broken Cross " is locally said to mark the place of a battle with the Scots. It stands by the shore on a green mound, of which a great part has been hollowed out and carried away; but the top of the bank remains, with the cross upon it, overlooking the ford that leads through the river Wampool and over the sands to Newton Arlosh.

It is of red sandstone, so thickly encrusted with lichen that the stone is hardly visible. The part above ground is 24 inches in height; the arms are 19 inches across; the girth of the shaft is 39 inches. The shaft is rudely rounded on one side (the side to the left hand in the sketch) and squared on the other. The whole has an odd resemblance to a *torso*, with some rough anatomy of trunk, shoulders, and neck, hardly larger than the size of life. The resemblance, however, seems to be accidental, and the stone intended for a cross, though there is no distinct trace of ornament, and nothing to fix the date or the significance of it.

ARTHURET.

" I N the churchyard there is a plain obelisk of stone with a cross like that of the Knights Templar cut on the upper part of it in bas-relief."—(Lysons' *Cumberland*, p. ccii.)

" In the churchyard is . . . a rude cross, with a pierced capital, near to which tradition says lie the remains of Archy Armstrong, jester to James I. and Charles I."—(Whellan's *Cumberland*, p. 626.)

A glance at the sketch will show how these discrepant statements are both correct. In the Lysons' time, only the shaft with its Maltese cross was visible: by Whellan's day the fragments of the head had been put together and clamped to the shaft with the Y-shaped iron, and a bit of hoop on the under side to the left.

This is not a pre-Norman relic, but it is one of a series of high crosses which were developed in the Middle Age out of the earlier type. They preserve, in some instances, the wheel-cross head; sometimes, however, they have a cross-head with free arms. Their shafts are less ornamented than those of the pre-Norman period; most commonly chamfered, but not always; here decorated on the face, at Lanercost notched up the edges. Their socket-stones are important; larger in proportion than those of the earliest high crosses; sometimes remaining alone to prove the existence of the cross. For comparison, therefore, we describe a number of these, and illustrate two or three, under the headings of the places where they occur.

This at Arthuret is of red sandstone. Its head is in fragments, clamped together, and wanting the top limb. Across the lateral arms it measures 24 inches. It was originally a sort of bastard wheel-cross, being square in general outline, but with the arcs of the wheel distinctly shown, and the arms separated by four holes. In the centre it had a low boss, sunk in the face: and similar bosses on each of the lateral arms.

The shaft is 61 inches in height, not counting the tenon which holds it into the socket; for the whole thickness of the shaft is not sunk into its pedestal, as in the earlier crosses. The hole is about 16 by 9 inches, and the tenon a trifle smaller; while the shaft at base measures 23 by 9, tapering to 12 by 6 inches at the neck. The edges are not chamfered; one side is without ornament, the other

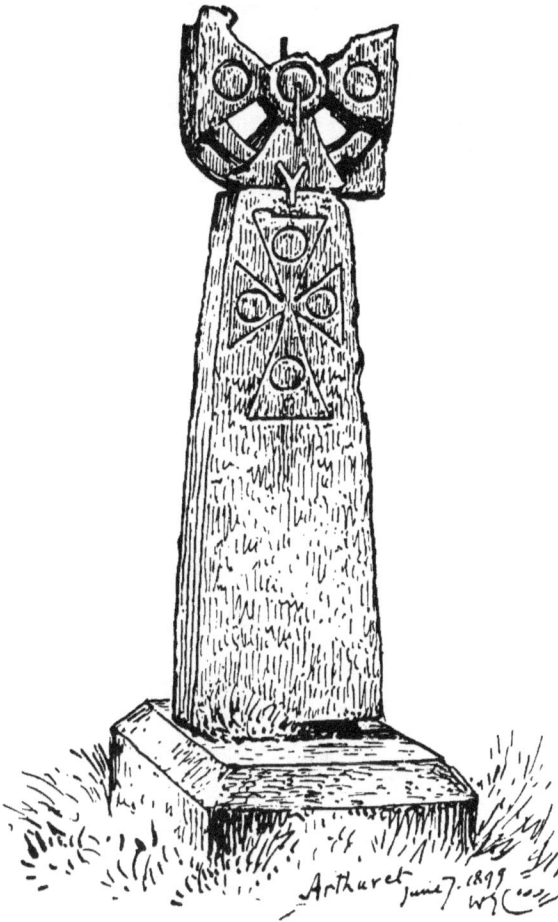

THE CHURCHYARD CROSS,

ARTHURET.

bears the Maltese Cross with four circles incised, like some mediæval grave-slabs.   This, however, is not a grave-slab, but has evidently been made for its present position, unique as it is in our district.

The socket-stone measures 29½ by 28½ by 13 inches ; it is bevelled on the four upper edges like the similar socket at Lanercost ; and stands, as many of these later crosses do, on a platform built of smaller blocks.

ASPATRICK EAST FACE. In situ.

(TO FACE P. 11.)

ASPATRIA.

(I.) THE STANDING CROSS.

ASPATRIA Cross still stands in its own socket stone, measuring 30 by 26 inches level with the ground surface in the churchyard, forty yards to the south of the church. Height 4 ft. 6 in. ; width at top beneath the curve of the circular head, which has been destroyed, 14¼ inches ; width at bottom where the shaft enters the socket, 18 inches ; thickness at top 7½ inches, at bottom 8½ inches. Red sandstone.

The circular head, the curve of which may be seen, and which would be something like the head of the Dearham standing cross, has been purposely knocked off, but the stem was so strong that it withstood the mad storm, and, indeed, served for long (it is said) as a pillar to which horses and cattle could be tied, to be claimed on the Sunday. Even this usage failed to overthrow the silent witness of the Truth of ages, the monument which stands firm to-day in its own native red sandstone socket.

Whoever set up this cross quarried a great block of living stone ; they did not even weaken it by squaring down to get a perfect surface, but worked upon the face almost as it left the quarry. Notice the hollowed surface beneath the north-east shoulder.

The north edge bears broad rings, with two crossing bands as its ornament. At the base of the east face beneath the tangled strands and convolutions which appear to have been woven into a pattern or web (of life) which might have been copied from one of the ancient MS. Gospels, we see the devouring wolf-like progeny of mankind's enemy (death or hell, Fenrir or Helia) bound, unable to hurt where the cross triumphs.

This cross has been copied and set up at Bowness in memory of the Rev. S. Medlicott.

Of the western face, sketched by him in the plate opposite, Mr. Calverley wrote further in the *Aspatria Parish Magazine*, May, 1890:—

The pattern of knotwork which you see here filling up all the western face is repeated on a red sandstone cross, part of which has been lately dug up in Bromfield churchyard by the Vicar, the Rev. R. Taylor. The same pattern also appears on the white sandstone shrine tombstone at the east of our church. Aspatria and Bromfield churches are both dedicated to the memory of the Apostle of Strathclyde, St. Kentigern, who was sometimes called, as at Bromfield, St. Mungo—the "dear friend."

At each place there have been found the remains of the white sandstone crosses of the earliest periods of our British church history, and also the remains of red sandstone crosses of the period immediately following this very early time, and dating several centuries before the time of the Norman conquest.

In his paper on *Early Cumberland Saints* Mr. Calverley said:—

The Ven. Precentor Venables, noting with surprise the scanty traces of early Celtic Christianity and the complete absence of the dedications to early native saints, of which Wales and Cornwall are so full, concludes that the Christianity of Cumbria was far less vigorous and reproductive than among the other Celtic tribes.

But surely other causes may account for the loss of traces —which may yet be found—both of Celtic art and of native saints: namely the ever-fluctuating ecclesiastical and political allegiance of the district, together with the constant change and interchange of races in the inhabitants themselves.

Ousby and Patterdale claim as patrons St. Patrick, whom we may, I think, call a Cumbrian Saint, as well as an Irish missionary ; for did not he come from the western end of the North Wall, kidnapped and taken over to Ireland in one of those many raids which devastated the land after the Roman legions had been withdrawn ?

I myself hold a benefice named after St. Patrick; for the name of Aspatria is but Aspatrick, altered during the last hundred years to please the ear or fancy. As far back as the

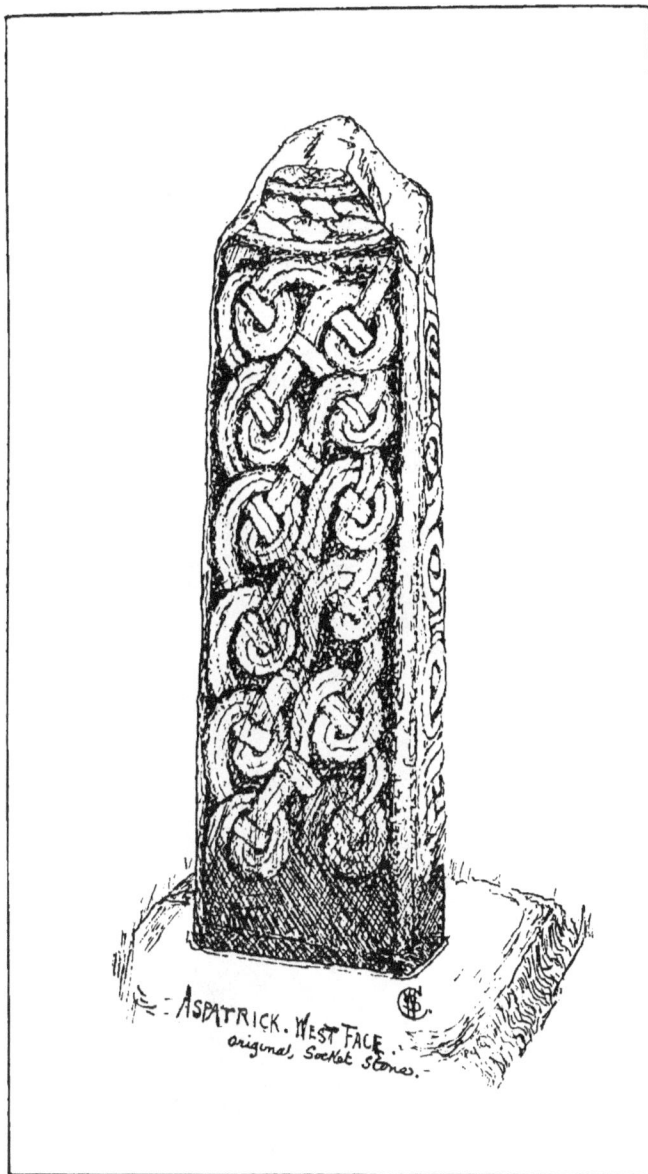

ASPATRICK. WEST FACE.
original, Socket Stone.

(TO FACE P. 12.)

reign of King John the name is Aspatrick, and a wath named St. Patrick's Wath is mentioned in the boundary of this part of the west ward of Inglewood Forest.

The Christian faith was, I believe, formed here in these very early times, and the cultus of the saint—the Holy One— Patrick, was probably strong, or at least alive when Holy Kentigern passed along this way.

St. Patrick, St. Bridget, St. Begha, leave their names then at Aspatria, Patterdale, Ousby, Bridekirk, Beckermet, Brigham, Moresby, Bassenthwaite, St. Bees : at nearly all of which places are many—very many—traces of Celtic Christian art.

From this group of what may be called Irish saints we must proceed to the Apostle of Strathclyde—St. Kentigern or St. Mungo, whose dedications are eight :—Aspatria, Bromfield, Caldbeck, Castle Sowerby, Crosthwaite, Grinsdale, Irthington, and Mungrisdale.

He is the great agent in the revolution which again Christianized Cumbria. His vast diocese extended from the Clyde to the Mersey, and from the Irish Sea to the Eastern watershed. He restored St. Ninian's Church.

Born in this country, that is to say, in the land of the Cumbri—on account of the plot against his life by his pagan enemies, "a generation of vipers excited by the sting of intense hatred and inflated by the poison of the devil," he was obliged to flee into South Wales.

He would follow the great road from Glasgow to Carlisle, and thence into Wales by Chester ; but turned aside to the mountainous districts, where, in one place, he set up a cross, as was his custom afterwards wherever he sojourned, as the sign of Salvation. Thence "directing his steps through the places by the sea," at length he reached St. David's safe and sound. Years afterwards he came back, at the call of King Rhydderch Hael, who had been established as the Christian head of the kingdom of Strathclyde by his great victory over the pagans in 573 at Arthuret, and settled at Hoddelm near Annan. It was not until near the close of his life that he removed the head-quarters of his see to Glasgow, where he died in 603.

Thirty years of work by such a bishop must have produced

great results, and maybe many of the lost dedications may
have belonged to churches which he was instrumental in
founding or resuscitating.

⁂   ⁂

With these two famous Saints, then, Aspatria Church is connected,
at any rate in name. Before the Norman building there must have
been an Anglian chapel, perhaps in some relations with the Irish
monks who settled in Cumberland in the 7th century. Earlier than
that there may have been a British Church, for the site was of
importance from the beginning. A Roman road passes near it.
Anglian remains, beside our crosses, have been found close by :—the
Brayton fibula, the great gold armlet (found in 1828) and—whether
Anglian or Viking—the grave-hoard of Beacon hill (found 1789).
It is to the later of these periods that the Standing Cross belongs.

The pattern on this cross has not been chiselled, but chipped out
with a pick in rude fashion ; the design is ingeniously planned and
carefully carried out. The east face is much damaged by weathering,
but the lithograph at the head of this chapter shows that it is conceived as one huge tangle of double-stranded cords, which are
perhaps more regular in their overlapping than the plate opposite
suggests. The lower part of this design is a great triple ring-plait,
woven together like a spider's web with radiating lines, whose con-
tinuity is most difficult to follow, and yet seems to be unbroken, and
strictly according to the laws of this school of interlacing ; in which,
without absolute symmetry, the ground is filled up with regularly
interwoven straps, flung in bold curves, but knotted together into one
almost water-tight web. The west side is much more simple and
comprehensible.

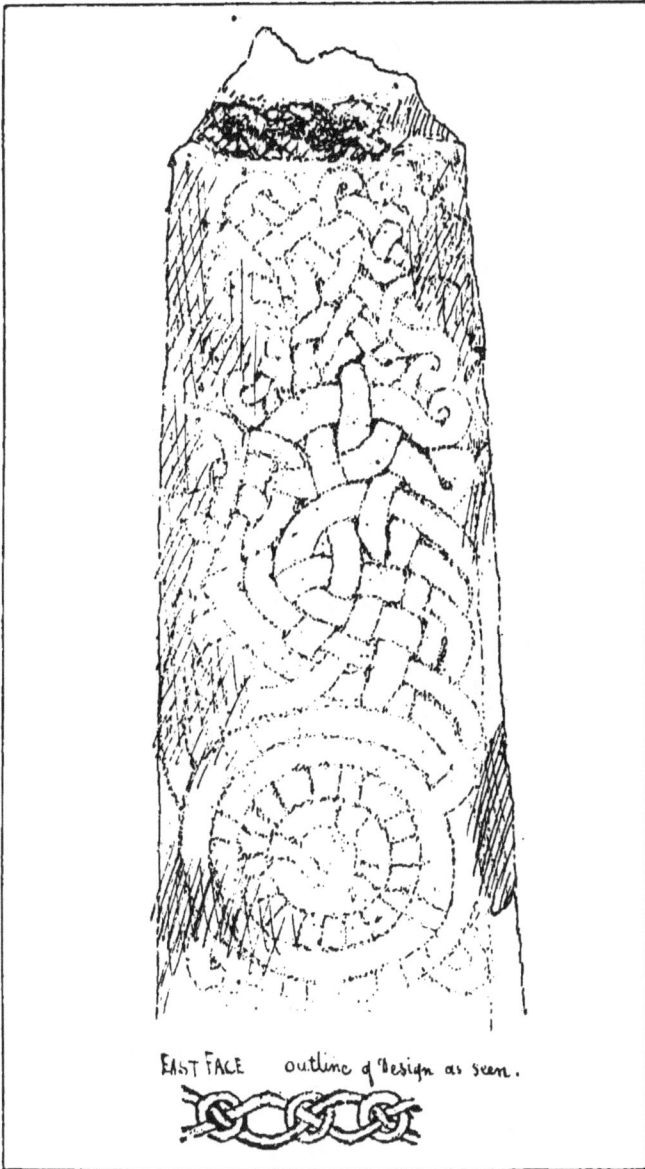

EAST FACE   outline of design as seen.

(TO FACE P. 14.)

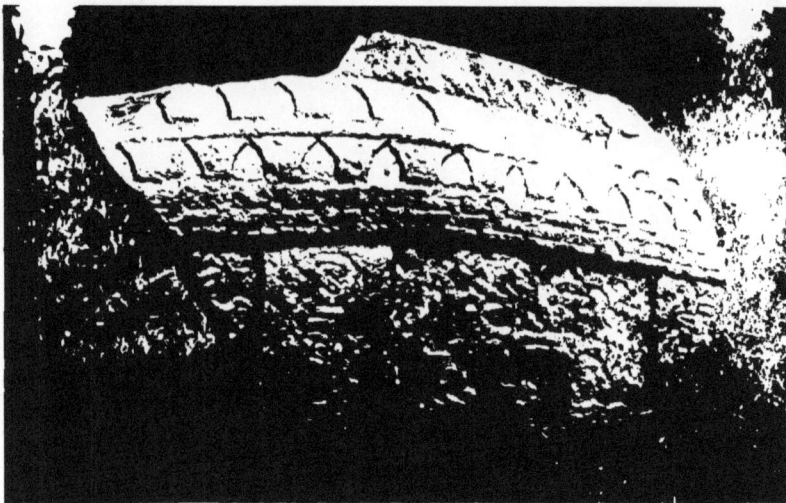

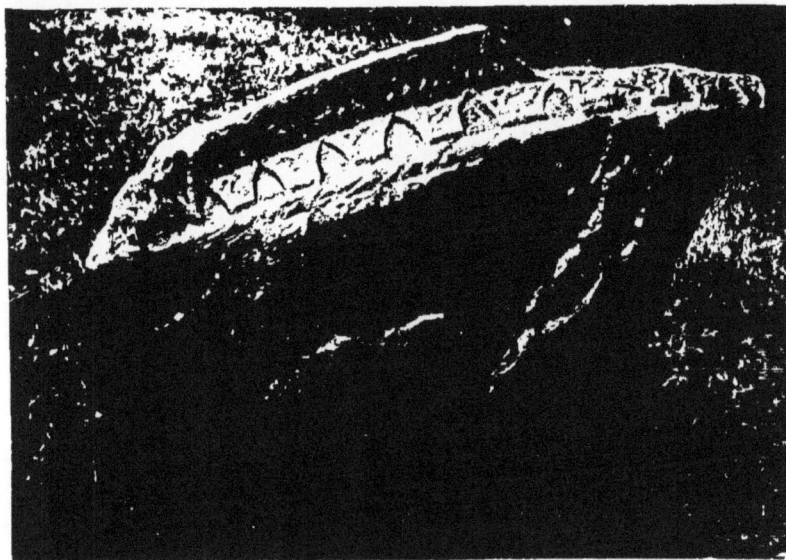

Two views of the Hogback,

ASPATRIA.

(TO FACE P. 15.)

ASPATRIA.

(II.) THE HOGBACK.

WE know that various races in different parts of the world have constructed their graves on the model of their houses, the idea underlying this kind of burial being that the dead live in these places in exactly the same way as the living live in their own houses : hence the chamber-tombs found in barrows or tumuli not only all over Europe, but very largely in the East. When, however, cremation was practised, a full-sized house was unnecessarily large, and models in pottery * were sometimes used.

Several hut-urns found in Germany are described by Dr. Birch in his work on ancient pottery, as being distinctly Teutonic, and occuring in sepulchres of the period when bronze weapons were used, and before the predominance of Roman Art. Similar hut-urns were discovered in Italy in 1817, in an ancient cemetery in the Commune of Marino (Province of Rome). Some of these urns are models of circular huts, with square openings in the sides as doors through which the ashes of the dead were introduced, and having imitations of thatched roofs. Some shew the beams which support the roof and the joists ; one has six columns on each side adhering to the walls, and small windows projecting out of the thatched roof. The roof of one is ornamented with devices of a modified key-pattern. Some large urns of thick pottery found with these hut-urns are beautified with the same pattern, as well as with a series of svastikas enclosed in panels.

In the York Museum are several Roman tombs roofed with tiles.† One is "formed of roof-tiles (*tegulæ*) and ridge-tiles

---

* Hut-Urns, *Archæologia*, vol. xlii, p. 99. Sir John Lubbock, Bart.
† Handbook to York Museum, p. 6, 61. I desire to thank Mr. H. M. Platnauer, of the York Museum, for his great kindness in sending me sketches of all the Roman Tiled Tombs in the Museum, with measurements.

(*imbrices*), which bear the impress of the victorious sixth Legion,* LEG. VI. VI."

The tiles of another tomb are " stamped LEG. IX. HISP., so that it is probable that the tomb covered a soldier of the ninth, or Spanish Legion." This tomb is set up in the exact form of a tiled house-roof, with the *curved ridge-tiles* placed upon the angle formed by the *two* side *roof-tiles*. It is No. 71 in the handbook.

Coped Tombs, commonly called Saxon Hog-backs, follow the idea of the grave being the Home of the Dead. I here give the two sides of an elaborately carved white-sandstone ridged and roofed house-shaped tomb of very remarkable character at Aspatria. It was brought to light from amongst the building material of the old church which was pulled down when the present church was built on its site. The fragment measures forty-six inches in length, twenty-seven inches in height, and eight inches in thickness.

At the top is a tall, thin, highly decorated ridge three inches thick, having two zig-zag flat bands worked upon it, standing up about three inches from the roof below. Then comes, on a curved and bulged surface, an ornamented roof with recessed work, looking like two rows of delicately moulded tiles richly adorned with a simple Triquetra on each tile, only that the tiles could never be made to sit on such a rounded surface, and, moreover, between the two rows of this recessed work is a rounded band or *syme*, with a narrow flat riband twined gracefully round it, plainly intended to bind down and hold the thatched roof, with its decorations, in its place. Along the eaves is a broad band worked with a kind of key pattern.

At the upper sinister corner of the higher figure, and the dexter corner of the lower figure, under the ridge and upon the upper row of devices, there is a raised portion and traces of an enlargement of the stone. I have sometimes thought the figure of a stag could be seen.

The upright sides of this house are covered with inter-lacing flat bands on one side, and the walls are strengthened

* Engraved in Llewellyn Jewitt's Grave Mounds.

with pilasters highly ornamented—there has been a central broad pilaster and a narrower one at each end—one end has been broken away—the whole of this side has been covered with work done with a narrow or pointed tool. The other side has suffered by the stone having split off. Sufficient of the surface remains to show that it was covered with knot-work of double strands. The broad band at the eaves has disappeared, but sufficient of the roof and tall ridge remains to shew that both sides of the roof were of like design, though the walls differed in their ornamentation.

In imitating the home of the living as a memorial of the dead it was but natural that the Church House should be taken as the model; and it may be that the mud and wattle-woven shrine, done in stone, with its carefully con-structed roof and graceful ridge, all richly decorated and covered with the sacred sign of the Holy Trinity, is nothing less than a survival, and may indeed carry us back to a time before there was any stone church on these shores. He for whom such a tomb was not too costly must indeed have been noble in the eyes of those who reared this monument.

※　　※　　※　　※

In his lectures on "The Church in these Islands before Augus-tine" (p. 46) the Bishop of Bristol (Prof. G. F. Browne) notes the tradition about the wattled walls at Glastonbury, now re-discovered by excavation, and comments on the extent to which this art of wattling was carried by the Britons. What is even more to our purpose, he quotes Archdeacon Prescott's information from the Lanercost Chartulary that there was a *capella de virgis*, a chapel of wattle-work, at Treverman (Triermain), where Divine Service was celebrated by consent of Egelwin, the last Anglo-Saxon bishop of Durham. This, says Chancellor Ferguson, in *Carlisle* (*Diocesan Histories*), p. 219, is "the earliest ecclesiastical building we have record of in the land of Carlisle."

The hogback is badly weathered; its details could hardly be better represented than in the photographs. The plait-work seems to have been rudely picked out; but the tegulated roof is very well carved, with curves truly and strongly struck, and the ground cut away fairly clean and flat.

ASPATRIA.

(III.) THE SPIRAL SHAFTS.

(A) White sandstone cross shaft, broken across, length 3 feet 9¼ inches by 16 inches in widest part.

(B) Two pieces of a white sandstone cross shaft, the lower fragment 16 inches by 15 inches; the upper one 20 inches long by 15 inches across the lower, and 13½ inches across the upper end; thickness, 6 inches.

One shaft (A) shows spirals near the bottom, massed in a manner reminding one of the curved svastika on the Dearham fragment, with two pieces of plaitwork of three double strands having bosses worked in every available space; this seems to have been a tall, broad, and thin cross fixed in the ground without a socket stone. The line marking off the carved from the uncarved part is not horizontal, and the work is irregular. It is the lower part which remains.

The other shaft (B) has two broad bands passing round bosses similar to the back of the Dearham stone, along each side of a central scroll; in the lower part are the body and legs of a man above a svastika of solid form; the man is hoisted up in the air, a sacrifice to the God of heaven; to heathen minds it might be a victim hurled to Odin; to Christians, the God man (the sun of righteousness)—the svastika is the sun sign—raised on the cross. In the upper part the scroll enlarges, and the space to the left is filled with spirals which take the place of the bands and bosses. A portion is missing between the two pieces of this shaft. The scroll work in the centre of the upper fragment, if continued downward, would appear like the work on the Dearham stone before named. A precisely similar raised scroll ornaments the edge of this cross, and the reverse is covered with spirals.

This work is such as might be the result of the free working of British native artists, following their idea of the scroll

W.S.CALVERT

W.S.CALVERT

CROSS SHAFTS ASPATRIA FORMERLY ASPATRICK

· PART OF SMALL HEAD LATER

(TO FACE P. 18.)

work and plaited patterns on Roman pavements, &c., in the years following the decay of the Roman civilization consequent upon the retirement of the legions.

The very small piece of redstone interlacing shewn is probably of much later date.

           ＊   ＊   ＊

The two shafts, now built into the wall of the vestry, inside, are of inferior design and rough, chipped workmanship. The ground is not cut away flat, nor is the space filled up with pattern, as in the better designs of this class. The peculiar *sham* double-strands of the plait-work connect these with a series of similar style, in which the true effect of a double cord, braided or interwoven, is not preserved. Each separate bit of the plait is disjointed from the rest, and the furrow that splits it lengthwise is not continued to the intersection. This forgetting of the original naturalistic intention is a mark of decadent or derivative art; (see the chapter on Spiral Crosses in the Editor's Afterword, below.)

The *svastika* mentioned, in the right-hand sketch, might possibly be understood as a Maltese Cross; and the legs of the figure have something between them which might be a tail, but may be a sword. On the shaded part, beneath the figure, tools have been sharpened at some time or other, as upon one of the Gosforth hogbacks. The stone is a yellowish white gritstone; that of the piece with the figure seeming more decidedly yellow than its companion fragment.

The red sandstone fragment is very neatly chiselled ; the ground of the interlaced pattern cut carefully flat.

ASPATRIA.

(IV.) THE SPIRAL FRAGMENT AND
(V.) THE SVASTIKA FRAGMENTS.

Writing on April 15th, 1898, Mr. Calverley said :—

I send you a picture of a new find, a fragment taken out of a dyke-side in my field at the back of the Vicarage, and on the side of the Priest's Lonning. I have had it walled into the north wall of the new vestry.*

It is a fragment of a very early British Cross, such as have been at St. Bees, Dearham, Cross-Canonby, Aspatria (several), Bromfield, Isel and Bridekirk, and maybe others we don't know of. The ornament chiefly consists of spirals, and sometimes the *svastika*, the sign of Buddha, on the soles of whose feet it appears to Eastern sages as they gaze heaven-wards, and the sign of Thor and his thunderbolts to the Northern warriors who looked forward to the fighting and feasting of Valhalla, and the sign of the sun and the perpetual astral motion to Roman civilization and the Mithraic system. It is figured on an altar now in the altar-house at Birdoswald, to represent the sun on the left-hand side of the sacred focus, and on the right-hand side appears the crescent, the Lady of the Night. It is also engraved on what I believe may be a Romano-British Christian cross, taken out of the foundation of the twelfth century church of " Aspatrick," which is another form of " St. Patrick," and which people pronounce to-day " S'Patrick " ; as witness, what many folks remember, when the Maryport and Carlisle Railway ter-minated at Aspatria, and the porter, now deceased (rest his soul in peace !) used quite politely to show out the first-class passengers, but, coming to the third-class carriages, threw open the doors and shouted " S'Patrick, get out ! "

---

* The work, as the photograph shows, is roughly picked out, and similar to that in the Spiral Shafts.

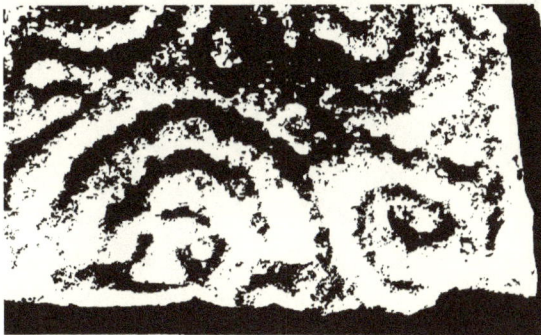

SPIRAL FRAGMENT,

ASPATRIA.

(TO FACE P. 20.)

The Svastika Fragments,

ASPATRIA.

The *svastika* or *fylfot*, or, as it is sometimes called, the *gammadion*, on this stone is carved * between certain circular objects which I take to represent the Holy Breads; the upper one of which is stamped with the sign of the Cross, plain, and represents the Host, just as I have seen it figured in some representation taken from the Catacombs at Rome. The person buried here was a priest of " S'Patrick " in the early days; perhaps even before St. Patrick was taken into slavery from " the town at the west end of the North Wall," which must have been either near Bowness on Solway or ·Dunbarton on Clyde, and in any case within the limit of our old kingdom of Strathclyde of the Britons.

St. Patrick himself very likely stayed here when preaching his doctrine of the Trinity to the many superstitious nature-worshippers among the natives, who dreaded the powers of nature in fell and flood, instead of serving the Lord of those powers.

The early British cross with the spirals is of quite a different character. Its sculpture is in relief, whereas the *svastika* is incised. The spirals are quite characteristic. The fragment is a relic of the times when the cross was set up to mark a preaching-station, and bears us far back to the British period. :

These crosses sometimes have traces of Roman ornamentation, as though the designer had in his mind's eye the regular riband-and-boss ornament of the Roman pilasters and pavements.

They must have been quarried from quarries lying open at the time. Those of the next period, such as the great crosses with such marvellously designed scroll-work and fruit and foliage and animals, such as are to be seen at Bewcastle and at Ruthwell (where, no doubt, the place has taken its name from the waters of Holy Baptism, close by the preaching station of the Holy Rood) must also have been won from ·open quarries. It is impossible to suppose that any building ·was going on at the time in the neighbourhood, which would require the rudding and removal of so great a depth of super-incumbent deposit as would be necessary to expose a post of

---

* Neat'y chiselled with a narrow or pointed tool in soft red sandstone.   -

living stone from which could be hewn, by means of grooves
a foot deep picked out, or by the use of wedges, a piece of
rock fourteen or sixteen feet long, two feet wide, and more
than a foot thick, such as would be required from which to
cut Ruthwell or Bewcastle Cross. These crosses were each
a solid piece of rock. Their heads have been broken off, but
there remain two whose heads are still upon their shoulders;
the one at Irton and the one at Gosforth. This latter I have
reproduced in order that I might, if possible, attain the
masonic mystery of the work.

We have a freestone quarry which supplies by many
steamers huge blocks of red sandstone for the ornamentation
of the fronts of New York buildings, built of the brown stone
of America. The red sandstone is sawn into and used for
lintels, jambs, bands, and in other ways as a variation in
colour.

The quarry-master, my much regretted churchwarden, Mr.
Henry Graves, helped me with his experience in my designs;
and, in about a year's time after my first acquainting him
with my wish, he took me down to the quarry and showed
me what he considered to be a good post of rock for the
purpose. This was very deep—the bottom post worked. The
men took every care to win the stone perfectly. They
wedged it away from its bed, two feet wide, two feet thick,
sixteen feet long; and they brought the great rock into my
cart-shed, where a local mason who had worked for Mr.
Graves a long time, who was now getting old, whose work
may be seen in the churches around and in the tombstones
in churchyards, set to work to level one side of the stone
and find the centre of the plinth. He said the stone was
just big enough, and therefore the cross was in it, if we could
only bring it out. He set to work, and after a while we had
a straight edge boasted off, and an end, and a centre found.
Then we began the real work, and soon had the head of the
cross worked into its proper thickness, and the boss formed,
and the shaft cut out, and the base squared and worked into
a cylinder. Then we proceeded with the carving.

Thus I became, so far, one of the initiated.

The ancient carved stones in our churchyards are often of
a different colour from the stone now generally used in the

district. They are often of a colour similar to the walling stones of the church, which have been quarried by the early folk from the ruins of Roman buildings,—camps, stations, etc., of the neighbourhood. These quarries may now sometimes be found; vegetation, denudation, cultivation of land, not having quite obliterated all traces. I have found some of them where none thought a stone-quarry existed.

This sometimes accounts for the colour of the stones; and when it does, is good evidence.

Where did the stone of the Beckermet crosses come from?

At Aspatria there are many crosses and several colours; it must have been a pretty permanently occupied station.

At Bromfield there are two very ancient crosses of different colours.

The earliest ones are always of the light coloured sandstone; the next are red.

* * * *

A very remarkable parallel to this *svastika* fragment exists in a slab from Gillespie, Glenluce (now in the Edinburgh Antiquarian Museum), to which Mr. Calverley's attention was called by Mr. Robert Blair, F.S.A. It bears crosses and semicircles, with a *svastika* incised, like this at Aspatria; and also (what does not appear here) groups of dots in threes, which connect it with the early incised cross from the Mull of Sunnoness, Wigtonshire, (Dr. Joseph Anderson's *Scotland in Early Christian Times*, second series, p. 90), and others of the archaic series from St. Ninian's country.

BECKERMET : St. Bridget's.

The Inscribed Shaft, and its Partner.

A T Beckermet are two churches, one on either side of the river, and both very ancient sites. It has been suggested by Canon Knowles (*Transactions C. & W. A. & A. S.*, vol. iv., p. 143 ; 1879) that St. Bridget's was a nunnery, St. John's a monastery, perhaps as early as the seventh century,—a double foundation like those at Kildare, Whitby, and elsewhere.

In the churchyard of St. Bridget's, locally called "the low church," there are two headless shafts ; one with the famous inscription, and a companion much resembling it. They are of the type best known in the Pillar of Eliseg, near Valle Crucis in Denbighshire ; being cylindrical below and square in section above. Mr. J. Romilly Allen (on the Llantwit pillar, *Archæol. Cambrensis*, 5th series, vi., 24, and on the Early Christian Monuments of Lancashire and Cheshire, *Transactions Hist. Soc. of Lanc. & Chesh.* ix. N.S., 1894) says that the type is chiefly found in Cheshire and Staffordshire, and that its origin seems to him to be Mercian rather than Northumbrian ; it is not found in Ireland and Scotland, and only once in Wales.

These Beckermet shafts most nearly resemble those at Chulow in Cheshire, two that have been placed in the Public Park at Maccles-field, Stapleford Cross in Nottinghamshire, and Eliseg's, in having panels rounded at the bottom but set above a ring or rings finishing the cylindrical shaft. In this they differ from the Gosforth shafts, which have the round bottoms to the panels, but no strongly marked rings just below, placed as if to conceal the junction of round and square.

In this inscribed pillar, however, the cable-moulding is interrupted by a vertical groove just beneath the inscribed panel, a little like the groove in the Llantwit pillar. The lower part is not truly cylindrical ; the corners of the original block of stone have been rounded off, leaving flattish faces, and in the middle of each a hole has been bored,—a larger hole under each of the two narrower panels of the upper parts, and *vice versa*.

The inscribed pillar is of red sandstone, now 51½ inches high ; the greatest girth of the round part is 68½ inches ; the square part measures 15 by 10 inches near the top. The socket-block in which it stands is also of red sandstone, measuring 35 by 30 by 15 inches.

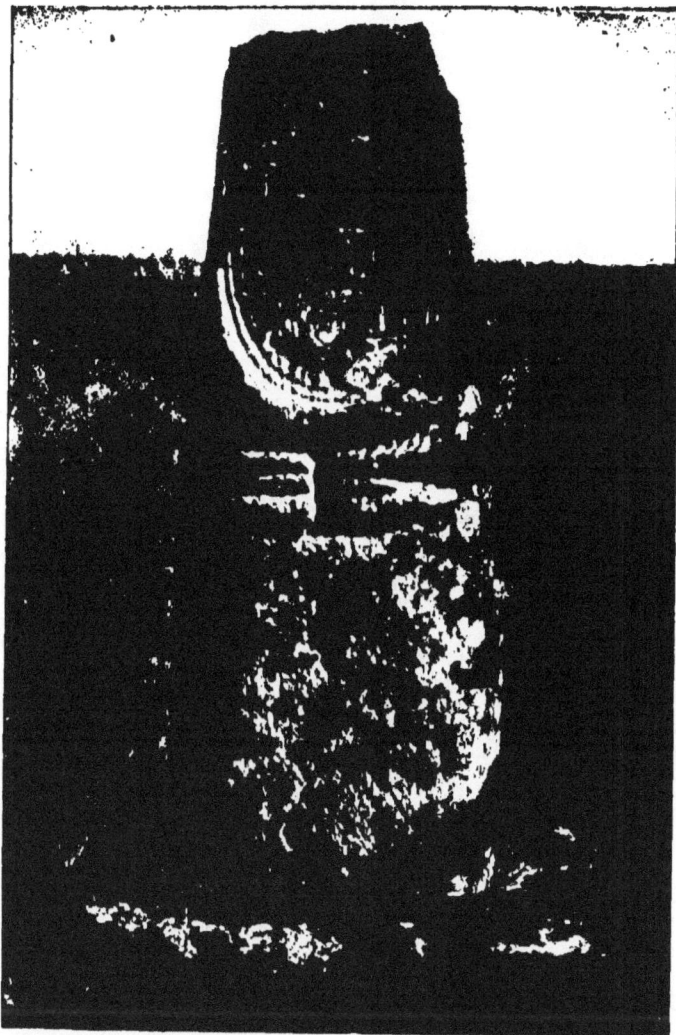

THE INSCRIBED SHAFT,

BECKERMET, St. BRIDGET'S.

(TO FACE P. 26.)

The panel containing the inscription is now 24 inches high, by 16 in greatest width. One or more lines of inscription are evidently wanting, as can be seen from the corresponding panel on the east side of the stone, where the floral scroll is obviously incomplete. The pattern to the south side is much damaged : on the north the ornament resembles the spirals which are so often seen on a certain class of our monuments, here looking like ill-drawn floral scrolls, but with a tendency to settle into the irregular cells which characterize the type. (See over leaf.)

The inscription has puzzled many antiquaries. Chancellor Ferguson has kindly looked up the various notices, beginning with Lysons' *Cumberland*, p. cci., in which no reading is attempted: followed about 1857 by Father Haigh's celebrated *Tuda* reading (*Archæologia Æliana*, N.S. vol. i., p. 149, in a paper on " The Saxon Cross at Bewcastle ").

Canon Parkinson of Manchester, Principal of the St. Bees Theological College, had made a rubbing which Father Haigh read as English in Roman characters, thus :—

HIR TÆGÆD
TUDA SCÆAR
QUÆLM TER
FORAN FÆLS E ·
RXNAUUANG ·
AS ÆFTER

and translated :—

" Here enclosed
Tuda bishop :
the plague-destruction before,
the reward of Paradise after."

The life and death of Bishop Tuda may be read in Bede's *Ecclesiastical History*, book III., chapters 26 and 27: how he was the last of the Scotish bishops of Northumbria, and died of the plague in 664, and was buried at Pægnalæch or Pægnalæth. Father Haigh argues that Beckermet is Pægnalæth,* and the date of the monument 664.

---

* The Anglo-Saxon Chronicle says that Tuda died at Wagele; and as the letter Þ is almost identical with the Anglo-Saxon *Wen* or W, the name in Bede might be read Wægnalæth, of which Wagele is a shortened form. Now the island over against Barrow-in-Furness was formerly written Wagheney, Latinized Wagneia; and though now spelt Walney, is called Whanney. By analogy Wagna-leth, Wage-le, would become Whalley. The place of that name, however, in Lancashire is *Wallei* and *Watelei* in Domesdaybook, though the presence there of Early Anglo-Saxon crosses reminds us that it was an important burying-place in pre-Norman times.

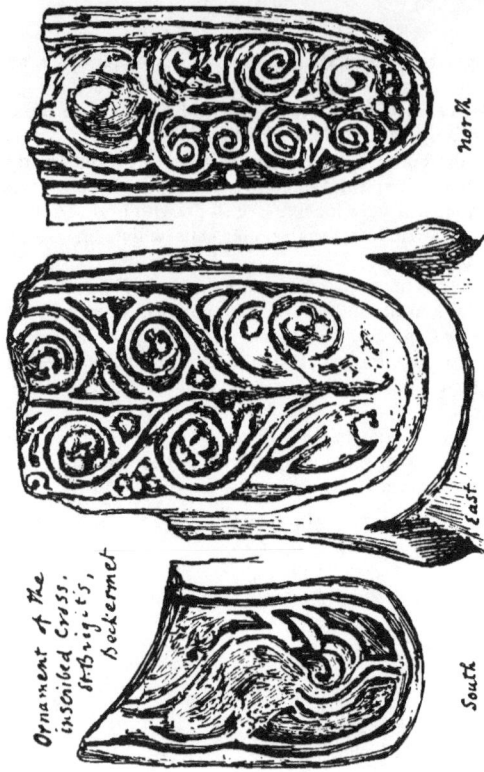

Ornament of the
inscribed Cross.
St Bridget's,
Beckermet

North

East

South

BACK AND EDGES OF THE INSCRIBED CROSS.

BECKERMET. ST. BRIDGET'S.

In 1859 the Rev. John Maughan gave, at the Carlisle Congress of the Royal Archæological Institute, this reading and translation :

HIR BAEKNE	" Here beacons
TUDA SETAH	two set up
QUHEN ARLEC	queen Arlec
FOR SUN ATHFE-	for her son Athfeschar.
SCHAR. BID URRA	Pray for our
SAULA.	souls."

(*Archæologia Æliana*, vol. VI. p. 61).

Next, in 1861 the Rev. F. Addison of Cleator exhibited new rubbings to the Society of Antiquaries of Newcastle; and concluded that the reading had not been discovered. In 1862 Mr. John Dixon of Whitehaven (*Arch. Æl.*, vol. vi., p. 124) gave two casts of the inscription to the same society. One cast was sent to Copenhagen; and in the following year Prof. George Stephens and Archivary C. F. Herbst sent readings (engraved in *Arch. Æl.*, vol. vi., p. 192) but no translations; Stephens remarking that the language can scarcely be English, or Runic, or Latin, but guessing it to be some old Pictish or Keltic dialect. The inscription does not appear in Stephens' *Old-Northern Runic Monuments*.

Finally, in 1866, R. Carr Ellison gave :—

HIU, BILEOFTIE	" O, thou loved
JUGIOTH EDIH '	Offspring Edith,
QINEL MIEC	Little maid, in
SŒF-SYNELLE	slumber waned.
J XII B.I. HIRE SAU	Years XII.. Pray ye for her soul.
J. M h. C. III	Year MCIII."

A copy of this reading, made by Mr. Calverley, gives HIH-BILEOFTRE JUGITHI and SWŒF-SYNELTRE ; translating " To beloved," etc., and in Latin " Dilectissimæ Proli Edithulæ," etc., in the dative case.

As so little success had attended readings from rubbings, it remained to make a fresh attempt by *tracing* the letters. The stone was not squared and smoothed before carving; and consequently the ordinary heelball rubbing brings into prominence all the irregularities of the natural surface, without sufficiently showing the marks of the chisel as such. The same difficulty attends photographs, as will be seen from our illustration. But by carefully following the marks of the chisel, feeling them through thin paper, and tracing the forms at leisure, a new reading came out, which resembled the old original transcription of Lysons' artist. The letters showed themselves as Irish minuscules, of a curious type, but very well and very distinctly formed, except where the surface is weathered in the streak of softer stone that runs down the middle of the panel, broadening towards the base ; which, being slightly turned up and not vertical, has caught the weathering more than the upper part.

Imitating the minuscules as nearly as we can in ordinary type, we get:

(line wanting)

rIntdIegne

Iudn : Icdir

qbre : Imiec

FOS : Fd : seIFe   (or SdFe)

î.Xst.·. rhn:sI

cr

The **d** in the inscription is evidently for **a**; **r** and **s** we have written for the unfamiliar forms which are their equivalents in the minuscules. Some letters are doubtful, but **iuan, cair, miec, Fos, selfe** or **safe**, and **xst** are quite plain.

The group *iuan* recalled the Norse name *Saudar Iuan*, "Sheep John," on the Cross at Maughold, Isle of Man, and the connection with Man was strengthened by the fact that Beckermet was in the lands of that Celtic and pre-Norman "castle of Carnarvon," *Caer-n-ar-mhon*, the castle over against Mona, which afterwards belonged to the Flemings. Juan is a Manx form which lasted down to the "Juan Jem Moore" of the election-ballad of 1837, quoted by Mr. A. W. Moore (*Surnames and Place Names of I.O.M.*, p. 123). The early Irish way of spelling John was *Eoan*, as in the Annals of the Four Masters *sub anno* 1171, where mention is made of Askulf Thorkels-son's Orkney Berserk, called "Johan le Devé" (not Dene) in the Anglo-Norman poem on the Conquest of Ireland. Before that date it was not a common name in Ireland ; very rare in the Annals. Among the Northmen, however, it was early adopted from England, and in the 11th century written Ióan. One of the name in Iceland married a granddaughter of Snorri Godi, who died 1031 ; another, born 1054, was bishop of Hólar. So that in Man we might expect to find the name in this form of Juan at an early date.

At first, as the upper part of the letters *gne* in the first line is broken, we thought the **n** might be **Il**, making Gile-Juan for Giolla-

Eoin : but this seems hardly possible. The *Cair*, followed by *qbre*, or what looks very like this odd combination of letters, naturally suggested the well-known name Cairbre. Mr. A. W. Moore, in his *Surnames and Place Names of the I.O.M.*, p. 208, says that what is now *Arbory*, or in Manx *Skeelley Cairbre*, was in 1153 called *terra Sancti Carebrie*. In 1231 a document calls it *terram Sti. Columbæ, herbery vocatam ;* for there were two chapels in the parish, *Keeill Cairbre* and *Keeill Columb*.

A member of the *C. & W. A. & A. S.* who is both a student of old Celtic and a Gaelic speaking native of the west of Ireland, Mr. John Rogers, visited the place and thought the inscription Manx Gaelic, written phonetically with omission of some aspirated letters; a feature in Gaelic writing which afterwards became common, and even at an early age was creeping into use. He instanced from the 9th cent. *Book of Deer* (Ed. Macbain) *Malbrite* for *Mal Brighite, Blienec* for *Bliedhenec, Fienasi* for *Fiedhnasi, Bead* for *Bethad*, etc.; and it must be remembered that regular scholarly spelling is not the rule in cross-inscriptions.

Rinta, Rinia or *Rinid* would stand for " made." *Le gne* = " for "; *gne* being " face," and the phrase idiomatically equivalent to " against " " for the purpose of." In *Cairqbre* he thought the *q* might be carved for *d* (that is *a*) and in pronouncing Cairbre a slight vowel is always heard in the middle of the word, as seen in the above quoted *Carebrie*. The *l* after *Juan* is so nearly like an *i*, and so impossible as an *l*, that he would read *Juan i Cairabre*, phonetic for *Juan (mh)i(c) Cairabre*, " John son of Cairbre " or perhaps " John of Carbery " (the place.)

The following words he expanded as *ithmigh aig fos fa selbh*, " gone to rest under the keeping " : *ithmigh aig* being pronounced as *imi ec*, and *fos*, a word for " sleep, rest," still used in Scotch Gaelic.

The *i Xst* might be a contraction for "in Christ" or " Jesus Christ." Then follows,—after a triple dot, as in the St. Vigean's Cross,—space for two letters, and a group much less plain to read. Mr. Rogers suggested *(Fo)rin-si Cr(ist air)*, " Be gracious to him, O Christ ! "

The whole might then mean :—

> (This cross was)
> made for
> John mac Cair-
> bre gone to
> rest in the keeping
> of Christ. Be gracious
> to him, O Christ !

THE SECOND SHAFT

ST. BRIDGET'S.

BECKERMET.

The companion pillar is of greyish white freestone; 68 inches tall from its base, 47 inches in girth round the cylindrical part, and 11 by 7½ inches near the top. It now stands in a socket much too large for it, cut in a block of red sandstone measuring 44 by 29 by 19 inches, never truly squared, and now split.

This shaft has a cable-moulding round it, like the other, beneath the round-bottomed panels. The west side is much weathered; the north and south sides are ornamented with simple plaits in double rows, and the east side seems to have borne the same design.

As to the cable-moulding, Bishop Browne remarks of the pillar of Eliseg (Archæol. Journal, XLIV. No. 174, 1887, p. 151) that it is no indication of a very recent date; for that pillar bears an inscription which no one is able to put later than the ninth century.

BECKERMET.

St. John's.

At this church, together with a number of mediæval cross-slabs, there are two white sandstone " spiral " fragments ; an interlaced, dragonesque socket-stone and five fragments of similar type, as well as another piece of rude interlacing, all of which were figured by the Rev. Canon Knowles in *Transactions* C. & W. A. & A. S., vol. IV., p. 139, 1879. For this book they have been re-drawn by the editor from the original stones.

The White Cross-Head and Spiral Shaft.

These two large fragments lie at present (1899) outside the porch. They are of white freestone ; the shaft (facing page 35) measuring 26½ inches in length, 13 in breadth tapering to 12, and 6 thick. The head is 33 inches long, by 15 broad, and 7 inches tapering to 6½ in thickness. One side and one edge of each have been defaced. The carving may have been partly done with the chisel, but in some parts it is evidently finished very roughly with the pick. The plates have been very carefully and successfully engraved, thanks to Messrs. Carl Hentschel & Co.

Canon Knowles compared these with two similar white sandstone shafts at St. Bees and with a cross at Kirk Maughold, Isle of Man, and assigned them to the British period and local workmen ; a suggestion which Mr. Calverley followed in treating sculptures of this type at Addingham, Aspatria, Bromfield, Dearham, etc.

The somewhat similar stone at Kirk Maughold we take to be the Rowler Cross, thought to be the monument of a bishop Roolwer (Hrolfr) who is mentioned in the *Chronicon Manniæ* about 1050 as buried at Maughold (P. M. C. Kermode, F.S.A. Scot., Saga-book of the Viking Club, vol. I., part iii., p. 364).

The other fragments are preserved on the window-sills of the north side of the church.

WHITE CROSS-HEAD,

BECKERMET, St. JOHN'S.

(TO FACE P. 34.)

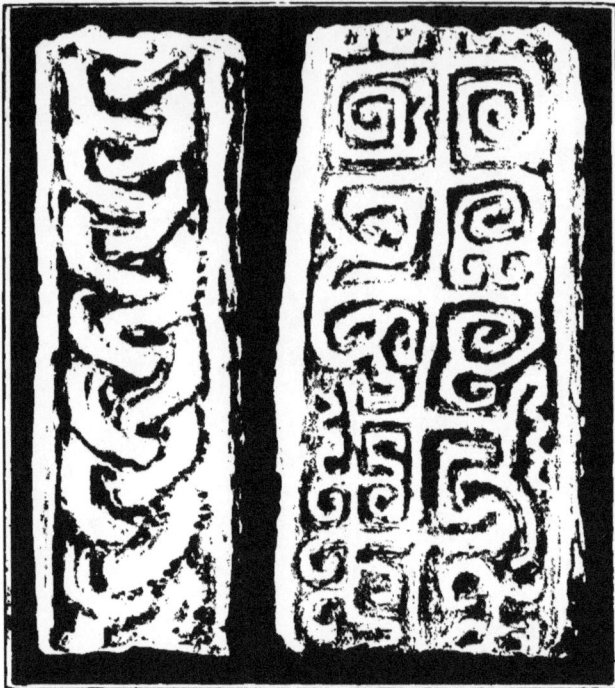

WHITE SPIRAL SHAFT,

BECKERMET, ST. JOHN'S.

(TO FACE P. 35.)

The socket-stone, assigned by Canon Knowles to the 11th century, is of red sandstone, 24 inches wide, 6½ thick, the breadth from the socket hole to the edge being 11 inches. The ornament is carved on a very rudely-prepared face : the block was hardly squared and by no means dressed flat, and the pattern follows the irregularities of the surface with unusual boldness. The relief is not deep ; the work partly chiselled and partly picked, getting by its sketchy handling a very varied and artistic effect.

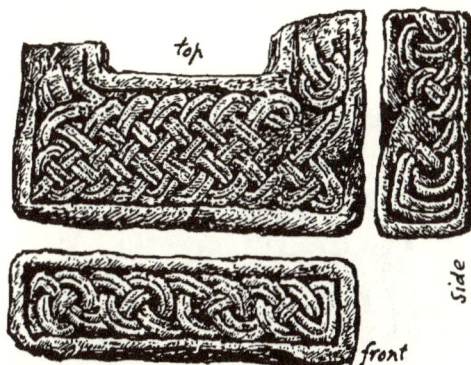

THE SOCKET STONE.

Three fragments, which can hardly belong to one and the same shaft, are connected with this socket by their manner of execution ; and two more, differing in execution, resemble these in pattern.

The fragment A, which fits best with the socket, is figured next. It is of red sandstone ; 36 inches in length ; 13 tapering to 11 in breadth, and 5½ tapering to 5 in thickness. The back and one edge are defaced, and the ornament is much worn, but shows the same carelessness of what the modern carver calls workmanlike execution, together with a free and masterly use of tools, and well closed though not symmetrically planned design. The little fragment (B) 9½ by 10½ by 4½ inches, which formed the neck of the cross, repeats the design of the side and edge of the greater piece. We have here the two ends of a shaft, which allowing for the rate of tapering, would have been nearly six feet long, to which must be added the cross-head now lost, and the thickness of the socket stone ; so that the original would have stood perhaps eight feet high,—one of the richest and most picturesque of all our later pre-Norman crosses.

a   b   c

FRAGMENT B.

a   b

FRAGMENT A.

ST. JOHN'S, BECKERMET.

The other fragment (C), from the same hand, as it seems, is also of red sandstone; 25½ inches long, 11¼ broad, tapering to 9½, and 5¼ thick, tapering to 4¼. Instead of the knots along the edges (b) and (d), it has a simple plait; but the dragonesque pattern of the sides, and the bold work, roughly picked out and finished in details with the chisel, are similar to (A) and (B). In the blank space of (a), defaced with a chisel, there are no signs of an inscription.

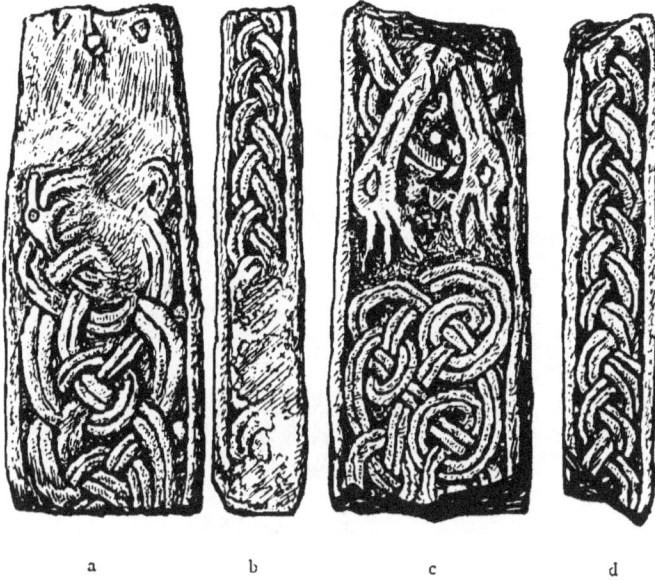

a   b   c   d

FRAGMENT C.

There was also an interlaced fragment of red sandstone in the garden of the Rev. J. Steele at Croft House, Beckermet, which by inadvertence was built into the wall of an addition to the house, on the south side near the east corner, where its edge, without ornament and measuring 22 by 7 inches, may be seen about 5 feet from the ground.

(D) and (E).   These two fragments are parts of a third cross, differing from the preceding in manner of work, though not at all in design.
In this the emphatic points of intersection are marked with deep
drill-holes, which is not the case with the others, or the socket-stone.
This use of the drill is very rare in our series; it occurs on the
Gosforth Cross in the bit of interlacing work on the north side, and
it recalls the drill-holes of the 12th century South French and North
Italian sculpture ; though it can hardly be derived from 12th century
teaching, and is an old Greek and Byzantine trick.   It is interesting,
as an evidence of artistic intention, that while the drill is used freely
to punctuate monotonous interlacing, it is not used in the more
varied " thunderbolt " pattern, which seems to have been thought
good enough to stand in quiet breadth without breaking up with dark
touches.   But the contrast got by the dark touches gives a curious
delicacy to the surface.   In this stone the " thunderbolt " pattern is
better set out than in (A), but pellets are freely used in both to fill
gaps.

These two are also of red sandstone; the lower fragment (D) is 24
inches long by 13½ broad, tapering to 13, and 6 inches thick.   The
the upper piece (E) is 23½ inches in length, 12¼ tapering to 11 in
breadth, and 5½ in thickness.   Some parts have been defaced with
a chisel, or perhaps used to sharpen a tool upon, like the Gosforth
hogback.   This plate also is very successfully reproduced.

FRAGMENT F.

F is a piece of red sandstone, measuring 22¼ by 8½ by 6 inches,
with an ill-drawn square-cut plait, and a cable edge indicated
roughly.   It has been turned into a mediæval grave-slab, and has
a later cross on the back.

It may be added that in the early part of 1899, when part of
a cottage opposite the churchyard gate was pulled down, two stone
troughs were found, one oblong and the other roughly square; they
are now in the Jubilee Tower at Braystones.

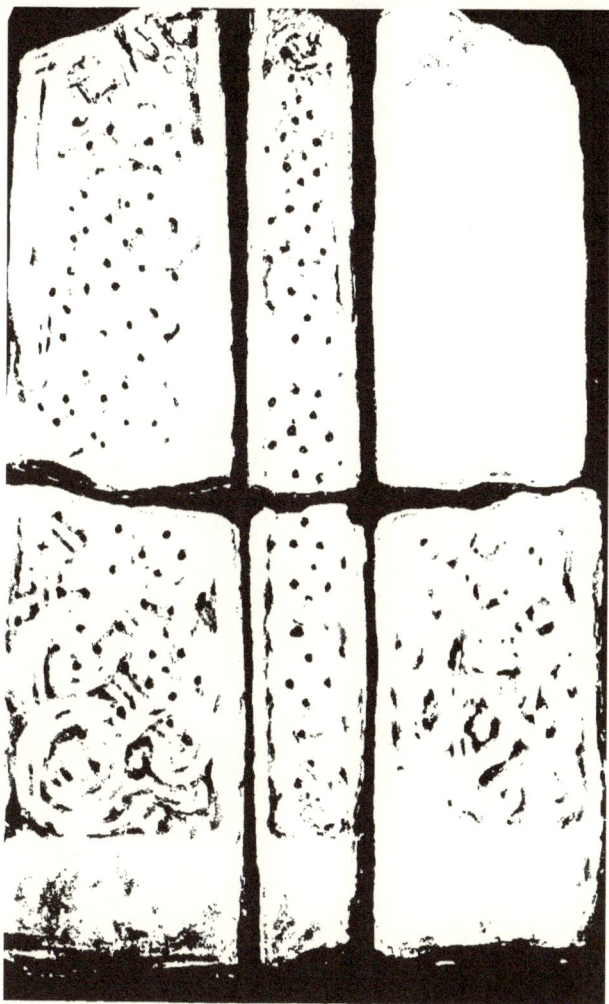

THE "DRILLED" SHAFT,

FRAGMENTS D AND E.

BECKERMET, ST. JOHN'S.

BEWCASTLE, WEST SIDE (TO FACE P. 39.)

BEWCASTLE.

The Cross.

THE two accompanying large illustrations are from Mr. Fletcher's photographs, and shew the west and south faces of the great cross at Bewcastle. The details are : *west face*, near the top, remains of runes* over an oblong square headed panel, containing the figure of S. John Baptist bearing the nimbed Agnus Dei. Beneath this panel and over a much larger central, oblong, circular-headed panel are two lines of runes, the upper line beginning with the sign of the cross and reading GESSUS (Jesus), the lower one reading KRISTTUS (Christ). This central panel contains the glorified figure of the Great Christ, robed as a priest, bearing in His left hand the sacred roll, His right hand uplifted to bless, treading upon the lion and the adder, and His holy head leaning slightly to the right hand surrounded with the circling halo. Below this central figure comes the principal inscription in nine lines of runes. Beneath this, in a wide circular-headed panel, standing a little sideways, and looking towards the spectator's right hand, is a man holding on his left wrist his hawk, which has flown up from its perch beneath. The stone is here much weather-worn, but the figure appears to wear a tippet or cape, and may hold something in the right hand, whilst the legs and feet appear beneath the tunic, and the head is uncovered. These three figures are the only human representations on the cross. The central figure is the Christ. Above we see S. John, who was sent to prepare the way of the Lord. Beneath surely the king or leader, by whose help this cross was set up, as a sign that the way of Christ was to be made plain in the wilderness of heathen

---

* Prof. Stephens thinks that these runes may also have recorded the Holy Name.

Northumbria. "It may have been," says Prof. Stephens, "the figure of Alcfrith himself," whose name appears in the inscription above the panel, which reads : " This sign-beacon (trophy) set up Hwætred, Wothgar, and Olfwolthu, after Alcfrith, once King, eke son of Oswiu. Pray for his soul."

The details of the *south face* are—at the bottom an intertwined knot-ornament ; above this a line of runes beginning with the sign of the cross; above this a very beautiful piece of double scroll-work, consisting of two grape-bearing vines with foliage and clusters, filling an oblong panel. Another line of runes appears above, and a smaller panel of knot-work above this, surmounted again by a panel filled with a single vine-scroll bearing near the centre an early sun-dial whose principal time-divisions are marked by a cross, and having rich fruit above. Another line of runes separates this panel from a third carving of knot-work, which, with some more runes, brings us to the top of the cross-shaft. Prof. Stephens reads the lines of runes on this face thus * : " In the first year of the King of this realm Ecgfrith," and he considers that this gives us the date of the cross, A.D. 670. Ecgfrith succeeded to his half brother Alcfrith in this year. Oswiu's first wife, a Celtic lady, bore him Alcfrith. King Ecgfrith's mother was Eanflæd, daughter of King Edwin of Northumberland.

The *north face* has also five panels. The central and largest panel, filled with chequers only, has above and below it and separated by a line of runes, a smaller panel, containing very elegant knot-work presenting elaborate specimens of the sacred sign of the Holy Trinity—the triquetra so constantly used in the early MSS. In the lowest compartment on this side are two conventional flower and fruit bearing vine-scrolls of perfect design and exquisite workmanship, more nobly conceived than perhaps anything of the kind which is known in the land. The uppermost compartment contains a single such scroll. The two divisions—at the top and at the bottom of this side—

---

* I quote Prof. Stephen's reading of the runes, and therefore his argument based upon them for the date given by him.

THE CHRIST.

BEWCASTLE.

(TO FACE P. 41.)

containing these three Paradise Trees are separated from the knot-work divisions each by a line of runes. At the very top, preceded by three crosses, is another line of runes—GESSUS (Jesus). The runes on this face appear to name three persons, Wulfhere, King of the Mercians and son of Penda, Künnburug, Alcfrith's Queen and Penda's daughter, and Küneswitha, the Queen's sister. It will thus be seen that the chief face of the stone bears three sculptured figures, the central one being the Christ; that each of the two panelled sides shew three divisions of interlaced work or geometrical design, and three conventional flower and fruit bearing vines; and that the knot-work displays in various ways the sign of the Trinity (on the south side—here shewn—the lowest panel has eight double, and the central and smaller panel eight single triquetræ joined in one). The sun-dial, with its rays marking the hours, and the hole for its gnomon, has been cut at the time of the making of the cross, and is part of the original design, so far as we can see.

It would be difficult to refuse to believe that the main object of the work was to teach the doctrine of the Trinity of the Godhead, with its manifestations of the Sun of righteousness—Jesus the Christ—the Lord of Life—the true Vine; whilst commemorating the triumphant dead at a period when the streams of Roman and Celtic art met and were harmonized by ornamentation of a general northern character, possibly under the influence of Wilfrid's foreign masons, and when the streams of northern and classic ideas also met and were being harmonized by the religious poems and scripture paraphrases of the first of all English poets— Cædmon—in the monastery of the Abbess Hilda at Whitby.

The *east face* of the cross is filled with one great vine-scroll rising boldly from below and bearing many fruits, which are being eaten by beasts and birds. A hound or fox devours a cluster near the ground; further up are two creatures of conventional character, and higher still two birds, hawk or eagle and raven, while the two topmost fruits are nibbled by two squirrels. All this is much like the scroll work on the two sides of the Ruthwell cross, as also is the figure of Christ treading on the beasts (swine

or lion and adder) on the west face, and the S. John Baptist
bearing the Agnus Dei which appears in the upper panel of
both crosses; but whilst the Ruthwell cross has ten panels
filled with figures and no other ornamentation than the two
similar scrolls worked on the two edges of the stone and
the runes which are cut everywhere along the borders of the
panels, the Bewcastle Cross apparently presents one commemoration surmounted by the Saviour and His forerunner,
and is rich in moulding and in design, calculated to present
and illustrate to a people saturated with northern ideas the
central thought of the Christian teaching alone.

*

We give here the Bewcastle and Ruthwell Crosses together.
At Ruthwell the arms and and centre of the cross-head are modern.
At Bewcastle the head is gone. Its socket is yet visible, though
now filled with cement to keep water from collecting and bursting
the stone when it freezes. Local tradition says that a cannon ball
of Cromwell's did the mischief. Another story is that the head was
blown off in a gale of wind. Camden records in an autograph slip
found in his own copy of the *Britannia* that a cross-head from
" Bucastle " was sent to him, through Lord Arundel, from " my Lord
William," that is, the so-called Belted Will, the antiquary of
Naworth. Camden died in 1623, so this must have happened earlier.

The whole monument must have been about 21 feet high from
the base of the pedestal; which is itself a remarkable block.
When, in the winter of 1890-91, the cross had been damaged by the
attempt of an unskilled person to take a cast of it, Chancellor
Ferguson, with Mr. Calverley and others, visited the place, to report
on the damage,* and to repair it as far as possible. Mr. Baty of
Carlisle then estimated the weight of the pedestal at six tons. It
had been cut out of a square pyramidal mass, 3 feet 10 inches in
depth; 5 feet square at the base, and 3 feet 9 inches square at the
top, with a chamfer of 12 inches taken off each corner. About 3 feet
of the stone had been buried below ground.

The pedestal, which had long been in an unsafe condition, was
then fixed with cement and copper cramps, and concrete was put
under the turf round the whole of the socket-stone, to prevent any

---

* Report on the Bewcastle Obelisk, by Chancellor Ferguson. *Transactions*
C. & W. A. & A. S., vol. xii., p. 55.

BEWCASTLE.   RUTHWELL.

The two great Anglian Crosses.

(TO FACE P. 42.)

SCROLL-WORK.

BEWCASTLE.

(TO FACE P. 43.)

mischievous or inquisitive person from pulling up the part that had been broken.

The shaft as it stands is a square pillar like an obelisk, a single block of gray freestone, 14¼ feet high above the pedestal (into which it was fixed with lead) and 21 by 22 inches at the bottom, tapering to 14 by 13 at the top. At Langbar on White Lyne Common, five miles north of Bewcastle, a similar block 15 feet long, of undressed stone, is said to lie in the quarry from which this may have come.

At several places on the moor the outcrop of freestone has been quarried in a primitive way, by chipping wedge-holes along a line on the surface-rock, and rending off pieces of various size. Some of these pieces have never been carried away, though ready for use; in some cases the spot has been abandoned when it was found that the stone would not split straight. It would be easy to bring a block of any size on a sledge from this moor to the site of the church; for it is all downhill, and an easy gradient. The church (St. Cuthbert's) is in the ruins of a Roman Camp, close to the Maiden Way, and adjoining the castle now in ruins.

It has been said in popular gossip or tradition that Ruthwell Cross was the fellow to Bewcastle Cross; also that it was brought by sea, and, according to some, cast up by shipwreck; some say, left at Ruthwell because it was too heavy for transport inland. Mr. Maughan, however, seemed to think that the block on Langbar was meant for a second cross at Bewcastle.

It is true that at Penrith, and perhaps at Gosforth, high crosses were in pairs; but it is far from proved that this was usual. Ruthwell and Bewcastle are of the same school. Their differences make it plain that they are not from the same hand. Some of the runes are different; some details are rather more deeply cut at Ruthwell; and some of the Bewcastle motives, the sun-dial, chequers and plaits, are wanting. But their resemblances give them a place together far above other high crosses in our district or around it. The figures in both are well proportioned, well designed, and well carved; they are very fine sculpture, totally different from the caricatures on such crosses as at Halton and Leeds. Our sketch of the Christ in Blessing is not flattered by the reproduction, in which the dark lines are too violent and the modelling has vanished. The general forms, however, are better given even by this than in Stephens' plate. The floral detail, weathered as it is, can hardly be beaten by any work of its kind in the world.

How unlike this work is to 12th century carving can be seen at once by comparing the sketch of a floral scroll opposite with Bride-kirk Font. Both are English work under Greek-Italian influence; but many centuries and a total change of feeling separate one from the other. The mere fact of the use of a chequer-pattern does not

indicate Norman age. The chequers on Bewcastle Cross are a
variety of the step-pattern on Irton Cross; chequers also appear at
Bromfield, Kirk-Bampton, Torpenhow, and Long Marton, but these
are different in treatment, just as Norman interlacing, of which there
is plenty, differs from the regulated braids of Anglo-Saxon age.

As to the date of Bewcastle Cross, though Stephens is now somewhat superseded as an authority, and his reading of the runes has
been questioned, yet much weight must be given to the arguments of
Bishop Browne in his lectures on "The Conversion of the Heptarchy." He accepts the early date and contends strongly for it.
According to his view, the latter part of the 7th century was a
period of great artistic energy under Wilfrith and other Romanizing
leaders; and at that date these scrolls and interlacings were learnt
from Lombardy, not from Ireland. For example, the tomb of the
Irish Columbanus at Bobbio, which one would expect to find ornamented with the so-called Irish art, is decorated merely with the
patterns then in vogue at Rome; while in Lombardy, not in
Ireland, interlacing and scrolls were used early in the 7th century.

The Runes have occupied the attention of many scholars ever
since the beginning of antiquarian study in England. The late Rev.
John Maughan, Rector of Bewcastle, in "A Memoir on the Roman
Station and Runic Cross at Bewcastle" (1857), traced the successive
attempts of Camden and Lord William Howard (who both died in
1623); Sir Henry Spelman and Olaus Wormius of Copenhagen;
Wanleius and Hickes; Bishop Nicolson of Carlisle in 1685; Mr.
George Smith of Brampton in 1742; and Mr. Henry Howard of
Corby Castle in 1801, who, says Maughan, "although he failed in
his attempt to open the lock, yet was probably the first person to
point out the right key." Others worked at it, but we really owe
the generally-received reading to Mr. Maughan himself. The
account given by Stephens in "Old-Northern Runic Monuments"
(part ii, pp. 398-404) is practically an abstract of Maughan's memoir;
and other writers, up to Bishop Browne (in "The Conversion of
the Heptarchy," lecture vii) have followed his interpretation.

Stephens read :—

+ ThIS SIG-BECN	This victory-column
ThUN SETTON H-	thin (or lofty) set up
WÆTRED WOTh	Hwætred, Woth-
GAR OLWFWOL-	gar, Olwfwolthu
ThU AFT ALCFRI-	after Alcfrith
ThU EAN KÜNING	once (lately) king
EAC OSWIUNG	and son of Oswi.
+ GEBID HE-	Pray for the high
O - SINNA SAWHULA.	sin of his soul.

RUNES OF BEWCASTLE CROSS.   (TO FACE P. 45.)

This was adopted from Maughan, except the last two lines, which he had rendered

" Pray thou for them,—their sins,—their souls."

To show the Runes as they stand, we give a plate, photographically reduced from a squeeze-tracing, carefully made and repeatedly revised, with the help of the present Rector of Bewcastle, the Rev. Edward Walker. The photographs are less trustworthy, because the painting of the runes by Mr. Maughan, now in parts worn away, confuses the plain light and dark. There is no doubt that the cross has weathered of late; and visitors unknown have poked and scratched at the letters without mercy. Fortunately, the stone is so hard that an ordinary knife-point makes little impression ; but if the surface is broken the weather will attack the details more successfully, and change beyond recognition or re-construction the tiny touches upon which the value of the writing depends.

In the first line we may note how the second S and the I following have been crammed into a space too small for them ; as though the carver had cut " Thisigbekn," and, finding he had made a mistake, corrected it. Another mistake was made by beginning to cut the groove of the moulding, on the right hand side of the panel, too far from the edge of the stone. It still appears, though almost smoothed away, and with some of the letters carved over it.

The first words are plain. *This sig-bekn thun,*—" this tall trophy or standard " ; *thunian* meaning " to stand out " or " to be proud," and *sigbeacn,* " a banner," in regular Anglo-Saxon.

Hwætred (the *e* is broken) was thought by Maughan to be the Wihtred, afterwards King of Kent ; and *Olwfwolthu* he connects with Elfwold, King of the East Angles ; suggesting that they might have been followers of Alcfrith in their youth,—a guess which we have no means of verifying. *Hwætred, Wothgar,* and *Olwfwolthu,* however, seem to be the names of the actual designers or artists, and they are Anglo-Saxon names, not Irish. The cross is Anglo-Saxon work.

Æft Alkfrithu is plain, but the words following are a little doubtful ; for the E of *ean* is a distinct M ; and the first word of ' King ' is X, the rune certainly not the inverted pitchfork engraved by Stephens. As *an-cyning* is a poetical word meaning " unique king," one would like to tack the M to Alchfrith's name : but *æfter* takes a dative. Perhaps the accepted reading is the best that can be offered,—" late king " ; and the next line *eac Oswiung,* " and son of Oswiu," is plain enough, in spite of some breaks and blots.

In the last line but one we have the G : : ID of *Gebid,* followed by H. The last letter of the line has been read E, but looks more like A. The first in the last line is apparently the combination of A and N ; and the cross-stroke, making N, is not a mere fracture, but a chiselled mark. HEAN might mean " lowly."

What follows is very indistinct; the reading SINNA SAWHULA is not plain enough to support any argument, still less to afford the only basis for a severe judgment on the king's character.

Alchfrith, whose name is read on this cross, was the eldest son of Oswiu of Northumbria (Bede, *Ecclesiastical History*, iii., 14-25). In his youth he went over to Penda, the pagan King of Mercia. He married Penda's daughter, Cyneburg, and joined with Penda in an attack on Oswiu. But, later on, he was the means of the conversion of Mercia, when Peada, Penda's son, at his persuasion, was baptized with all his nobles " At the Wall " in 653 ; and in 655 Alchfrith helped his father Oswiu against Penda in the decisive battle of Winwæd, which was won by the Christians against great odds.

Then in 664 came the famous Easter controversy, the struggle between the Irish and the Roman missionaries. Bede says (*Eccl. Hist.*, iii., 25) " Oswiu, taught and baptized by the Scots, and understanding their language, knew no better than to accept their teaching. But Alchfrith had been taught by Wilfrith, and rightly thought his doctrine better than all the traditions of the Scots. It was Alchfrith who had given Wilfrith a monastery at Ripon," . . . and it was " King Alchfrith " who sent Wilfrith, after the successful issue of the controversy, to be made bishop in Gaul.

Bede calls him King Alchfrith, and it is evident that he was a king, reigning over part of his father's too extensive realm. But by 670, when Oswiu died, Alchfrith also was dead, and his younger half-brother, Ecgfrith, became king of Northumbria.

Another still younger brother, Aldfrith, had been educated in Ireland. There is a well known poem in praise of Ireland by him still extant. He it was who succeeded Ecgfrith, and has been confounded with Alchfrith. As Lappenberg (*Hist. Eng. under the A.-S.*, vol i., p. 187, note) remarks, it was common to have similar names in families: Penda and Peada were father and son; Oswiu's daughters were Alchflæd and Ælflæd; we have in this cross the name of Cyneburg, Penda's daughter and Alchfrith's wife, and her sister Cyneswith. The two sisters, with Wulfhere their brother, then become King of Mercia, re-appear in a legend of the Anglo-Saxon Chronicle (*sub anno*, 657) as the chief builders of the great abbey which was afterwards known as Peterborough ; and they eventually became the St. Cyneburga and St. Cyneswitha of local legend.

Bishop Browne, however, suggests that the Cyneswitha of the cross may be the mother of Cyneburga and Wulfhere, the widow of Penda.

But why, one may ask, are these names found in so out-of-the-way a spot as Bewcastle?

Cumberland in 670 was, at last, after 250 years of Celtic freedom, being invaded by the English, which was possible only after the battle of Winwæd. Since then, for fifteen years, Anglian families had been settling across the border as a dominant race and taking up Cymric land. Many struggles must have gone on during the process, and the young king must have been to the front in many a fight; in one, at last, may have fallen, not ingloriously.

The cross is called, in the Runes, "this *sig*-beacon,"—standard of victory. No doubt the word may refer to the Cross in its religious aspect—"*In hoc signo vinces*": but to the practical English mind it must always have suggested that the grave was the grave of a conqueror.

Our sketch of the Christ shows the GESSUS KRISTTUS in Runes. On the north side, seen in perspective in one of our photographs, the KÜNNBURUG is plain, and KÜNESWITHA fairly so. The name of Wulfhere, king of the Mercians, is not now easy to read.

On the south side, FRUMAN GEAR, "in the first year," is distinct. The rest of the legend "of the king of this realm, Ecgfrith," is hardly visible. But the date of the Bewcastle cross does not depend on its legend. The style and workmanship are surer proofs of its origin.

* * * *

A copy of the cross was placed, about 1840, by Miss Sarah Losh, in the churchyard of Wreay, near Carlisle, with Latin inscriptions instead of the Runes on the original.

CROSS HILL, BEWCASTLE.

At Cross Hill or Roman Cross, 2½ miles north of Bewcastle Church, there was formerly an ancient cross; a part of which, says Whellan (*Hist. of Cumberland*, p. 646) still exists.

The present Rector, the Rev. Edward Walker, says, "The Ordnance Surveyors have located the site of the cross, but there are *no* remnants of any kind to be found."

BEWCASTLE.

The Baronspike or Barnspike and the Hazelgill
or Hessilgill Runes.

In March, 1864, a shepherd named C. Watson observed an
inscription near the top of a hill two miles east of Bewcastle. There
is a cairn or pike, easily visible from the church, and set upon
a tumulus 24 paces in diameter, which is surrounded by a trench
76 paces in circumference.

A site of this kind is often called by the country folk a " borran,"
from the Gaelic *boireann*, a word perhaps imported by the Irish-
Viking settlers, and meaning a rough place with large stones lying
about. Sometimes the name is given to naturally rocky places
where animals find their retreats ; as, for instance, a " fox-borran."
But the Roman Camp at Ambleside used to be known as Borrans
Ring ; the famous camp in Dumfriesshire is Burnswark (not Birrens-
wark, but *borrans-virki*, as the Gallgael would have called any
" ruined fort ") ; the moor with the stone circles between Eskdale
and Wastdale-head is Burnmoor ; the ridge covered with cairns
between Eskdale and Corney is Barnscar (*borran-skör*), and farther
south, near Sheffield, a hillside with pre-historic remains is Barnside.
Many instances might be given to show how Burn and Barn have
this meaning in place-names ; and this Barnspike, with the ringing
R sometimes pronounced Baronspike, is merely the " pike on the
borran."

Close beneath the summit there is a broken escarpment ; and on
a particularly large and nearly vertical face of the rock, south of
the pike, the shepherd found writing, and brought the news to his
master, Mr. Little, who showed the runes to the Rev. John Maughan,
rector of Bewcastle ; already for many years well-known as the
diligent student of the Runes on the Cross, and local authority on
the Roman Wall, great in controversy with Dr. Collingwood Bruce
and other antiquaries in Northumberland and Cumberland. The
Dolfin runes had been found in Carlisle Cathedral not long before
(in 1855), but this was the first discovery of " rock-risting " in
England. What was more, the runes, when deciphered, seemed to

prove an old Cumberland legend in the teeth of Northumbrian criticism. He read :—

BARANR . HRAIT . AT . GILLHES . BUETH .
IAS . VAS . DAUTHR . I . TRIKU . RAB .
D . VAULKS . AT . FADRLAND . NU .
LLANERKASTA .

" Baran wrote this inscription in memory of Gillhes Bueth who was slain in a truce by Robert D Vaulks for his patrimony now called Llanerkasta."

Now this legend had been published by Mr. Maughan in his 1857 " Memoir," from John Denton's MS. *History of Cumberland*; and had been disproved by Mr. Hodgson Hinde in 1859, in an article " on the Early History of Cumberland," printed in the *Archæological Journal*, vol. xvi., p. 217.

The discovery was published, and Professor George Stephens of Copenhagen accepted it ; made some amendments in the reading, and printed the whole in *Old-Northern Runic Monuments*, part ii., pp. 648-654.

Dr. Charlton of Newcastle visited the place, and in spite of what he thought was tampering, found " two strokes filled with the old lichen," and so took it as genuine. Indeed there is no reason to believe that the inscription, once carved, was materially damaged.

Eight years later, in 1872, another shepherd, John Davidson, found another inscription on another hill-top, about half a mile to the north of Barnspike. The two summits are divided by a stretch of moor, up to which runs a dell called Hazel-gill, losing itself beneath an escarpment like that of Barnspike. On the top of this northern hill, marked by the cairn at 1211 feet in the one-inch Ordnance Map, is a grassy mound which Mr. Maughan thought was another ring-barrow. Fifty yards to south of it, just as before, on a vertical face of rock, appeared these words, as rubbed by Maughan and read by Stephens :—

ASKR HRITA HEIL KIL HIMTHIKÆ
HESSIL.

" Ask wrote this hill to Gil henchman to Hessil." (*Op. cit.*, part iii, p. 310).

Being in doubt about Mr. Maughan's rubbing, Professor Stephens applied to the late Canon Simpson, who sent someone to take a fresh rubbing. Professor Stephens laments that " this gentleman had forgotten to take the second line," HESSIL, which he conjectures should have shown a genitive or dative termination ; but printed Maughan's notes, connecting Ask with Askerton Castle, and Hessil and Gil with " Hessilgill." Stephens appears to have accepted the ring-mound above (which is by no means obvious, as that of Barnspike is) and thought it the grave of Gil ; though he demurred a little to the identification of a stone building with Gil's dwelling-place. He thought the inscription heathen, and dated it 10th century.

It was no wonder that Canon Simpson's friend did not include HESSIL in his rubbing, for it certainly does not exist upon that stone, nor anywhere near. At the foot of the written crag there is an old shepherd's bield, ruined, and lichened over, even in the niche cut in the rock for its roof-tree, but of the nineteenth century. On a rock beside it is " A.R." neatly picked out with the point of a mason's hammer ; and these letters, which may be the initials of the builder of the bield, are also lichened. Near the Barnspike inscription masons have been at work chiselling wedge-holes to rive lintels and gateposts from the surface-rock ; and there also are modern initials, " T.P." similarly picked, and similarly lichened over. Indeed, lichen goes for little in determining age on this rock.

" Hessil " is not to be found : but we give copies from tracings of the other words as they now appear.

They have been lately scratched over by some visitor, but the rock is so hard that the knife-point makes only a faint impression. The cutting is not broad and soft, like the runes on the cross ; it is just what we could imitate with a bradawl and mallet ; and the two inscriptions seem done by the same person, though perhaps at different times.

From simple inspection we should take them to be forgeries, and we notice that both are in crannies of the rock where a person could be safe from observation by shepherd or gamekeeper while he " risted his runes " ; and an hour would be ample for the longer job of the two. The position in the cranny would shield the fresh carving from immediate observation until it began to be lichened over. A little milk, too, hastens the growth.

By an examination of the wording our suspicions are confirmed.

With all respect for bygone authorities, we read in the Barnspike inscription :—

> Baranr hraita at Killhes Bueth
> is uas tauthr i triku Rab
> te Vaulks at Fetriana nu
> Llanerkast.

" Baran wrote for Gilles Bueth, who was killed (daudr, Icelandic for ' dead ') in truce [by] Robert de Vaux at Fetriana, now Laner-cost."

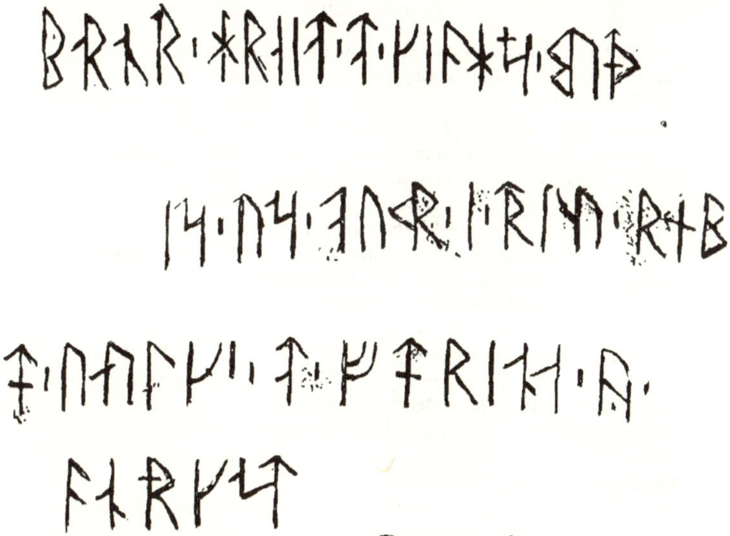

Barnspike

Hazelgill

THE RUNES ON THE ROCKS,

BEWCASTLE.

The writer has overdone his twig-runes, and put the short late S
at the end of *Vaulks*, while using the long early form elsewhere.
He had no D or G, and wrote *Killhes* for Gilles ; *tauthr* for dauthr,
and, we take it, *te* for de. The dialect is, as Stephens remarked,
strange. The shape of the runes, and the formula *hraita at*, are
copied from Maughan's (erroneous) transcript of the Dolfin inscription, given in the 1857 memoir.

We need not stop to ask whether Denton's " Gilles Bueth " was
a form of the name which a rune-writing 12th century man would
use ; or whether he would call Rɔbertus de Vallibus, Robert de
Vaulx, Hrodbert of the Dales, Dala-Hrodbjartr, by the broad Scots
' Rab ' ; nor again, whether he would spell the name, found as
Lanercost in the 12th century Charter, with this double L, antici-
pating by a few centuries a doubtful etymology from the Welsh.
But in his *Petriana* he evidently tried to write " Petriana," being at
a loss for the runic for P, which is an uncommɔn letter, not given
in the list of later Runes in handbooks. And Petriana was one of
the Roman Stations on the Wall. Previous writers had thought it
was Castlesteads ; Maughan thought it was Lanercost. *Petriana nu
Llanerkast* !

Now the curious thing is that Maughan himself did not see this
point. He was delighted to find that the inscription justified the
legend of Gille Bueth, but he did not notice this other confirmation
of his own theories, so kindly or so maliciously supplied. He, at
any rate, was not the forger of the inscription.

The other " rock-risting " we read :—

Askr hrita at Hesat el Kil himthika, in which perhaps the *t* of
Hesat and the *l* of *el* have been transposed, making " Ask wrote for
Hesal and (et) Gil his house-carle." Here is Hessil : he came into
another line, we suppose, by mis-copying. *Himthika* is known as
a word in Danish runes ; Cleasby and Vigfusson refer to Rafn 184,
185, 197, 217, and 218 (s.v, *heimthegi*). Ask and Hesal and Gil are
obviously got out of Askerton and Hazelgill.

Now it was characteristic of Mr. Maughan that he looked for
personal names in place-names, following the late Mr. Robert
Ferguson, whose book on *the Northmen in Cumberland and Westmorland* appeared in 1856. In the Beckermet inscription we have seen
how Maughan found his " queen Arlec " at Arlecdon and her son at
Frizington. In the same way we have had Baran evolved from
Barnspike : for the statesman family of Barron could not have got
their name from a 12th century Baranr ; that is not the way
in which surnames originated.

Mr. Maughan had been for years the enthusiastic Runologist of
the countryside, eagerly expounding the Bewcastle Cross, circulating

among his parishioners the story here retold, talking to all and sundry about his theories on Petriana and place-names. In some other antiquarian matters he is known to have been deceived. It was on his authority that the Maiden Way north of Bewcastle was laid down in the Ordnance-map, with many forts, etc., which recent investigation has shown to be imaginary. (Compare his paper on "the Maiden Way," *Archæological Journal*, no. 41, with *Transactions*, C. & W. A. & A. Soc., vol. XV., part II., p. 344, etc.) There is reason to think that he was the victim, especially in his later years, of a series of practical jokes. Old roads, pavements, ruined forts (cottages) were found for him, by the zeal or roguery of his neighbours; and these runes are their creation. They are not the work of a Runic scholar; they were concocted by a clever Cumbrian who had read the Rector's papers, heard his talk, perhaps used his books, and, like his countrymen, laughed at enthusiasm and loved a joke.

BEWCASTLE.

THE DIAL.

On the south face of the cross, in the middle of a panel containing a bas-relief of foliage, and under the name of Ecgfrith in runes, is a sun-dial. It is part of the original design and construction of the monument; for there has been no patching or piecing of the stone. The dial is in high relief, and the substance of it has been left unremoved in the first carving. The flow of lines and harmony of composition show that it was intended by the artist to fit in among the patterns of the cross.

If the cross dates from the 7th century, so does the dial; and this is not so extraordinary as it might seem, for sun-dials of Anglo-Saxon age are not wanting in other places. The Yorkshire dials were discussed by Father Haigh in the *Yorkshire Archæological and Topographical Journal* (parts 17 and 18, 1877). A portable dial with runes, found at Cleobury Mortimer in Shropshire, was dated by Professor Stephens from the 6th century (*Old-Northern Runic Monuments*, part iii., p. 161). The Kirkdale dial (figured by Bishop Browne, *Conversion of the Heptarchy* p. 195) puts the matter beyond dispute by its Anglo-Saxon inscription : " This is the sun's mark at every time."

Mr. Calverley, in his paper on " Some Ancient Dials in the Diocese of Carlisle " (1884) named and figured a series of examples from Bolton in Westmorland, Caldbeck, Dearham, Isel, Kirkoswald, Milburn, Newton Arlosh and Torpenhow, which, with one or two additional instances, will be found under their localities in the course of our work. It is not to be understood that they are all pre-Norman, but they are of the type which was known and used in pre-Norman days.

Figures and descriptions of rayed circles, and of circles without rays, and rays without circles, are given by Mr. W. Andrews in the *Archæological Journal.* He thinks they are not dials, because " the rays are equidistant, or nearly so, and consequently do not correspond to the hour-lines upon a dial. Also no figures are engraved." He connects them with cup-markings found in England, Germany, Switzerland and Sweden, " usually on the south side of churches, near an entrance, and not beyond the height of a man's

THE ANGLIAN DIAL.

BEWCASTLE.

(TO FACE P. 54.)

arm. These cups are believed to possess healing virtues." Of the rayed circles he concludes that " although they are not sun-dials, they may possibly in some way symbolize the sun."

In reply it might be said that accuracy was hardly needed in these ancient dials ; twenty minutes are nothing to people without trains or watches. Figures were not required, any more than they are on a watch ; one knows the time without reading the numbers. But considering that the mediævals and pre-mediævals continually used paint on their sculptures, we can hardly say how far these scratches might not have been completed with colour.

As to their present position, we know that in many cases the stones on which they were cut have been re-set ; which accounts for their being in groups, or upside down, or on the wrong side of a church. Where they occur on the evidently untouched jambs or capitals of a priest's door, they seem to be *in situ*, and intended as dials.

They must not be confused with a great variety of mason's marks ; for instance, the " pairs of compasses " at Kirkoswald, and perhaps some of the empty circles figured by Mr. Andrews.

Some apparent irregularity and rudeness in the figures may be taken as the result of the fact, found by experiment, that the wall on which the dial was to be made did not face due south. For instance, at Kirkoswald the wall faces east of south, and the noon-mark is therefore the ray which seems to indicate one o'clock ; at Caldbeck the little cross that seems to mark the noon is not vertically under the centre, as if the dial were intended to face a little to the west ; or was found to do so after it had been cut.

Mr. Maughan, and Professor Stephens following him, say that the principal time divisions on this Bewcastle dial are marked by crosses. Our sketch, however, represents it as at present visible to the naked eye, from the top of a step-ladder placed over against it.

Perhaps the little twig under the dial has been taken for a cross, or meant as an ornamental form of one.

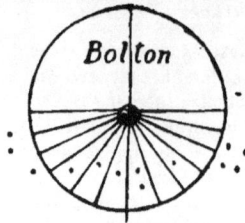

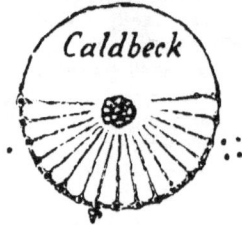

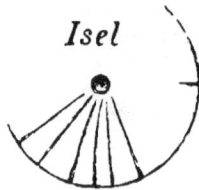

VERTICAL SUN-DIALS

AT VARIOUS SITES.

BOLTON.

(WESTMORLAND.)

THE DIAL.

In his paper on Dials, Mr. Calverley gave a sketch by Mr. J. G. Goodchild, F.G.S., etc., of one "built into the south face of Bolton Church, Westmorland; south-west angle"; adding, "this is not its original position."
As the illustrations to that paper are now out of print, we have re-drawn the dials mentioned, from new sketches on the spot. In this fine specimen at Bolton we have added the group of four dots opposite the ray marking 4 p.m., as at Caldbeck; compare also the " N " on the window-jamb at Isel Church (see under ' Isel ').

This dial is incised on a red sandstone block; the circle measuring 6 inches in diameter.

THE NORMAN CAPITALS.

All Saints', Bolton, is an early 12th century church, with a Norman doorway, interesting for its pattern of six-petalled rosettes, and for its rude capitals ; of which the western one bears a figure holding a hammer in one hand and an axe in the other ; and the eastern capital has a strange person with wings, perhaps an angel.

BOLTON.

The Norman Knights.

On the north side of the church is built into the wall, above a window, a bas-relief of which an illustration is given. It is of red sandstone, 26 inches by 16½, roughly chiselled, but cut deep into the stone, leaving a frame in high relief round the picture. The surfaces are flat and show no detail, but the contours tell the tale. Two knights in tall, pointed helmets, and with the kite-shaped shields and lances of the reign of Henry II., are fighting on horse-back. One, the smaller and inferior in rank, for his lance bears no banner, has broken the guard of the other, who flings up his shield and drops his lance to receive the point of the conqueror's full in his face, in the vulnerable spot under the nasal of his helmet. The horses are very rudely drawn.

The Norman Inscription.

Adjoining this slab is another, apparently the companion to it, built into the wall; measuring 21 by 13½ inches, and lettered in uncial letters with an inscription hitherto unexplained.

+ DS LVRREN DE.WERE

DVN:qS:HOM ES ·:· DE.BO

ELTVN: +· II ·OMRS:QV

SeAT IF MV·R·ESNE
LVRLAL VV R: OS
+ RA.T:O N V RAM
      D S L V R H E I

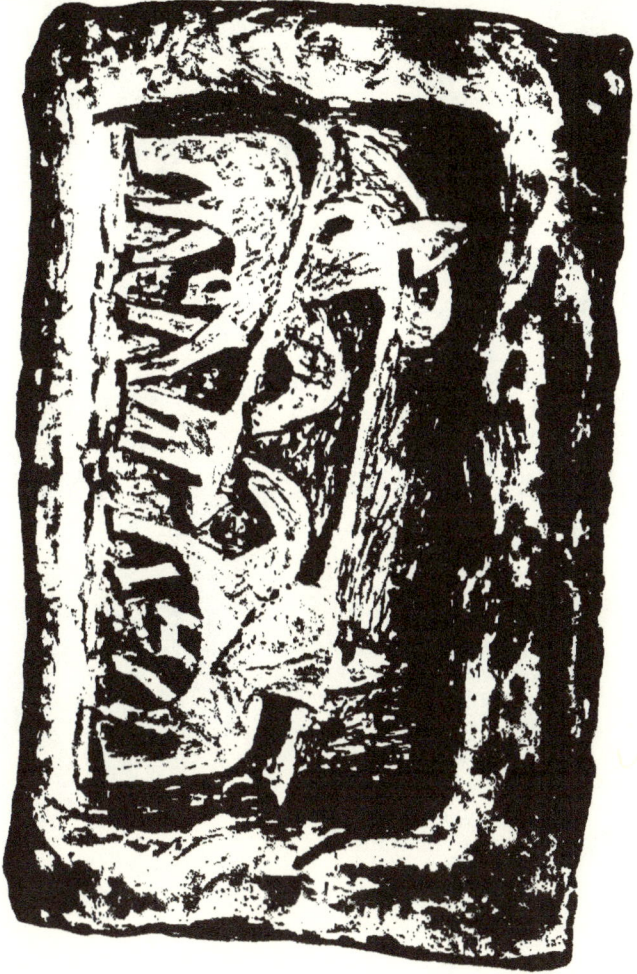

THE NORMAN KNIGHTS,
BOLTON.

(TO FACE P. 58.)

THE HOGBACK, AS SEEN FROM INSIDE THE CHURCH.

ST. MICHAEL'S, BONGATE, APPLEBY.

(TO FACE P. 59.)

BONGATE, APPLEBY.

HOGBACK.

THE church of St. Michael at Appleby stands to the east of the river, away from the castle and mediæval town, in the quarter called " Old Appleby " or Bongate, *i.e.*, the gate or road of the bondmen, or else of the *Böndr* (*plural* of *bóndi*, old Norse for farmer) —*Bónda-gata*. This was the original Scandinavian Apple-by which gave its name to Apelbiscire long before the Norman castle and its town were built; and the church of St. Michael is on a pre-Norman site,—the story of its removal from the Holme notwithstanding,— and its walls contain masonry thought to be " Saxon." The ancient north doorway is later, a 12th century arch of a curious horseshoe curve, built over a great stone used as a lintel, which Mr. Calverley, in 1885, recognized as a pre-Norman Hogback. Our sketch below shows the structure of this arch as seen from the outside, with the modern filling of the doorway. The Hogback, cut out for the voussoirs and split by the superincumbent weight, is of red sandstone, 75 inches in length, and 18 in greatest height, by about 8 inches in thickness. Some convolutions of its ornament and a few of the *tegulæ* of the shrine-roof can be seen, but most of the surface has flaked away, and before long all trace of pattern will disappear. On the inside, however, a part of the surface, measuring 38 by 16 inches, is visible, the rest being hidden by stones and plaster. The sculpture is bold work, picked out or very roughly chiselled.

BRIDEKIRK.

SPIRAL CROSS-HEAD.

O F what was once a cross only a part of the head remains ; but enough to show that it was of the early spiral-patterned type, in white sandstone. The boss is surrounded with a double raised ring, connected by an arm with a smaller boss, like the fragment here figured from Cross Canonby. The reverse has a flatter boss and a single raised ring.

The measurements are: radius from the centre of the boss 8½ inches ; thickness 3½ inches. The whole fragment measures 13 by 9 inches.

SUPPOSED HOGBACK.

There is also in the churchyard, among many mediæval grave-slabs and fragments of sculpture which do not come into our series, a stone which Mr. Calverley at one time thought might be a hog-back ; but on moving it he found that it bore no ornament by which it could be classed. It is, however, of a type which may represent, like a stone at Plumbland, the transition between hogback and grave-slab. It is rounded on the upper side as if semi-cylindrical, but coffin-shaped, tapering sharply from the shoulder to the head, and less sharply towards the foot. At the shoulder it is 14 inches broad and 8 inches thick ; 61½ inches in length.

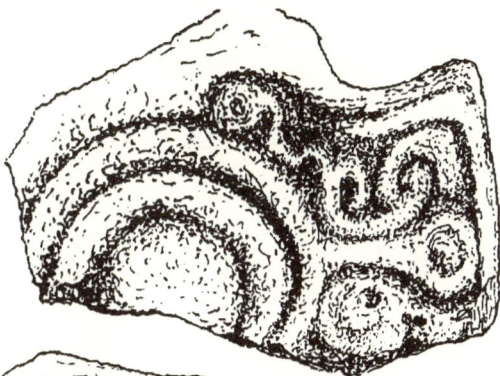

FACE.

REVERSE.

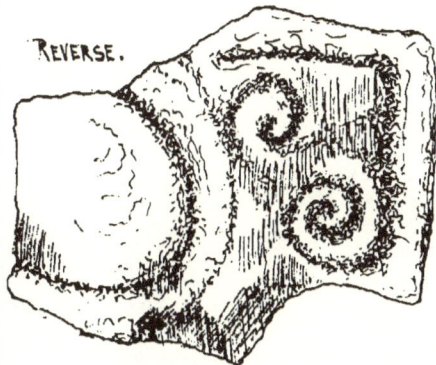

FRAGMENT of CROSS-
-HEAD at
BRIDE KIRK.

CROSS-
CANONBY

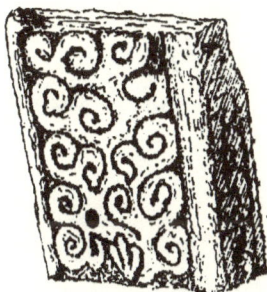

FRAGMENT of CROSS SHAFT. two sides.

ISELL

(TO FACE P. 60.)

BRIDEKIRK.

The Tympanum.

The south doorway of Bridekirk Church was, with other arches and doorways of the old church, carefully removed and re-inserted in the new building to the west of the ancient site. In the circular head of this doorway is the sculpture, for the sketch of which we are indebted to Mr. W. G. Collingwood, who says that the bas-relief is like others of the eleventh century in France and Italy, but ruder. Comparison with well-known Saxon manuscripts of early eleventh century shews that the double peaked beard was then in fashion, and went out when the Normans came. But it came in again for the image of Christ, in the thirteenth century, as alternative with the full beard. The soft red sandstone has perished, so that we can scarcely pass judgment on the original state of the work, but at first glance it appears to be too rude for thirteenth century. On the other hand, what evidence have we of Saxon art such as this appears to represent in the early eleventh century in Cumberland ?

The Byzantines put a glorified Christ over the door from the porch to the church, but the Christ is throned with gospels opened.* We should hesitate to name the Bridekirk Tympanum an ascension or a resurrection scene, being only certain that it shows the Christ in glory, with double beard and divided locks flowing over either shoulder, nimbed and fully draped, in the attitude of blessing and within a vesica. The stone is too much decayed to shew whether the Book of the Gospels was held in the left hand or to give us the exact display of the right hand; and the lower part has been cut away, so that it is impossible to say whether the figure is or is not "throned," seated on the rainbow.

It was not carved for its present purpose, the lower part

---

* Byz. Guide to Painting. Didron (Ed. Stokes) II. 390.

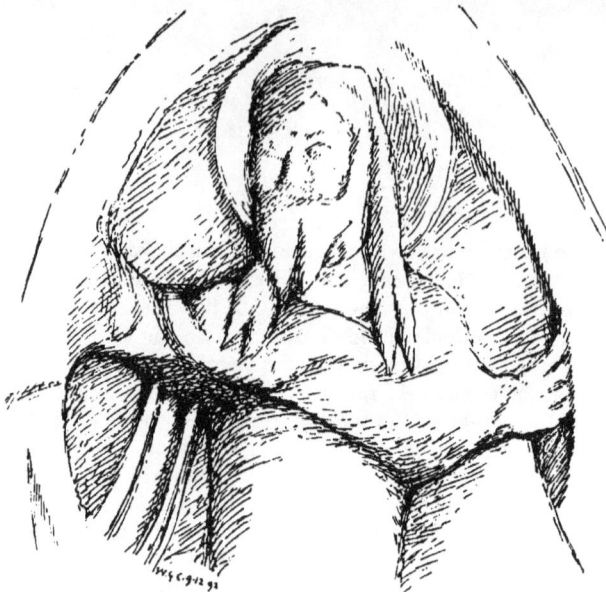

The Tympanum, BRIDEKIRK.

having been cut away to suit a door with flattened circular head at some period before its removal from the old building. It measures 5 feet 9 inches across the bottom, is 7½ inches thick, and is broken through the right shoulder vertically. The line of a more pointed arch seems to have been cut on the left side up to the right arm, as though the mason had begun to make the whole stone into the heading of a pointed arch. The material is red sandstone, whereas the other mason work of the old doorway is of light coloured sandstone. The foreman of the builders of the new church says that it was taken out of the wall of the old church, about the centre of the building near to the chancel arch, out of the walling stones, not out of the foundations; that it was buried for some time in soil to remove the whitewash; that very little, if any, chiselling was done to it before re-fixing in present position, and that the work was done by the foreman him-self, Mr. T. Robinson. The only chisel marks which appear are a few slight marks on the under side to the right hand.

In vol. XXIII. of *The Antiquary*, Feb., 1891, there is a short account of a Tympanum at Elstow, Bedfordshire. The writer, Mr. Geo. Bailey, records his impression and conviction that this old stone must owe its origin to the period embracing the latter part of the tenth and the early part of the eleventh centuries, and states that the draperies and general character of the work are almost identical with those of the Benedic-tional of St. Æthelwold, written for him during the time he was Bishop of Winchester, between the years 963 and 984, by Godemann, afterwards Abbot of Thorney, 970 (I find), and finely copied in vol. XXIV. of *Archæologia*. On con-sulting these drawings I find no less than eight illustrations in which the chief figures are included within the *vesica piscis*. In six out of the eight this figure is the Christ, the Son of Man in triumph, appearing to Stephen, His Baptism, appearing to the Apostles, the Ascension, and Christ in glory with flowing locks; the other two being the descent of the Holy Ghost and the Holy Trinity. The semi-circular arch is another characteristic, even though the particular arch at Elstow or Bridekirk may not be of the same date as what it encloses.

By the friendly aid of Mr. Senhouse, of Netherhall, and

the kindness of the brother of the compiler, Mr. Wigram, of Elstow, I have become the possessor of the *Chronicles of the Abbey of Elstow*, in which I find an illustrative plate and a description of the principal entrance to the Church. It is situated in the wall of the north aisle, and "consists of a semi-circular arch of five archivolts, resting on a curiously moulded *abacus* of attic type, which is ornamented with a deeply-cut chevron moulding, simple but effective in treatment, and in the angles of the piers are columns with cubical capitals, carved with bossed flutings. Above the arch, resting on a simple square cornice (and within another semi-circular arch) is a very quaint but beautiful carving, representing our Lord in the attitude of blessing, seated on the rainbow, and surrounded by an aureola, or glory. The right hand is raised, the fingers being held as in the Latin form of benediction, and the left holds a book; the dress of the figure consists of the *peplum*, or outer robe, plaited with small plaits, as was usual in the 11th and 12th centuries, and an inner robe with large sleeves; the head is environed with a cruciform *nimbus*. On the right of the central figure of the Saviour is that of St. Peter, holding the symbolic keys; on the left that of another Apostle, probably St. John. Each of these figures holds a book in the left hand, the right being raised, with the fingers extended in the attitude of admiration, and their heads are inclined towards their Lord as shewing reverence and deep attention. The whole of this carving is executed in low relief, and it is most probable that, like most other sculptured subjects of the period, it was richly coloured, and the background gilt. This remarkable portal, with its bas-relief, belongs evidently to the same original structure as do the early semi-circular arches of the nave; and it is most likely that, on the extension of the church in the thirteenth century, it was, as is the case in many other instances, spared by the masons of the period, and re-inserted, on account alike of its interest and its antiquity. Immediately over the carved tympanum is one of the small windows of the earlier aisle, and several fragments belonging to the older portions of the church are built into the walls."

The central figure at Elstow and our Bridekirk sculpture agree ; the nimbus, the flowing locks on either shoulder, the outer garment with its many folds, the inner garment seen at the neck and at the sleeves, at Bridekirk, and the *vesica*, as far as the waist, where the later mason has cut out his door head. Whether there were other figures on either side which have been hacked away to fit an arch for which it was not intended, or it was originally the centre of a gilded and coloured reredos, tomb, tympanum, or other structure, it is a remarkable relic to be found in this part of the country, and its likeness to a sculpture which can be pretty certainly dated as being at latest eleventh century, and situate at Elstow, adds greatly to its interest.

The Benedictine abbey,* convent, or monastery of Elstow, was founded about 1078 by Judith, niece of William the Conqueror. She was the widow of Waltheof, Earl of Northhampton and Huntingdon, and there is reason to conjecture that she was actuated by a desire to make such atonement as she could by the founding of the abbey for her share in causing her husband's death.

Waltheof, who was the son of Siward, Earl of Northumbria, in 1069, with his brother Cospatrick, joined the Danes in an attempt to subvert the recently established dynasty. This proved fruitless. In 1070 he submitted to the king, who, in the following year, confirmed him in his rights as Earl of Northampton and Huntingdon, and gave him his niece in marriage. Waltheof's brother Cospatrick, Earl of Northumberland, having, on some new disgust from William, retired into Scotland, where he received the Earldom of Dunbar from the bounty of Malcolm ; Waltheof had been appointed his successor in that important command, and seemed still to possess the confidence and friendship of his sovereign. In 1074 another conspiracy against the king was set on foot amongst the English nobles, and great pressure was brought to bear on Waltheof, in order to induce him to join it. This, however, he refused to do, though at the same time he pledged his word that he would not betray their design. The plot somehow reached the ears of Judith ; she

---

* *Chronicles of the Abbey of Elstow*, by the Rev. S. R. Wigram, M.A.

informed her uncle, and he had the unfortunate Waltheof imprisoned at Winchester, where, after the lapse of a year, he
was beheaded, May 31st, 1075. Fifteen days later his body
was, by the king's permission, obtained through the inter-
cession of Judith, disinterred by Ulfketyl, Abbot of Crowland,
and buried in the chapter house of that abbey. The Earldom of Northumberland at this time embraced Cumberland,
which was a principal abode of the Danes, and it would
seem that the earls had, of necessity, strong seats here
between the mountains and the Solway. Uchtred,* Earl of
Northumberland, not long before Canute's assumption of the
English Crown, in alliance with the Danes, began to commit
depredations in Cumberland, but was defeated after a sharp
combat, near Burgh-upon-Sands, by Malcolm, King of
Scotland. The site of a castle is still pointed out at Ough-
terside, in the parish of Aspatria, known for several centuries
as *Uchter-sat* (Uchtred's seat). Cockermouth Castle appears
to be the chief stronghold in Allerdale-above-Derwent, but it
was not until the parcelling out of the lands after the Conquest that the baron shifted his residence from Papcastle to
Cockermouth Castle, which is said to have been built largely
out of the ruins of Papcastle. On the high ground between
Aspatria and Papcastle is one of the ancient beacons so
necessary in early times on these borders, Moothay or Moota.
The wardens of these marches never rested long from the
days of King Rhydderch Hael to those of Edward I., and it
is not likely that Judith's husband could succeed his brother
and his father Siward in the earldom without Judith herself
becoming acquainted with so important a position. Bridekirk Church is the parish church of Papcastle, where
Waltheof must have had a strongly guarded seat not far
from the mountains, as nearer the sea he would also have the
seat still bearing the name of a former earl, Uchtred.

When Waltheof had become sainted on account of the
wonders done at Crowland Abbey immediately after his
burial, as well as for the holy life he had led during his

---

* Lysons, from Fordun. [But Uchtred had done much more ; in 1000 he had
given Malcolm a crushing defeat: see Freeman's *Norman Conquest* I., p.
329 and Skene's *Celtic Scotland* I., p. 385, quoting the Ulster Annals and
Simeon of Durham, " de obsessione Dunelm."]

imprisonment at Winchester, and the honour in which he
was held by all the English (of whom he was looked upon as
the last champion), what wonder can there be if Judith
his wife should make amends as far as possible for his loss,
and lighten a little the burden of the Norman yoke, by re-
building or beautifying the ancient church of Saint Bridget,
which had suffered much in the many ravagings and
plunderings from the effects of which none had escaped in
those terrible days.

BRIDEKIRK.

THE FONT.

As an interlaced and Runic Monument, the Font at Bridekirk comes into the scope of our work; and beside being a fine piece of 12th century work it is worth including, if only for comparison with the other forms of art which we have in review.

It was beautifully engraved by the Lysons for their History of Cumberland; but, like all the illustrations of the time, their pictures give it rather too classical an aspect, and lose something of the grotesque vigour of the old Northumbrian craftsman. It was described also, with a woodcut, by Prof. George Stephens, in his *Old-Northern Runic Monuments*.

Quoting from Mr. Henry Howard's paper, read to the Society of Antiquaries on May 14th, 1801, he says that there was a tradition of its removal from Papcastle to Bridekirk. Father Haigh and Professor Stephens agreed in the main in the reading of the runes, which have been variously translated by earlier students.

+ RIKARTH HE ME IWROKT(E)
AND TO THIS MERTHE GERNR ME BROKTE

i.e., " Richard, he me wrought, and to this beauty carefully me brought." The inscription, he says, is a mixture of Scandinavian Runes and Early English, and points to a strong Scandinavian element in the population. The dialect and style make it 12th century. Our fac-simile is reduced from a careful tracing which may be verified in the photograph (facing page 71.)

THE FONT.

BRIDEKIRK.

(TO FACE P. 68.)

DETAIL OF THE FONT.
BRIDEKIRK.

(TO FACE P. 69.)

In his third part, Stephens noted that a certain Richard of
Durham was a famous architect and sculptor, living about 1120-1180.
Of him Reginald of Durham tells the story that he owned a relic,
a bit of St. Cuthbert's chasuble, and carried it about with him
in a silken bag. One day while he was working at Norham Castle,
a French priest stole the bag, and opening it was disgusted to
find nothing but a scrap of rag. He threw it on the fire, but it
would not burn; and when Richard came back after two hours, there
it was! Richard was a man of substance, and the most famous
artist of his time in North England. Stephens was therefore
inclined to believe that it was he who carved this font, and wrote
the Runes upon it, somewhere about 1160. When we come to consider the rarity of highly artistic work in our district, at the period
to which this beautiful sculpture belongs, Stephens' attribution
seems less and less unlikely.

The top of the font measures 21¼ inches by 18; the narrowest
part below, 20 by 16; the base 27 by 23½. Its height is 34 inches.

Of the four sides, one bears the usual scene of the Baptism
of Christ, who is half immersed in the water rising up, as
it were, around him. St. John Baptist, with moustache and
camels-hair cloak, is pressing Him down to dip Him in the waves,
and the Dove reaches down from fruited intertwined boughs, very
like the treatment of contemporary work on the facade of St.
Martin's at Lucca, and elsewhere. Above is a two-headed dragon,
in which it is difficult to see any definite symbolism; and the
pellets, some plain, some petalled, and some revolving (like
svastikas grown by a gardener into composite flowers) seem to be
inserted with no further intention than to break up the background,
which 12th century taste, unlike the closed-up composition of
earlier art, often left vacant.

Part of the carving on the opposite side of the font has been
sketched on a larger scale, to show how the artist made use of
the spaces of background as throwing the delicate patterns into
broad relief. This is a development of the use of drill-holes in
our Beckermet St. John's fragments. As Richard treats it here
it is a very successful trick. The creatures and the orb they
are supporting—the griffin with firmness and the water-monster
with apparent spite—stand out in wonderful softness and substance;
and the Greek-Italian leaf-moulding which frames them gains
an almost transparent delicacy from its contrast with the deep-cut
blackness of the cornery patches of ground.

The Adam and Eve side we have sketched as well as it can now
be done while the font stands so near the wall. Lysons' engraving,
fine as it is, gives no wavy edge to the flaming sword, and

prettifies the faces and figures quite out of their "Gothic" character. The story is the usual and obvious one: "As in Adam all died," so in Baptism the new life is given. Perhaps the two monsters with the orb symbolise this also. The griffin, though said in a bestiary (J. Romilly Allen's *Christian Symbolism*, p. 370) to signify the devil, elsewhere (*ibid.* p. 285) carries souls up to heaven. In Dante's vision (*Purgatorio XXIX*) a Griffin draws the heavenly chariot; Didron says it means the Pope, others intrepret it as the Christ; Ruskin, in his famous passage on the Griffin of Verona (*Modern Painters*, III., chap. 8) shows that it means simply the Divine Spirit in regenerate man, which here upholds the Sun of life. So also does Cetus, Leviathan, the nature-power of water; but in spite of itself. See it writhing into knots, gnawing fiercely at the fire it would extinguish and yet compelled into service! For what says the gospel? "Except a man be born of Water,—and of the Spirit . . ."

That is hardly straining interpretation. A thoughtful artist, in an age when symbols were used and understood, might well have intended something of the sort. But the Adam and Eve panel contains a bit of artistic imagination which marks our Richard as a real poet. You must not mind that the hands are too large, or that the anatomy is childish: there is expression in the attitudes and faces; and that is what people looked for in those days. The tree is not natural, but it is the old typical tree of life,—the date-palm of Oriental Eden in Mesopotamian tradition, come down through generations of Greek art,—Cypriot, Attic, Byzantine, and somehow wandered overseas to Northern England: the date-palm without the soma-tendrils and without the serpent; not the temptation of knowledge and intoxication of power, but the Heaven-on-Earth that was lost at the Fall.

These things being understood, we can feel how freshly and powerfully the old tale is told. Our artist has seen it all: the angel, no winged shadow; there are dreams enough to play with elsewhere in our work; this is how it was: a real person, dressed like a queen, beckons them away, menacing, but not smiting, with the flickering blade. Adam comes forth in his coat of skins, deprecating, and very much afraid of the sword. But Eve, in a passion of regret, has fallen on her knees under the tree, and flings her arms about it with a bitter cry; do you see how her lips are parted, and brows drawn together in pain for her Paradise Lost? She does not care for the sword; she wants to stay!

Now the man who invented this knew a great deal more than most carvers of wood and stone; and even if our Richard learnt the motive from some Italian master, he was a true artist to have felt it so deeply and rendered it so strikingly.

ADAM AND EVE PANEL.

BRIDEKIRK.

(TO FACE P. 70.)

THE FONT.
BRIDEKIRK.

(TO FACE P. 71.)

For pure handicraft of stone-cutting, the last side, given from a photograph, is enough to show the way to many a modern carver. Its beauty is in the delicate surface, so gently undulating and crisply contrasted with deep-cut ground ; and on that surface such dainty curves so lightly struck by the same hand that drove the chisel elsewhere vigorously into the stone. Its design, too, is full of decorative invention, and no wonder it has been placed in full view as though it were the front of the font. But as it bears the artist's name and inscription and no direct religious teaching, it must have been meant for the back, or least prominent side of all. It is a wilderness of quaint notions, far different from the Anglian and Scandinavian motives of our earlier crosses. The little person munching grapes off the bough, and the many grotesque details, which are not *fairy* grotesque but *goblin* grotesque, show that we are now on the brink of mediæval Gothic : far away from the flowing robes and happy innocence of the Bewcastle Tree of Life imagined by Hwætred and his friends, five hundred years before Richard's more passionate and more complex art was so eagerly—*so gern*—" to this mirth brought."

BRIGHAM.

THE CROSS-SOCKET.

THE Brigham cross-socket is a peculiarly interesting
fragment, and, associated with other early monuments,
may be of value in the reading of one page of our history.
The stone is of light-coloured sandstone, and measures two
feet eleven inches by two feet six inches, with a thickness of
thirteen inches. It is cracked through the middle longitu-
dinally.

The top of the socket (A) has a cable moulding running
round it, similar to the one round the pedestal of the
Dearham font.

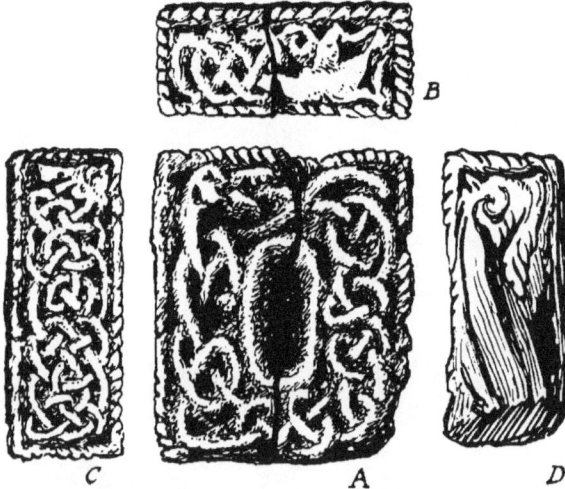

The place for the reception of the cross stem has a raised edge, and measures sixteen inches by eight inches, perforating the stone. Around it coils the serpent, with wolfish mouth and teeth and swollen throat, the tail of whom, after many windings and wanderings, finds refuge only in its own mouth. On the shortest of the three sculptured sides of the socket (B) is a strange figure, composed of a wide distended throat, over whose cavernous depths fang-like limbs appear to close with ominous strength, and the twisted tail of the serpent, which is partially restrained by an eight-shaped knot or bond.

On another side (C) the head of a horse takes the place of the wolfish head and wide throat of the two figures which I have already noticed, and the serpent-like intertwinings seem to consist of two bodies issuing from the neck of the horse, and becoming incorporated each with the other. These are also bound by a knot.

On the other side of the socket (D), part of which has crumbled away, there still remains the head of a wolf, nose resting on tail, which is curled round, not rampant, shewing teeth and claws, and having tail erect, as on the Dearham Font, yet certainly not dead, though calm, and under subjection. All the designs on this socket shew vigour, and at the same time restraint.

In connection with these symbols I would place the following extracts from Grimm's *Teutonic Mythology* (Stallybrass, vol. I., pages 244 and 312-315) :—

" Loki, in punishment of his misdeeds, is put in chains, but he is to be released again at the end of the world. One of his children, Fenrir, *i.e.*, himself in a second birth, pursues the moon in the shape of a wolf, and threatens to swallow her."

" Hel is no other than Loki's daughter, and, like him, a dreadful divinity. Rån receives the souls that die by water, Hel those on land, and Freyja those that fall in battle.

" The O.N. Hel (gen. Heljar) shows itself in the other Teutonic tongues even less doubtfully than Frigg and Freyja; only the personal notion has dropped away, and reduced itself to the local one of (Gothic) halja, (O.H.G.) hellia, (A.S.) hell, the nether world and place of punishment.

" Originally, Hellia is not death nor any evil being; she neither kills nor torments; she takes the souls of the departed and holds them with inexorable grip. The idea of a place evolved itself; the converted heathen applied it to the Christian underworld, the abode of the damned; all Teutonic nations have done this, from the first baptized Goths down to the Northmen, because that local notion already existed under heathenism.

" In the Edda, Hel is Loki's daughter by a giantess; she is sister to the wolf Fenrir, and to a monstrous snake," (the serpent Jörmungandr, which lies coiled around the world ash of Yggdrasil).

" Her dwelling is deep down in the darkness of the ground, under a root of the tree Yggdrasil, in Niflheim, the innermost part of which is therefore called Niflhel, there is her court (rann), there her halls. Her platter is named *Hûngr*, her knife *Sultr*, synonymous terms to denote her insatiable greed. The dead go down to her, *fara til Heljar*, strictly those only that have died of sickness or old age, not those fallen in fight, who people Valhalla.

" The unpitying nature of the Eddic Hel is expressly emphasized; what she once has she never gives back. She is of wolfish nature and extraction; to the wolf on the other hand a *hellish throat* is attributed.

" In the Danish popular belief Hel is a three-legged horse, that goes round the country, a harbinger of plague and pestilence. Originally it was no other than the *steed* on which the goddess posted over land, picking up the dead that were her due.

" A passage in Beowulf shows how the Anglo-Saxons retained perfectly the old meaning of the word. It says of the expiring Grendel, ' Hel took possession of him.'

" In Germany, too, the Mid. Ages still cherished the conception of a voracious, hungry, insatiable Hell. It sounds still more personal when she has *gaping yawning jaws* ascribed to her, like the wolf; pictures in the MS. of Cædmon represent her *simply* by a wide open mouth.

> " The raging tyrant
> he was like the Hell
> who the chasm (steep descent)

be-yawneth with her mouth
from heaven down to earth.
And yet to her it cannot hap
that she ever become full;
She is the insatiable cavern,
that neither now nor ever said
' that is what I cannot (manage).' "

Now there is such a representation in one of the windows of the Carlisle Cathedral. Also, such representations were usual in the miracle plays of mediæval days; and in the Brigham cross-socket we have a full representation of the incarnations of Loki, Fenrir, the Midgard-Snake, Hel, and the horse, all under bonds. And the cross-head, in similar symbolism, represents the victory over the powers of evil.

❊ ❊ ❊ ❊

The socket-stone, upstairs in the church tower, is carved with deep and smooth chiselling in high relief; unusual if not unique in execution.

BRIGHAM.

The Cross-Head at the Vicarage.

The cross-head (now over the vicarage porch) is of red
sandstone, and measures one foot nine inches across the
arms, and one foot five inches from the top to the fracture
at the waist of the figure. It is sculptured on both sides and
at the ends. The front (A) shews the head and body of a man

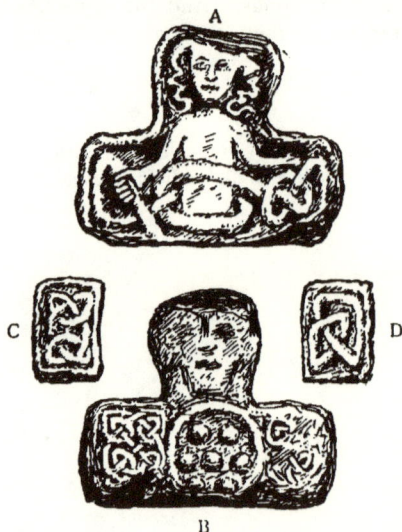

having long wavy hair, and grasping with his right hand
a serpent, whose body is coiled around his waist, and twisted
into the usual knot in the opposite arm of the cross; above
this knot the left hand of the figure is raised with open palm
in an attitude of victory.

On the reverse (B) seven small bosses, within a circle, a
head and two patterns of knot-work.

On the ends of the arms (C, D) knots.

BRIGHAM.

FRAGMENTS AT THE CHURCH.

We add notes on the fragments now (1899) in the chancel of Brigham church.

A and B represent two sides of the broken shaft of a rather late cross. The edges are ornamented with a double strap braided into the common plait of three. The fragment is of white freestone;

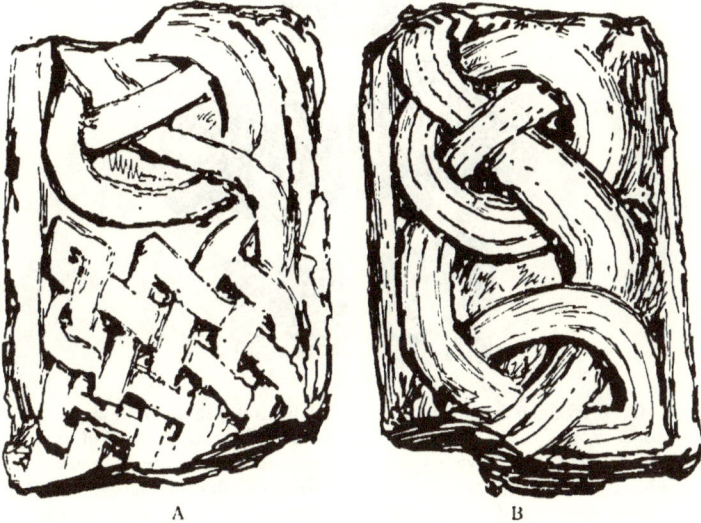

A   B

13¼ inches broad at the widest part, tapering to 12 inches; 4½ thick, and 18 inches long. It is neatly and smoothly carved, in low relief, with a flatter and emptier effect than is usual. The design of the interlacing is very degenerate. The bands vary greatly in breath, and they do not "follow on" as they ought. The ground shows in broad spaces, cut away flat.

The other pieces are :—

a. A cross-head of the hammer-head type, with incised cross on the uppermost limb. It is of limestone, 18 inches across the arms.

b and *c.* Two sides of a wheel cross-head, of which the three arms are left. Red sandstone; diameter, 16¼ inches; thickness, 7 inches. On one side is a central boss and ring, with a simple knot of interlacing on the arms. On the other the central boss is flatter and the ring incised; and incised double lines mark out the arms. It is rough picked work, not chiselled.

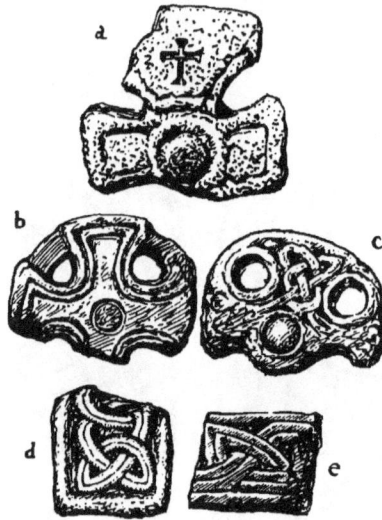

d. Interlaced fragment of very gritty and pebbly yellow sandstone, 7 by 7 by 5 inches. It has a double strap braided into a ring plait, the division of the strap lengthwise being marked with a fine line, but the edges of the strap are deeply marked; the whole very neatly chiselled, considering the roughness of the material, which is like the stone of Reycross on Stainmoor.

There is another bit of red sandstone, measuring 7 by 4 by 3½ inches, with a similar pattern in clean chiselled work. This is not figured, being like *d.*

e is another fragment; fine-grained stone; 6¼ inches long, 5 broad at the greatest breadth, but slightly tapering, and 3¼ thick. It is beautifully chiselled in low relief with a double strap in a plait of four on one side; on the other side a similar double strap in a plait of three; and on the edges single straps in plaits of three. There is the same angular character at the ends of the pattern, as in *c* and *d*.

These are all pre-Norman relics. The Norman apse and nave were assigned to 1080, and the font to 1250 or thereabouts, by the late Isaac Fletcher, M.P., F.R.S., in a paper contributed to *Trans.,* C. & W. A. & A. S., 1879.

Of this Norman church some sculptured bits are kept in the chancel; among them, a capital with the loose 12th century interlacing, and a snake with its tail hanging over the edge of the stone; very characteristic of the turn which decorative design took in transition to mediæval Gothic.

Both within and without the church there are many interesting grave-slabs of later date.

BROMFIELD.

The White Sandstone Cross.

ON the south side of the church of St. Mungo, in Bromfield churchyard, is a raised quadrangular platform, ascended by four red-sandstone steps. There is no cross-shaft, dial-pillar, or any other erection upon the platform, which was, in the last century, used for crying sales, things stolen or lost, &c., and giving notice of local and parish affairs.

Three of the steps were above ground ; one step was covered by the churchyard sod. The top of the platform was covered with turf, the growth of many years. At the south-west corner and in the south side of the second step had been cut a rectangular hole, into which had been fixed the stem of what seemed to have been a holy-water stoup. This remains *in situ*. The fragment, sometimes locally called "the chair," stands eleven inches high, and consists of what appears to be the base of a circular bowl, whose rim has been entirely demolished, supported by a rectangular pediment (sides, seven inches by eight inches) with a bead at the corners. Possibly a lower portion of the original pedestal has at some time been broken away. Hutchinson's History mentions the platform "of four or five quadrangular steps of stone that formed the base of the cross, long since destroyed," and also notices the "stone stool heretofore used and probably put up that public notices and proclamations might thence be given with more advantage."

The Rev. T. Lees, F.S.A., suggested that in earlier times, when the cross stood in its place, the reliquary might be placed upon this stone during the ceremonies which took place on the Sunday before Palm Sunday, or other processionals of the cross, when the children sang hymns, and a halt was made at different stations around the church.

White sandstone Cross Head.

W. S. CALVERLEY.

Fragments of British Cross,
S.t MUNGO,
BROMFIELD.

(TO FACE P. 80.)

There is a similar fragment fixed in an isolated red sandstone block lying in the churchyard of St. Kentigern, Aspatria. I have looked upon these remains as being holy water stoups, for use at early mission preaching stations, where crosses had been erected. In Cutts' *Sepulchral Slabs and Crosses*, plate V., fig. 2, is engraved a slab from Marisk, Richmondshire (date given as twelfth century) having four symbols ; on the right hand beneath the cross head, the textus or gospels ; on the left hand the chalice. Beneath the book is a symbol which Cutts says "may be the corporas case." " The remaining symbol," *i.e.*, the one beneath the chalice, he says, "is unexplained ; it may, perhaps, be a pyx." Now this figure is not as the others are, complete in itself, but it appears to be a square ornamented case, perhaps leather, with a curved loop on one side, by which it might be carried, and it is fixed upon a thin upright staff by which, as by a handle, it might be borne aloft in processions. This staff is placed in a square unornamented pediment, apparently resting upon the second step of the Calvary and rising a little above the highest step, thus well elevating the " pyx " or the reliquary, whichever it may be, in a position possibly alongside the holy water stoup, beneath the church-yard cross.

This memorial slab of a Richmondshire priest of the twelfth century seems to illustrate very clearly the uses of the fragments still preserved near the crosses which marked the sites of Christian mission stations of the time of SS. Ninian, Patrick, and Kentigern at Bromfield and at Aspatrick, now euphonized into Aspatria. Thinking that some of the stones used in the formation of the steps of this platform might prove to be portions of the ancient cross, and might still bear sculptures, the vicar of Bromfield, the Rev. R. Taylor, and I determined to examine them, and did so on June 4th, 1888. For this purpose we pared off the sod lying upon the top and raised the upper steps, which we were surprised to find presented the chamfered edges of old grave covers, and bore crosses incised and in relief of a plain or decorated character, with Calvary steps or window tracery, or both, and having the sword, the shears, the arrow, or parts of inscriptions appearing alongside.

These upper layers of stones were all grave slabs,
generally lying face downwards, but as each stone has
a broad end and a narrow one, and as one side only of each
is square with the ends, the other side making at the
head an acute angle with the end, and an obtuse angle at the
foot, some ingenuity was needed in fitting together the
material as a stepped platform, and so the stones were *sometimes* placed with the figured surface uppermost, in which
cases the chamfers and carvings were generally almost worn
away or were hidden under the superincumbent step. We
thought that some of the lower steps, the long stones of which
were hollow with foot wear, and especially those of the south
side where stood the stoup, might prove to be other than old
grave-covers used up again; but inspection shewed that the
socket into which the stoup was fitted had been worked in an
ancient grave-cover, six feet eight inches long, placed as the
second step from the ground. The whole platform was
formed around a core of earth and stone fragments. There
were twenty-three covers of different sizes, designs, and
dates, ranging from two to nearly seven feet in length, and
from the eleventh or early twelfth to the end of the fourteenth
century in date. The best of these were fixed erect against
the west wall within the church by the vicar; the others
were re-arranged as a platform as before.*

On excavating the core of the structure we found several
very small tomb slabs, about two feet long, some of them
bearing lines for the guide of the masons, as though fresh
and unfinished from the stone-cutter's yard. There were
also the two halves of a cylindrical pillar, split lengthwise
down the middle. These may have been the lower part of
a red sandstone pillar cross, or they may possibly have
been part of a column from the church. There were no red
sandstone sculptures which could be recognised as belonging
to such cross. Beneath these buried fragments we found
a mass of harder earth and *white* sandstone fragments. These
pieces of white sandstone, about a dozen in number, shewed
traces of sculpture, and beneath them we turned up the

---

* The mediæval grave-covers are figured and described by Mr. Calverley in
the *Transactions* of the C. & W. A. & A. S., vol. XI., article 12.

complete head of a white sandstone cross of the very early type, with central boss and ring, and a raised beading round the edges, the solid head and arms in one piece, the stone very much worn and weathered before being buried here.

The smaller pieces were put together and revealed the shoulders and part of the shaft of the cross. The cross had not only been broken up, but split down the middle sidewise before burial. One very small piece, which will be seen under the arm on the right hand in the drawing here given, being placed upon one of the pieces of the back part of the cross, revealed the curve beneath the arm containing the moulding. Further down, a solid piece of stone completed the relics which we were able to fix into place. These have been cemented together and placed by the vicar in the church, affixed to the wall behind the reading desk. The cross, as we now know it, is thirty-one inches high. The head is nine inches wide at top, fourteen inches across the arms, and six inches thick. The neck is nine inches across. The shoulders fifteen inches. The greatest thickness is seven and a half inches. The lower parts of the shaft have been worn away, as if by the sharpening upon it of a scythe or other iron implement.

The whole must have been exposed to the weather many hundred years before it was broken up and buried. This may, indeed, be the identical cross around which the British were gathered to listen to the Gospel and receive baptism before any stone church was raised, and even two hundred years before St. Kentigern the apostle of Strathclyde, whose name the present church bears, journeyed this way on his road into Wales in the sixth century.

Another fragment of pre-Norman times, a house-shaped (hog-back) tombstone, its roof ornamented with triangular tiles, has been built above the Norman arch inside the west doorway, as at Bongate, Cross-Canonby, and other places.

[The hog-back is too defaced to illustrate or describe in further detail.]

BROMFIELD.

The Interlaced Cross-Shaft.

At St. Mungo's Church, Bromfield, we meet with quite another type of cross-ornamentation. The stone is cut away so as to leave a series of horizontal projecting bands. The small fragment, one face and one edge of which is here given, was found by the vicar, the Rev. R. Taylor, broken up and buried beneath much mason's rubbish and the remains of the very ancient weather-worn white sandstone cross (figured above), in the centre of a platform surrounded by steps, which no doubt marked the site of the churchyard cross in its better days. The sculptor has had some type in view, but he has not been skilful enough to form the designs correctly. Interlaced or knot-work appears upon the face, upon the bands, down the sides, and in the ends of the horizontal bands. The edge is better done than the face, and the rosette, formed of two double rings with an interlacing knot, seen in the end of the upper horizontal band, has been perfect. The design in the end of the lower horizontal band is similar to one on the edge of the Rockcliff cross, that on the edge of the stone itself is similar to one on the standing cross at Aspatria. These remains consist of three pieces and have been fixed within the church porch for safety, by the vicar.

*   *   *   *

The dimensions of this shaft are : height, 30 inches; breadth across broadest band, 13½; thickness of broadest band, 5¼ inches. It is of soft red sandstone, and the work is not chiselled, but hacked out rather roughly.

In Mr. Calverley's drawing of the face (the left-hand figure in his plate,—not the edge of the shaft) the upper panel represents a different side from the lower panel, while the separate bit of ring-and-knot pattern is the ornament of the other side of that upper panel.

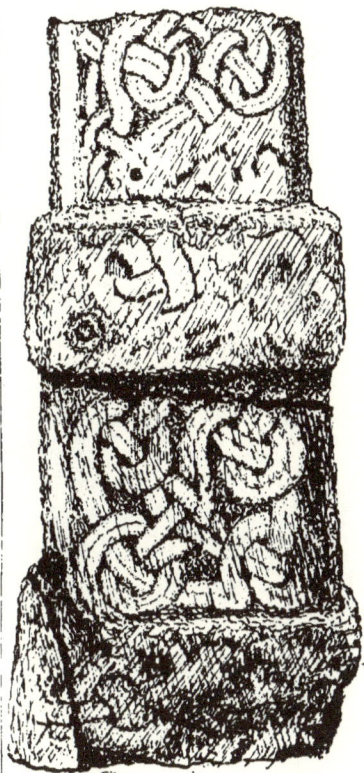

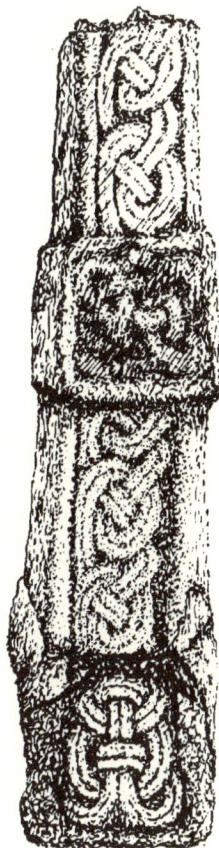

Bromfield. S! Mungo.

(TO FACE P. 84.)

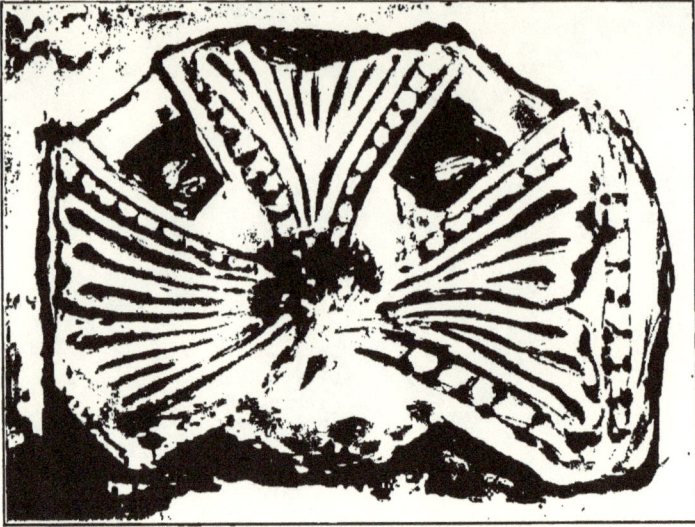

RED-SANDSTONE CROSS-HEAD.

BROMFIELD.

(TO FACE P. 85.)

BROMFIELD.

Two Cross-Heads.

Into the wall of the outbuildings (tool-house) on the left as you go through the garden gate to the Vicarage, two cross-heads have been built ; one of which is figured opposite. It is of red sandstone, 12 by 7 inches, finely chiselled ; and may be compared with a cross-head at Kirkby Stephen. It is probably one of our series of post-Norman " Resting Crosses."

The other, measuring about 12 by 14 inches, is a plain Maltese cross with a circle in the centre ; flat surfaces, no interlacing, and of the mediæval period. Among the grave-covers there are two instances of rudely incised ring-crosses of a very early-looking pattern ; which nevertheless are seen to be mediæval by the shears, etc., at the sides.

The tympanum of the Norman doorway, on its outer side, is ornamented with chequers like those on Bewcastle Cross ; only the little spaces alternately raised and sunk are not square, but oblong.

It may be mentioned that a well in the field to north of the church is known as St. Mungo's Well.

Bromfield church was restored in 1861 and again in 1894. On the former occasion it was found that the Norman church and its Norman chancel had been greatly altered when the transepts were added, and the chancel arch widened. At that time, no doubt, the 13th century tombstones were removed from their original positions and built up in the form of steps around the place of the cross in the churchyard. The Norman builders had already used the hog-back tombstones of some pre-Conquest lord to make a permanent centre, over which to build the arch of their south doorway. So that St. Mungo's at Bromfield offers a good instance of the continual re-modelling which so many churches have undergone.

BROMFIELD.

CROSS-HEAD AT HIGH AKETON, FROM BROMFIELD.

The cross-head, of which I here give a sketch, was
noticed by the Rev. Richard Taylor, Vicar of Bromfield,
on passing through the farmyard of High Aketon, in that
parish. It is of light-coloured sandstone; measures twenty-
one inches across, is four inches thick, and is built into an
outer wall. The arms of the cross pass through a circular
band ornamented with plaitwork of three strands, and they
protrude slightly. The head has been broken from the
shaft close beneath the circle. Instead of a boss occupying
the centre as at Dearham, the head of whose standing
cross this one much resembles, the head of a beast stretches
upwards and is held by a ring through the snout, within the
upper arm or limb of the cross. Each of the side arms
contains, as at Dearham, a design which may have been
intended to represent the Triquetra.

If reference be made to the great cross at Gosforth
the head of the beast will be seen on the shaft of the cross,
attacking the holy forces above the Triquetra in the arm
immediately over its open jaw. At Aketon the beast has
pressed upward and swallowed the holy sign and the boss
itself, even as the wolf swallowed Thor and Odin in that last
fight, but he is overcome at length, and we can hardly help
but be reminded of the wolf gagged and bound as represented
in another carving on the Gosforth cross, when we look at
the ring in the nose of this last aid to the reading of our early
Christian sculptured stones. The time has not come at which
we need date each work; rather let us gather together every
fragment as being of priceless value towards elucidating some
of the obscurities of our history.

Mrs. Dykes, of Red House, Keswick, kindly allows me
to say that the property, together with Crookdake Hall
adjoining, and once the home of Adam of Crookdake,

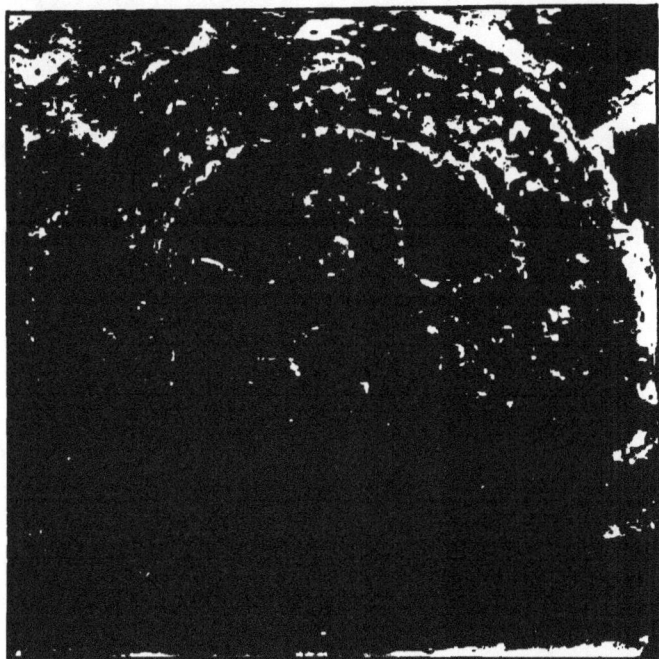

CROSS-HEAD AT HIGH AKETON

FROM BROMFIELD.

(TO FACE P. 86.)

whose tomb is in the transept of Bromfield Church, belongs to Mr. Dykes, of Dovenby Hall, and that she has no doubt that the cross-head was taken from Bromfield Church, but not from devotion to antiquities, as it is known by writings and by tradition in the family that the north transept of Bromfield Church, called the Crookdake Chapel, was utilised for the repairs of the farm houses on the estate by two possessors successively in the early part and middle of the last century. Mrs. Dykes has reason to believe that the chapel was in ruins, which might somewhat excuse the plunder.

These facts supplied by Mrs. Dykes are valuable, inasmuch as by their means we now know that there have been, in pre-Norman times, at least three crosses of different types at Bromfield Church; one of white sandstone,—the cross whose head we have here under consideration, and a red sandstone cross, smaller but somewhat of the same character as the Rockcliff cross.

The Vicar of Bromfield tells me that the chapel, sometime called the Crookdake Chapel, now the north transept, is the Lady Chapel, and that the chapel to the south of the chancel is the St. George's Chapel.*

---

* On this chapel see *Yorkshire Diaries & Autobiographies in the XVII. & XVIII. Cents.''* (Surtees Soc., 1886) pp. 45, 61, and 71.

BURTON IN KENDAL.

At the parish church of St. James, during restoration in 1844, was found the head of a wheel-cross. It was seen by Mr. T. Wilson in 1874 or 5 in a stable near the church. A shaft with figures in panels and on the reverse incised interlacing designs, a fragment supposed to be the neck of the same and another fragment were also photographed by Mrs. Sutcliffe, of Burton.

⁂

So far Mr. Calverley's notes. He afterwards took plaster-casts of the fragments, and Mr. Chalmers of Burton School made drawings. It is to Mr. Chalmers that the present safety of these relics is owing; he looked them up and placed them in the church, after long neglect. The shaft was not entirely cleared of mortar until 1899, when Mr. Chalmers and the present writer treated it with dilute acid, and brought out the pattern of the fourth side, shown in the plate facing page 89.

THE CROSS-HEAD.

Yellowish-white freestone; 14 inches in diameter; 6¼ in thickness. The holes are deeply sunk but not pierced; the designs is anything but symmetrical and regular; the execution rude, and hacked, not chiselled. The reverse is like our view, only the centre is sunk, not raised into a boss; making this a five-hole cross, which is rare in our district.

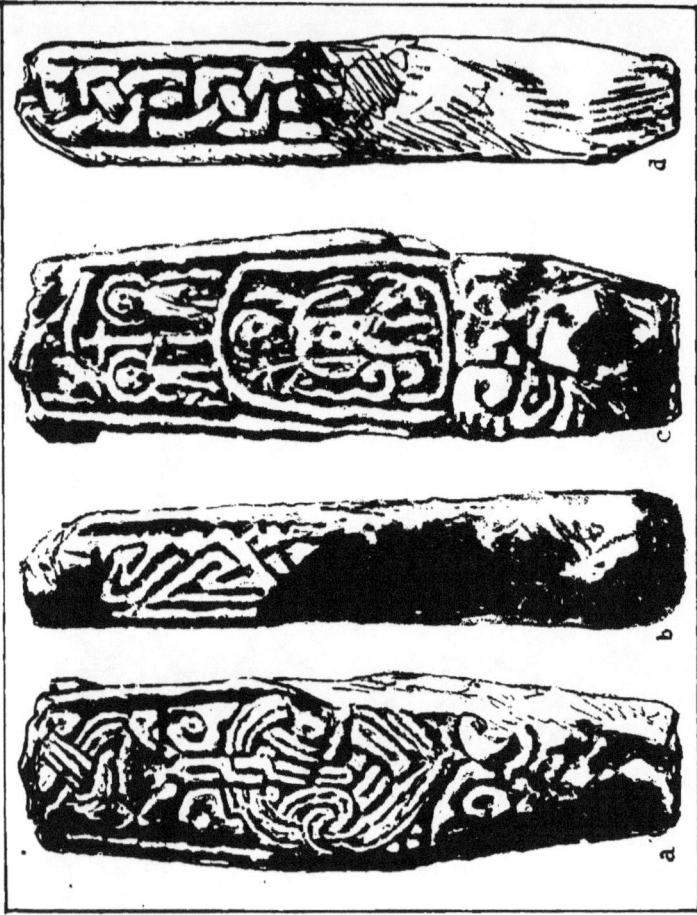

PRE-NORMAN CROSS-SHAFT.
BURTON-IN-KENDAL.

(TO FACE P. 89.)

BURTON.

THE SHAFT.

This greater shaft-fragment is of the same yellowish-white
freestone; 38 inches long by 10½ broad in the middle, tapering to
9 at the narrower end; 6½ inches thick, tapering to 6 at the top. The
work is also hacked out with the pick; key-pattern and chain-plait,
and florid interlaced devices of a late Scandinavian type, resembling
fibulæ of the Viking age.

The figures on the face of the shaft, though not well drawn
or well carved, seem to have been suggested by good work, as if
in reminiscence of good models; and they are interesting in their
obvious symbolism and "literary subject." In the middle is Christ,
risen or rising from the tomb, which is expressed by the arched
roof of the panel,—the cave of Gethsemane. He tramples on the
old serpent, whose feeble wings flutter at its neck, while its
head writhes round to bite the heel of Christ, and the tail twists
into knotted rings. Christ is naked, except for the loin-cloth,
which one can just make out in a good side light, though these
details are much worn. Even the anatomy of the figure is hinted
in rude touches, and a beard and long hair; there seems to be no
nimbus round the head. In the left hand He carries the palm of
victory, and in the right His symbolical sceptre-cross (as usual
in Resurrections), which here is bursting into leafage,—Aaron's
rod,—the Resurrection symbol.

Above, a male and female figure, John and Mary, as at Halton,
which this work in many points resembles, or perhaps two angels,
stand by the untenanted cross; one pointing to it as much as to
say "He is not here; He is risen."

Such, as one sits the morning long before this ancient grave-
stone, studying it with care, seems to be the meaning of its dumb
language: to forgotten mourners the hope of glory. One would
like to know who of the ante-Norman thanes or ladies of Kentdale,
Vikings from Galloway, it would seem,* in origin, and surely
stirring folk in a stirring time, deserved such kindly remembrance.
Or is this only one of the courtesies of the grave? It is hard to
think so.

---

* By the name Ninesergh,—the chalet of Ninian, a name brought from the
land of the Gallgael; and by their connection with Gospatric's house.

BURTON.

THE NECK FRAGMENT.

This is similar to the cross-head in material and execution; and measures 13 inches in length. Across the narrowest part of the neck it is 9 inches wide and 5 thick. It is not a part of one cross with the great shaft, for both have the spring of a head; but this head may belong to one or other of them; so that, as elsewhere, there must have been two (or more) similar crosses at Burton. It does not in the least follow that they were a pair, one at each end of a grave. Indeed a slight difference suggests that they were not closely contemporary, but one made in imitation of the other, as at Beckermet St. Bridget's. What is more natural than that a dying person or his friends should wish for a monument like one already known and admired?

BURTON.

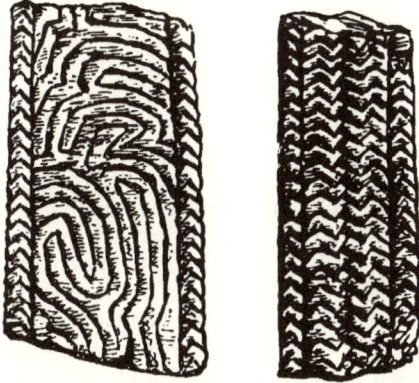

THE ZIG-ZAG FRAGMENT.

The last bit of a shaft we have here is evidently much later. It measures 15½ by 8 by 6 inches, and is of a finer-grained stone, very neatly chiselled; but cheap and poor in design, as if to get as much appearance of ornament as possible with the least expense of invention. The reverse and the other edge are like the edge shown, a mere zig-zag; suggesting Norman date, though seeming to belong to a cross of Saxon type. It is curious how the worm-cast style of the face anticipates the ugliest rustication-tricks of Renaissance architects.

At Burton there is also an old market-cross; which, however, does not come into the scope of our work.

CALDBECK.

SUN-DIAL.

A DIAL is cut on a stone built in the wall, to the east of the lintel of the priests' doorway, in the south side of the chancel of Caldbeck Church. The stone has been removed from some other window or door, or other place, and put in its present position when the lancet window was restored. I first discovered it on August 23, 1883. This is a most remarkable and interesting dial, and I hope this notice of it may lead to further profitable research. The circle is clearly cut, and each ray in the lower half is marked by a round hollow drilled into the stone. In the centre remains still the iron of the gnomon, which has been broken off; the lead which has been rammed well around it to keep it in its place has nails hammered into it. The centre ray, downwards, proceeds beyond the circle and takes the form of the cross. To the right, outside the circle, are four drill marks which remind one of the N on the Isel dials. To the left also may be seen one of these round drill holes, which appears to be of the same date as the dial, and intended for some real purpose. The number of rays and stops is *seventeen*, but one ray is evidently marked *beyond* the diameter, as in the lowest dial on the window at Isel (see *Isel*) making the number of divisions in the real half circle *sixteen*, in the whole "day-night" thirty-two, and thus bringing us into contact with the "octaval system" of time division, common among the Angles (*Yorkshire Dials*, p. 159), in which daynight is divided into eight equal parts, sub-divided into sixteen, and again sub-divided into thirty-two.

❊   ❊   ❊   ❊

The dial is figured in the plate opposite *Bolton*. It is 7 inches in diameter.

The church is of the 12th century, dedicated to St. Mungo whose well is shown hard by, in the steep bank of the rocky Caldbeck.

CARLISLE.

The Dolfin Runes.

IN 1855 Mr. Purday discovered a Runic inscription under the plaster and whitewash on the western wall of the south transept of the cathedral. Mr. Maughan, in July, 1855, suggested that it should be translated : " Dolfin (raised) this stone in sorrow for the soul of his son." In November of the same year Dr. Charlton of Newcastle read "Twelve idlers cut these marks on these stones." In 1857 Mr. Maughan amended his reading to : " Dolfin wrote this stone in memory of Ulfar," *at Ulfhara*. It was Prof. Stephens who cleverly read and rendered : (*Old-Northern Runic Monuments*, part II., p. 663).

TOLFINÆ (or H) ÜARAITA ThÆSI RÜNR A ThISI STAIN.

" Tolfinæ wrote these runes on this stone."
There was a famous Dolfin of Carlisle who governed the country until William Rufus drove him out in 1092; but it seems more likely that this Dolfin was a less important person. The inscription is not monumental, but only slightly scratched ; a *sgraffito*, in fact ; and may be the idle scribble of some " Norman" builder ; a Northman, it would seem by the dialect and form of lettering, and 11th century, Prof. Stephens thought, from the *üa* of *üaraita*,—" the only gradual melting away of the *w* or *gi* into the *y* or *i* of the Early English." Maughan's transcript, *hraita*, is like the similar word in the Barnspike and Hazelgill runes, which were evidently imitated from Maughan's woodcut of this.

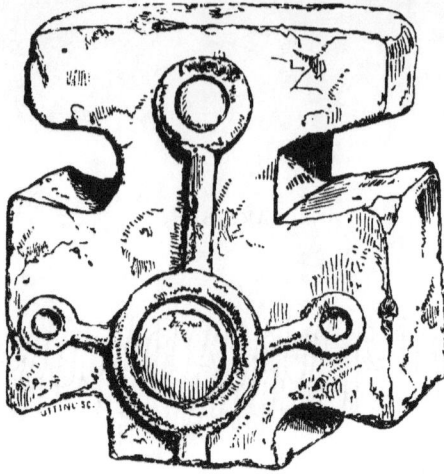

CROSS-HEAD, FOUND 1855.

FRAGMENT, FOUND 1857.

CARLISLE.

(95)

CARLISLE.

Two Anglian Cross-heads.

At a meeting of the Archæological Institute, February 3rd, 1855, a communication was made from Mr. C. H. Purday about the recent discovery of a sculptured cross or head-stone at Carlisle Cathedral, in the course of works then in progress. It lay imbedded in the masonry, in the south wall of the transept, which is Norman; though several alterations were made in this wall about the year 1300, when the Chapter House was built against the south front. Mr. Purday stated that the cross seemed to him to have been quite a low one, probably placed over a grave; the upper arrises were completely rounded off, as if by friction; the workmanship was extremely rude and irregular; the back of the cross was plain, with the exception of a small round knob or boss in the centre. Some persons had been disposed to regard this cross as of Saxon times, subsequent to the re-building of the church and city of Carlisle by Egfrid, King of Northumberland, in 680.

Mr. Westwood, in discussion, remarked that he was unable to recall any cross of pre-Norman date bearing resemblance to this fragment, and considered that it might possibly be assigned to the 12th century.

This cross-head is now in the room over St. Catherine's Chapel, Carlisle Cathedral.

It is of light coloured sandstone; 16½ inches in height, 15¾ in breadth, about 6 in thickness. It is evidently one of the series known at Bridekirk, Cross Canonby, and St. John's, Beckermet, which last connects it with the " spiral " type of which we have so many examples.

Our cut is from the *Archæological Journal* (vol. XII., p. 180), kindly lent by the Royal Archæological Institute through the Hon. Sec., Mr. A. H. Lyell, F.S.A. To the same source we are indebted for permission to copy Mr. Purday's illustration of the second cross at Carlisle (*Archæological Journal*, vol. XV., p. 85.)

At a meeting of the Archæological Institute on December 4th, 1857, Mr. Purday showed a drawing of another cross-fragment found in the cathedral precincts, Carlisle, in digging the foundations for an addition to Canon Harcourt's house. It bore part of an inscription which appeared to have been continued on the two sides of the head of the cross. The material is a light-coloured sand-stone, which, Mr. Purday remarks, had been used only in the oldest parts of the fabric of the cathedral. Its dimensions were : width, 12¾ inches ; height, 4¼ inches ; thickness, 3 inches ; being only the lateral arms of a cross-head.

Mr. Westwood dated it about 700. The forms of the letters resembled those of the Durham Book, the gospels in the book of St. Chad at Lichfield, and the gospels of MacRegol in the Bodleian Library, all of these being MSS. of that period. The peculiar form of *S* to be seen on one side of this fragment, after the cross which precedes a word, probably the name of a female, occurs in the Durham Book and in the great illuminated pages at the commencement of each gospel in the Book of St. Chad.

This fragment is now in the Fratry, Carlisle. It was no doubt rightly dated by Westwood, but the inscription has not been satis-factorily explained as yet.

FRONT.   BACK AND SIDE.

THE STANDING STONE

(Sometimes called Barbon Cross)

CASTERTON.

(TO FACE P. 97.)

CASTERTON.

THE Standing Stone, or Cross, is on the top of a green hill, the most considerable *howe* in this part of the valley of the Lune, not reckoning the great fells that form the dale ; and it commands a wide prospect, though it cannot be seen as you travel the road that passes it from Barbon to Kirkby Lonsdale. The site is a little to the south of the entrance to Whelprigg, and just above a level crossing on the railway line ; it is close to the boundary between the townships of Casterton and Barbon, and just within the former. According to Whellan (*Hist. of Cumb. and West.*, p. 890) it was found in a field and erected near the spot where it was discovered some time before 1859. There is no church near it ; a Roman road passed close by.

The cross is made of a rough slab of freestone, 4 feet high from the ground at the back ; its front, or carved side, is 44 inches tall. The carved part bearing the cross is 21½ inches high and 15¼ inches across the arms of the cross. The neck of the stone is 8 inches broad at its narrowest and 6 inches thick; higher up it thickens to 7 inches. The ordnance mark is cut on the top of the stone.

As to the intention of the carving, it was thought at one time,—and Mr. Calverley acquiesced in the theory so far as to read a paper (which was not published) on that view,—that the stone was at first rudely hacked into the semblance of a heathen symbol, and afterwards sanctified by the carving of a cross to obliterate the pagan device.

A careful examination shows, however, that all the carving visible on the stone has been done at one time and with one intention. The shape of the cross has been skilfully picked out with a multitude of hacking touches, leaving a dotted and pitted surface, with which the smooth natural face of the split stone contrasts effectively and picturesquely, as in the manner of 17th century wood-carving. The arms are indeed more deeply outlined above than below, but this is natural ; the obvious requirement in cutting a cross is to get the head free ; and there is no trace of cutting on the *face* of the upper limb of the cross, just above the arms, as there must have been if the whole were originally intended to represent a cone on the top of a pillar. The work was continued round the edges of the stone both above and below the arms, and on the back of the slab, evidently with the intention of carving a similar cross on both sides. For some reason, this was not carried out ; but the sculpture is certainly left incomplete.

This cross is unique in our district. It bears some little resemblance to that figured by Dr. Joseph Anderson in *Scotland in Early Christian Times*, second series, fig. 60, at Hawkhill, Alloa, near which a number of interments were found :. and though it has not the so-called Celtic hollows at the intersection of the arms, it is of the shape of the early incised crosses at Laggangarn, Wigton-shire (*ibid.* p. 89).

The situation suggests the interment of a chief after battle, for which this is a likely spot ; and it might reward exploration.

CASTLE SOWERBY.

" TWO stone crosses, called Corpse Crosses, formerly stood on the common, and it is stated that when a body was being carried to the parish church for interment, it was usually set down here while a prayer was said for the repose of the soul of the deceased " (Whellan's *Cumberland*, p. 520).

On enquiry, the vicar, who has been at Castle Sowerby for more than twenty years, said that he had no information about these crosses, which may have stood anywhere on the high ground to the east and north-east of the church. At a spot marked in the six-inch ordnance-map ' Stone,' about half a mile north-north-east of the church, there is nothing but the last remains of a heap of road-metal.

It seems from Whellan that the crosses stood together in a pair, unlike the resting crosses of mediæval age at Rheda, etc., but like the twin crosses of several pre-Norman interments.

We may note that Castle Sowerby church is an early foundation, and dedicated to St. Kentigern. The stream that runs by it is called Gilcambon or Gilcolman beck, which seems to point to some early *Kil* or Anglo-Irish chapel of Caman or Colman, rather than to the Norse word *gil* in impossible combination. And we may hope that some remains of the crosses may still be found.

CLIBURN.

Dial and Cross.

THE church of St. Cuthbert was given to the abbey of St. Mary at York, and the appropriation was confirmed by Athelwold, first Bishop of Carlisle. The ancient building was restored in 1849. In the porch are built up two Roman stones, with an inscription about the re-building of a bath.

On the eastern jamb of the Norman doorway there is a dial, not yet cleared of plaster or whitewash (July 1899). It has evidently the hole for the gnomon in the middle; rays for tierce, sext, and nones (9 a.m., noon, and 3 p.m.), with one ray between each; but no circle. A sketch of it is given in the plate facing " Bolton."

Over the doorway is a tympanum, but without carving.

On the south side of the church, in the churchyard, is a cross. The shaft is modern, and dated 1887; but the base or socket is ancient. It is a great block of a warm-grey gritstone, more than 2¼ feet in height from the turf in which it is sunk. Its width at base is 33 inches, tapering to 29 at the top; its thickness is 29 inches tapering to 24. The hole for the cross is 18 by 14 inches.

This socket resembles that of the mediæval cross at Arthuret, and the series of late high crosses. It does not seem to be pre-Norman; and the modern shaft has been very judiciously left without interlaced ornament.

CROGLIN.

THE Lysons, in their *Cumberland* (p. ccii.) say, " In Croglin churchyard is a stone cross raised on steps, on one side of which is a braid, on the other a cross florée."

The same story is repeated by Whellan (p. 522), but a standing cross does not now exist.

A number of curious and interesting grave-slabs in the churchyard and at the rectory are later than the period with which we are now dealing.

CROSS-CANONBY.

A S giving Mr. Calverley's own description of the place, and his
views on its history, we reprint part of a paper contributed
to the *Maryport Advertiser* in January, 1888.

The earliest name of this place, Cross-Canonby, of which
we have any record, was probably ' Stænanby.' Very soon
after the Roman soldiers left the country Christian missionaries settled here, as they did as Aspatria, Dearham,
Brigham, Bridekirk, Beckermet, and St. Bees, and set up
a white-sandstone cross at the sacred place at which they
gathered the people together ; and the place in after times
got the name of Cross-Stænanby and Cross-by. The head
of such a cross, of early British date, was found when the
church was last restored, and a more perfect one is built up
in the vestry wall of Dearham church.

About that time the natives and colonists believed that
the goddess Helia, who gave her name afterwards to the
place of the dead,—the grave-home,—had her dwelling
beneath the surface of the earth, and gathered into her cold
halls all those who died of sickness or old age, and thus
when any of their great folk died they placed over the grave
a stone formed like a small house or the roof of a house.
There is such a tombstone (called " hog-backed," because
the ridge is curved, being highest in the middle as we see
the ridges of low-walled thatched cottages), now lying on
the south side of the chancel wall in Cross-Canonby churchyard. It used to be in the corner of the old churchyard
wall before the church was enlarged and the lych-gate erected
during Mr. Bower's incumbency.

The Christian usually placed a cross at the head and foot
of such tombs, and covered both cross and stone with
sculptures suggestive of the hope that the dead man would
rise to a new life in a brighter "home" guaranteed to him by
his belief in the ever glorious Trinity of God. There is such

a cross standing in Dearham churchyard, carved with the identical pattern which is found on this "coped" tombstone at Cross-Canonby. More elaborately carved tomb-fragments are at Aspatria and Plumbland, and an uncarved one at Bridekirk churchyard.

In course of time the mud-and-wattle and wooden churches, which were used in these very early days when the A.B.C.D. of Christianity was being taught about here, at Aspatria, Bridekirk, Crosby, Dearham, and all along our Solway coasts, gave place to stronger built stone structures, and probably about the year 1100 a simple Norman structure with nave and chancel was built. The builders used almost any good material which came to hand. They carried the nicely squared red-freestone blocks from the walls of the buildings which had been erected by the Romans at their camps and villas and mile castles, and even stones off their altars; and they took up the great grave-block of the British chief or Saxon head-man of former days, and placed it on the top of the jambs of their doorstead as a lintel. Such a lintel I discovered over the south doorway of Cross-Canonby church a short time ago, a fragment of the moulding of the eaves of the coping of the tombstones still remaining to tell of the far distant past, and the men long dead. A similar grave-block lintel, covered with interlaced carved bands, I discovered over the north doorway of S. Michael's church, Old Bongate, Appleby, last year; and a somewhat later and most beautifully carved grave-block lintel, with a prayer in Runic writing, and the name of the buried man, was taken from the old north door of the Dearham church when the new aisle was built in 1883, and is now preserved in one of the windows of the church. The "hog-back" first mentioned has escaped the builder's greed, and remains intact.

In the thirteenth century this little Norman church was enlarged by the addition of a very narrow lean-to aisle; the builders underpinned the south wall, took away as much of it as was thought necessary, threw a wide-pointed arch over the opening, actually leaving the upper courses of the old wall in their original position, and people may see to-day the upper part of one of the ancient Norman round-topped narrow windows over this new archway.

When the church was renovated in 1880 several carved stones turned up to tell the history of the place. One seemed to speak of the presence of the Christian faith here, even whilst the soldiers of the Roman Empire remained; and another told of the prevalence of the beliefs of Saxons, Danes, and Norsemen, and had upon it a representative of the man-wolf of the old Scandinavian Edda, where the offspring of the evil one, the treacherous deceiver, the old serpent, is represented as having the head of a ravenous wolf and a wolfish tail, but the body forms itself into a coiling knotted worm with another tail, that of a serpent, proceeding from it, whilst the wriggling body further takes human shape and divides into the legs of a man, which are bound at the ankles with an iron ring, showing the binding of the incarnations of evil by the faith of the cross of Christ.

Nearer our own time the church was attached to the St. Mary's priory, Carlisle, and was served by its canons, and the place got the name of Canonby; but the memory of the old cross and the early missionaries of, perhaps, fourteen hundred years ago will not die out, and even yet remains in the name of Cross-Canonby.

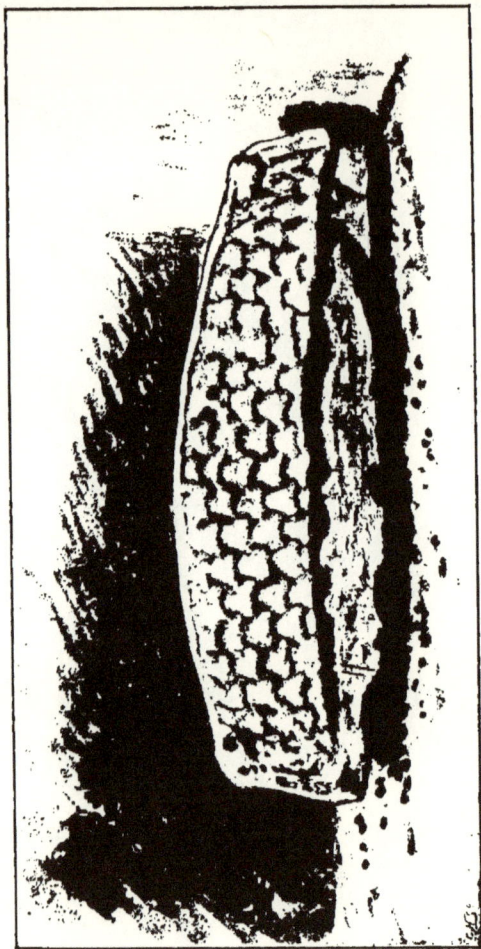

THE HOGBACK.

CROSS-CANONBY.

(TO FACE P. 103.)

CROSS-CANONBY.

THE HOG-BACK.

The Cross-Canonby red sandstone " hog-back " is 6 feet 1 inch long, 21 inches high, and 17 inches broad. It has escaped destruction possibly by reason of its massiveness. It formerly stood on the top of the churchyard wall, near the old entrance, and was in this position when I first discovered its character in 1874. It now lies at the east end of the south aisle. Over the south door of the church another massive stone of similar character does duty as a lintel. The Norman builders have thus utilized the memorial stone of their predecessors; they threw an arch over just as a builder now builds his arch over a *wooden centre*, only they left this strong *stone centre* on the top of the jambs, for it made a very good and permanent lintel.

The curve of the tomb-roof springs from an enlargement at either end of the stone. The whole surface of this roof is covered with the same pattern as that on the lower part of the crosses at Gosforth and Dearham, and which represents the intertwining branches of the world-tree of Yggdrasil in Scandinavian thought. The home of the dead, where Helia holds sway, is deep down in the earth beneath a root of the tree of Yggdrasil. Above ground and beneath the rainbow-arch the Tree of Life fills every space, and beyond is the bright home of the Blessed. There are Midgard and Asgard, the world home, where life's battles are fought, life's deeds done, and the home of the holy ones.

The uncarved surface on the lower portion of the stone would be nearly hidden by vegetation, only the roof over the dead,—as in the case of a Roman tiled tomb-cover,—would remain above ground, and at either end a sculptured cross, such as the one now standing in Dearham churchyard, carved with the identical device. The gables in this case are quite plain, as though the intention had been to complete the monument by erecting crosses at the head and the feet. The faith of the dead man was Christian. The ornament is one continuous symbolism of the doctrine of the Holy Trinity. The prevalent thought of the community appealed to is Northern or Scandinavian.

The arch of heaven descends at the horizon into Hel's dark home,—the jaws of death,—the grave. It was down the rainbow that Odin rode when he sought knowledge concerning the fate of Baldr; thither has the dead man been borne by those messengers who do the bidding of Helia; but for the Christian there is deliverance from " the cords of Hel," for the roots of the Tree of Life and the presence of the Trinity of God penetrate even into the Nethermost world —Nifl-hel,—as well as reaching upwards to the God's seat— paradise. When the crosses stood at head and foot, this was an imposing and instructive Christian monument, speaking plainly to all who looked upon it. At Heysham, Lancashire, the curved surface of the " hog-back " descends at each end into the huge jaws of a widely gaping monster, whose great eyes and " slaughter-craving throat " and head form the enlargement of the ends of the stone. The body and legs of the beast are quite insignificant. It is the *jaws of Hel*, " Hell-muth," which is portrayed.

✻　　　✻　　　✻　　　✻

No pattern remains on the "wall" of the shrine-tomb, that is, under the eaves of the roof, on the side shown in the sketch. On the other side the "wall" is divided by two upright bands,—one can hardly dignify them with the name of pilasters,—forming a panel, in which is some trace of a figure. Other figures seem to have been carved on this side, which may have borne the scene, so frequent in early monumental sculpture, of the Raising of Lazarus.

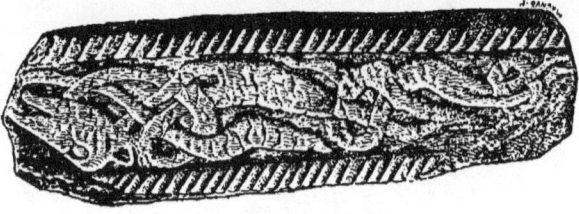

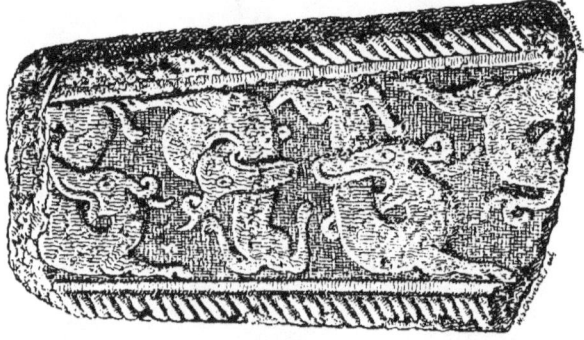

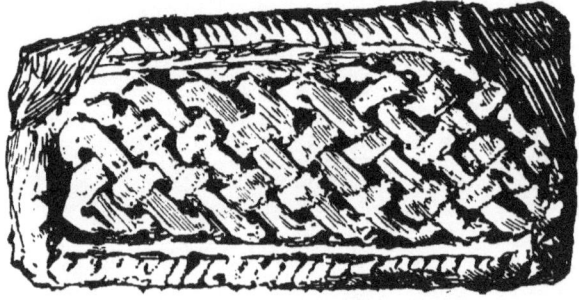

THE RED SHAFT, CROSS-CANONBY.

CROSS-CANONBY.

RED SANDSTONE CROSS-SHAFT.

This fragment of the shaft of a red sandstone cross was taken from the walls of Cross-Canonby church during the restoration in 1880. It is 21 inches high, 12 inches broad at the bottom, 10 inches broad at the top, and 6 inches thick. The engravings are by Prof. Magnus Petersen of Copenhagen, from my drawings, and photographs kindly taken for me by Mr. W. L. Fletcher, Stoneleigh, Workington.

The face of the stone (c) has sculptured, in relief, in a recessed panel, bordered on each side by a raised plain fillet and a moulding which leads our minds to the many Roman altars found in this neighbourhood,—a series of vigorously drawn animal figures, each having only three legs, and apparently spinning round and grasping their bodies in their jaws. The action of the creatures is wonderfully full of life, especially as it is seen in the fore leg and paw pressed against the edge of the panel, as the beast throws its body and hind legs high over in the air and seizes it with powerful jaws. Here are Fenrir's progeny sporting themselves.

East Sat the crone,
in Jarnvidr,
and there reared up
Fenrir's progeny :
of all shall be
one especially
the moon's devourer,
in a troll's semblance.
He is sated with the last breath
of dying men, &c.   [Völuspá, Strophe 32.]

The reverse (a) has, enclosed in a similar recessed panel, a flat fret or plaitwork pattern in low relief. One edge (d) of this fragment has, sculptured in the same fashion, a representation of one of the offspring of the Evil One, the treacherous deceiver, the old serpent, Loki. His head is that of a ravenous wolf, and a wolf's tail * is flourished by him, but the continuous body forms itself into a coiling knotted worm with another tail, that of a snake ; and still continuing this body further takes human shape, and divides below the loins into the legs of a man bound at the ankles with a ring, shewing the binding of the incarnations of evil by the faith of the cross of Christ.

I at first took this figure to be intended for the Mánagarm of the Edda (Völuspá, strophe 32), but I find that the head of the monster is downwards, at the lower and thicker part of the stone, and probably near the bottom of the cross, so that he is not here attacking the "God's seat," or the heavenly bodies, or the holy signs—as the cross or the Triquetra—but he is the Hell-wolf, Fenris wolf. Professor Dr. George Stephens says that this is the first time we see a local tradition that the Fenris wolf, though a kind of wolf-snake, still had a man's legs and feet, for—his father was Loki ! The fetter with which his nether limbs are bound is Gleipnir. This fetter with two interlacing bands ornaments the opposite edge (b).

The stone has been properly squared and worked with a broad chisel, and looks like such work as would be done by men imbued with the Northern thought, but having the art of their Roman predecessors.

*   *   *   *

Fenrir was another name for Loki ; his offspring the wolf is there-fore Fenris-úlfr, or Loki's wolf. We add figs. (a) and (b), showing the reverse and edge of the stone. The outlines of the plaited ornament are very neatly defined with the chisel; the ground and raised surfaces are but roughly worked over, giving a spirited contrast of sharp contour, and varied, irregular texture.

---

* The wolf on the Dearham Font carries such a tail.

THE "LAWRENCE" SLAB.

CROSS-CANONBY.

(TO FACE P. 109.)

CROSS-CANONBY.

WHITE SANDSTONE CROSS-HEAD.

This is figured in Mr. Calverley's lithograph of fragments from Bridekirk, p. 60. The fragment consists apparently of the lateral arms, without the crown and neck, of a cross-head, like examples at Bridekirk, Bewcastle, Carlisle, and Dearham, in having a large boss in the centre, surrounded by a raised ring, from which extend spines reaching and enclosing smaller lateral bosses.

Canon Bower, in a paper read to the C. & W. A. & A. S., on June 17, 1880, says that this fragment fell out of the interior of a wall in repairing a window, at the restoration in 1880. It had been used as rubble in the (Norman) church wall.

It is of a bright white sandstone, 18 by 9 by 7½ inches in size, and chipped out rudely with the pick.

Another portion of a cross is mentioned by Canon Bower as having been found at the same time, together with a quern, a half quern, and an old corbel. Other fragments, he says, are to be seen here and there in the churchyard.

EARLY GRAVE-SLAB. ("LAWRENCE" CROSS).

Noticed by Canon Bower (*Trans.*, C. & W. A. & A. S., vol V.)

Canon Knowles pointed out the "almost Roman broaching," and suggested a date as early as the sixth century.

The Rev. T. Lees thought the square on the dexter side was the *textus* or book of the gospels; "and if the device above the man is a gridiron, the human figure may represent St. Lawrence, who was in deacon's orders,"—an idea adopted by Mr. Calverley in his paper on *Early Cumberland Saints.*

It is of red sandstone; 31½ inches long; 10½ inches across the broadest end, and 3½ thick. The back is roughly dressed with the point, and the edges with a broad chisel. The front is neatly cut, but very poor in design and drawing.

CROSS-CANONBY.

a   b   c

THE "THUNDERBOLT" STONE.

Close to the early grave-slab was found a block of red sandstone, 8½ by 8 by 4½ inches, of which three sides are here shown. One bears a figure like that on the grave-slab; another has a rudely drawn cross, rather 'Maltese' in form, but evidently done without care; the third side bears a few scratches of the chisel in the shape of a thunderbolt, as the symbol is usually drawn in ancient art. All the designs are but slightly incised, the stone having been already squared, with diagonal tooling. It may have been a Roman building-stone; the road ran past the site, and an altar has been found in the churchyard. This is not the fragment of a shaft, or of any monument, but looks rather like a trial piece or carver's sketch, roughly done before setting to work on the grave-slab.

THE "BOLSTER STONE."

CROSTHWAITE.

(TO FACE P. 111.)

CROSTHWAITE. (Keswick).

JOCELIN of Furness, in 1180, writing from Irish documents the life of St. Kentigern, who died more than five hundred years earlier, tells us that the saint at Carlisle, hearing of the paganism of the mountain-folk, turned aside into the forest, and, having preached there for some time, erected a cross in sign of the faith, whence it took the name of Crosfield in English; " and," he adds, " a basilica has just been built there, dedicated to St. Kentigern."

It is generally supposed that the Crosfield here named is Crosthwaite, which is its equivalent in Norse; for the " basilica " of St. Kentigern can only be the Norman church still standing there and dedicated to that saint.

Bede tells us (*Eccl. Hist.*, IV., 29) of St. Cuthbert's friend, Herebert, who lived as a hermit on an island of the lake from which the river Derwent flows; and died on the same day with Cuthbert, 19th March, 687.

We have then at Keswick two saints and an early foundation, but little in the way of remains. From a recent number of the *Proceedings* of the Society of Antiquaries we extract a short notice of the stone represented in our photograph opposite; 11¼ by 10½ inches in size; 2¼ inches thick; and sometimes quoted as the Crosthwaite Bolster-Stone.

" The Rev. H. D. Rawnsley, M.A., exhibited a rough slab of sandstone, with a cross rudely carved thereon, said to have been dug up some twenty years ago, below the usual burying depth in Crosthwaite churchyard, Cumberland.

" A very early date has been claimed for the stone, and a suggestion made to associate it with St. Herebert, the friend of St. Cuthbert, but who is not known to have been buried at Crosthwaite. From the fresh chisel marks on the stone, which are clearly done with tools of various sizes, the opinion of the meeting was in favour of a comparatively recent rather than an early date for the stone." (*Proc.*, S. A., 2nd series, vol. XVI., p. 4).

With this may be mentioned Adam's Cross, at the head of Shoulthwaite Moss,—a cross cut in the rock, and sometimes pointed out as ancient.   Mr. William Wilson of Keswick, whose knowledge of the countryside is authoritative, tells us that the *name* of Adam's Cross is old, meaning the place where a cross-road leads up to a farm once known as Adam's ; but the carving is modern, and was cut about the middle of the nineteenth century to mark the boundary between the manor of Dalegarth and Mr. Marshall's property.

Such items as these are worth noting, to forestall errors.

CUMWHITTON.

A T the ancient church of St. Mary there is a cross-head of red sandstone, 16 inches across the arms, and 6 inches thick.

It is a Maltese Cross of which the arms stand free from a large central circle, which has no boss in the centre, but a depression like the nave of a wheel; and the spokes and tyre here carry out the resemblance. It is very like C in the plate of cross-heads at Gosforth, but has no bosses or circles on the arms. There is no interlacing, and no ornament at the back or edges, which are square in section, quite different from the pre-Norman type.

This may have been a finial, or it may have been the head of a tall mediæval cross, as at Arthuret and Cliburn.

DACRE CROSS SHAFT

(TO FACE P. 113.)

DACRE.

THE CROSS-SHAFT.

THE Dacre stone, of which I here give a drawing, is the shaft of a cross almost complete. The head has been broken away. The sculpture of the whole face of the shaft is seen. The plaitwork of three strands on the edge terminates correctly. We may not say what form the head and arms took, but the upper figure, which is a lamb, corresponds in position, and very closely also in form, with the upper figure on the much larger and very differently shaped cross at Penrith, the head of which is itself decorated with a raised cross having a central boss. The head, and it may be a few inches of plain stone at the bottom, is all that is wanting of this remarkable and most interesting piece of work, perfect in proportion, and of very great merit in conception and design.

The artist has divided the surface of the stone into four panels above each other. In the lower panel he has figured the Temptation. In the centre stands the tree bearing fruit in groups of threes, a fruit-bearing branch hanging down on either side; to the left Eve, draped, takes the fruit, while one apple falls, and the serpent, raising itself with open mouth, appears as the tempter; to the right Adam stretches out his hand to the tree.

In the next panel the stag is hunted by the hound, a fit picture of the life of effort of a fallen world. The hart has held its place in symbolism through all the ages. In the panel above two men join hands in peaceful compact over a square stone font * standing on two short supports, and over them the sun-sign, or a three-limbed sign, is seen : this part of the work is damaged. In the uppermost division the Lamb walks triumphant, for the world, the flesh, and

---

* Such a square stone font may be seen in Gilcrux church.

the devil may not compass the abiding death of him who is alive through Christ.

This, I think, is the reading of the picture-writing. The regeneration of Christian baptism is placed in apposition to the fall; the Lamb, once slain but ever living as our blessed Lord, is placed in apposition to the hunted stag. Baptism and the resurrection of the dead is the teaching. Outside the real design there is no attempt at ornamentation, or very little indeed.

The workman, whose skill may be seen in his treatment of the horns, shape, and movement of the stag, and in the general proportions of his figures, has not cut away the stone at the sides, between the legs of the animals, and in other places; but has left his work in simplicity, to tell its own story without adornment of any kind.

In searching for facts which might bear upon the history of the Penrith crosses, the circumstances of Athelstan's visit to Cumbria were forcibly brought to my notice, and about the same time Canon Matthews sent me his notes* upon this Dacre cross-shaft, which I had not seen. Now that I have seen the stone I find no reason to alter my opinion, namely, that the whole thing is Christian, that it commemorates the compact of the kings, and that the date 926 is not too early for its production.

* * *

The shaft is of white, or rather warm-grey sandstone, 38 inches in length, which seems to include the whole of the cross except the head, of which the spring is seen, and the uncarved part, if any, at the base. Its breadth is $14\frac{1}{2}$ inches, tapering to $11\frac{1}{2}$ at the neck. About an inch in thickness has been split off the back; the remainder is 4 inches thick; the original thickness would have been about 5.

The work is not chiselled but picked or hacked, with a good deal of irregular background left round the raised pattern. The contours of the patterns and figures are steep, and their surfaces flat. There is no roundness or variety of surface, and the execution suggests a decadent and late period of the style; that is to say, some time in the decline of the Anglian power.

The edges of the shaft are alike, with an ordinary plait of three strands.

* Printed in *Trans.* C. & W. A. & A. S., vol. XI., part I. (1890).

CROSS-SHAFT.

DACRE.

(TO FACE P. 114.

On the face, above Adam and Eve, the hart has a bough growing out of its head, in front of his horns. This must be an early form of the mystic stag of St. Julian, or Eustace, or Hubert, which bore the crucifix; and it fits in with the notion of Stephens, that the stag means Christ. Here, however, he is persecuted by the wolf or dog.

Above it the smaller figure stands apparently on a boat; the larger figure has no club, and therefore the subject is not Cain and Abel, as has been thought. They are taking hands, the smaller with evident reluctance, over a square something,—altar, book, or font.

The proper antithesis to Adam and Eve is the baptism, as at Bridekirk. Here it seems to be a baptism, but not the baptism of Christ, which lends much colour to the idea that it is meant for the treaty between Athelstan and Constantine, one part of which was the baptism of the Scottish king's young son, with the English king as his godfather,—more likely, perhaps, that the Cumbrian king Owain is shown here. The objection to this is partly that we are by no means certain that the treaty took place at *this* Dacre; it might be Dekker in Yorkshire; and that it was not usual to carve historical pictures on crosses. To the first objection one may reply that the circumstances of the campaign, and the geography of tenth century Britain, make this as likely a spot as any for the meeting; while the limitations of early Christian art have been far too tightly drawn. There are certainly portraits and heathen scenes; there are some hunting and battle scenes at Heysham and Gosforth which cannot fairly be interpreted as symbols; and some late Anglian work, as at Halton and here, may have exhibited the very natural tendency to embody current events, as in the sixth century mosaic of Justinian and Theodora at Ravenna, the seventh century mosaic " Granting of privileges " at Ravenna, the ninth century battle and hunting mosaics at Byzantium (Kügler's *Handbook of Painting*; Ed. A. H. Layard, I., 43); and many battles, portraits, etc., in early Italian sculpture.

If this is to be dated shortly after 925 or 6, as the tombstone, say, of Owain, and to be classed as Anglo-Cymric, the art becomes extremely interesting; since this is closely allied to the series of spiral white crosses which are characteristic of our neighbourhood. We have here the rudimentary spirals and triple pellets, with a plait on the edges, which, though wanting in spirit and invention, is far from being so debased as the plait-work of the white shafts at Beckermet St. John's, etc. Taking these last, with the Rowler cross (Maughold, I.O.M.), as eleventh century, we might well believe that the Dacre stone is a specimen of tenth century art; transitional between the earlier and the latest Anglian work.

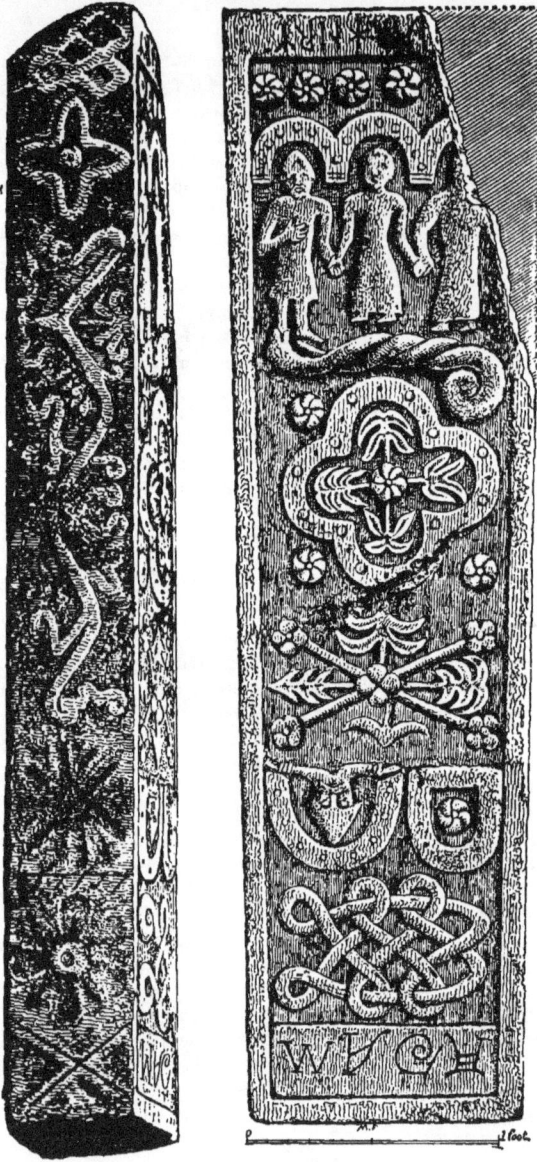

THE "ADAM" STONE,
DEARHAM,

DEARHAM.

The "Adam" Grave-Slab.

Dearham church, in the Diocese of Carlisle, stands on a howe something more than 100 feet above the sea level and at a distance, in a direct line, of two miles from the shore of the Solway and two miles and a half from the mouth of the river Ellen, eastward. This neck of land slopes quickly down on the east and north sides to Rowbeck, whilst on the west and south two little ghylls, running into the beck, almost divide the peninsula from the main land. The position is naturally strong. On the opposite side of Rowbeck, and facing the east of the church, is a farm-house, Dearham Hall, formerly the home of the Dearhams and probably fortified. At the west end of the church stands a massive, square, battlemented tower, built on to the old church late in the thirteenth century or early in the fourteenth. It is 40 feet high, or thereabouts, so that, standing in the hollow of the projecting neck of land, it commands the tops of the undulations over the surrounding district for a great distance, without itself becoming conspicuous. It would thus be a valuable shelter, beacon, and defence during the border troubles.

Many coffin lids or sepulchral slabs, bearing foliated crosses with Calvary steps and window tracery, and the sword and shears and book, are found built as copings to the churchyard wall and porch, and seats in the porch.* This last was added in the Decorated period.

The most easterly portion of the chancel has been added to a former chancel in the Early English period. That former chancel was added to the nave during the Norman period.

---

* *Trans.*, C. & W. A. & A. S., vol. V., Art. XVIII.; vol. VI., Art. XXII. These fragments, &c., have been preserved, and, together with many others which have come to light during the restoration and enlargement of the church, have been placed in the walls of the new aisle and of the porch that they may tell their hidden tale of the past once more to the people.

The two small original Norman windows of fine hewn masonry, which threw light upon the altar of that day, still remain. The original stone church probably corresponded in length to the present nave, which is now restored and enlarged by the addition of an aisle on the north side. This length was about 48 feet. The foundations of the eastern and western walls were found under the present chancel and tower arches during restoration in 1882. In the south wall towards the east end was a recess in the wall. In the place where the piscina should be, it still remains. Beneath this recess and inside the church, south of the altar of that early church, there had been many burials. Upon trying the ground with an iron rod and finding an obstruction at a depth of about 5 feet, and much water, it was determined to remove the soil carefully and prove the cause of the dampness, so as to remove it if possible. Close to the wall and only a few inches from the surface, a burial was observed facing eastward. No traces of any coffin or envelopement, a veritable illustration of " earth to earth." Each bone lay embedded in the mould in perfect order. The workmen, who were most careful and reverent, were ordered to step aside and excavate alongside the burial; but with a like result at a greater depth. A second time there was a new beginning, and now, at a somewhat greater depth and partially under the superincumbent death-heap (in its turn an earlier burial than the first), lay one who had been interred with a long straight wand, without bark upon it, adown his body, but in no coffin. At least no traces of such could be seen. There were wet leaves amongst the clayey soil, preserved through ages in the cold and airless humidity of this grave, so different from the dry pure earth of the upper ones. A bed of hazel or ivy leaves had been laid for the dead body, and probably his cross (an untooled hazel wand with a cross piece) was then laid upon him.

But what was the cause of the dampness and thus the preservation of these frail leaves, and this wand only half an inch in diameter? It was that beneath this grave and a little to the side was a coffin of oak; at each end its sides projected, having been cut away by an adze or hatchet, so as

to form at each end two handles. The lid had fallen in.
The iron nails were still to be seen. Of the body but few the
remains. The teeth were ground down close to the jawbone.
The burial had been placed in the clay, from which no water
could escape, and hence the preservation of the wood. This
I raised up, and beneath it, on the bottom of the grave, still
lay, apparently almost as perfect as when placed there, two
hazel wands, thus X, as a St. Andrew's cross, with the bark
still on them and the silvery light to show that they *were*
hazel when dry. Similar hazel wands were above the coffin,
flattened on one side and with the bark on, whereas the *first-*
mentioned wand was *round* and had evidently been purposely
peeled. Whether the crossed wands have any special
significance or were tied round the coffin, which was
evidently intended to be carried, I cannot say. I would only
remind you of the St. Andrew's cross and the thunderbolts
on the Dearham Runic slab, and of the four like crosses
at the foot of the famous cross in the Dearham churchyard.

In connection with these burials and hazel wands, I would
mention that St. Kentigern * was the apostle of Strathclyde.
There is a story or legend about him to this effect : "Some
one who had a spite against him put out all the fires
in the monastery. Hereupon St. Kentigern snatched up
a green hazel bough, and in the name of the Holy Trinity
blessed it and blowed upon it. Immediately, by fire sent
down from heaven, the bough produced a great flame,
and the saint lighted the candles for the vigils. On this, the
light ceased from the wood." I think these facts tend
to prove St. Kentigern's influence in connection with this
coast.

To return to the church. I do not know to whom it
was dedicated. The stones of which it was built are
the usual square-faced long wedge-like red sandstone blocks
used by the Romans at their camps. Many still retain the
Roman tooling. Amongst them, during the work of restoration, I have discovered the top of an elegant little Roman
altar ; but, unfortunately, the inscription is gone. The

---

* Died on the octave of the Epiphany, Jan. 13, A.D. 603.

Roman road from the station at Ellenborough on the Solway,
by Papcastle to Keswick, runs within a mile of the church ;
from this Ellenborough station, or from some nearer Roman
look-out, the stones of the old church would be carried.
According to his biographer, St. Kentigern journeys from
Carlisle to Keswick, and there erects a cross, whence the
place afterwards takes the name of. Crosthwaite.   He then
makes for the sea, and so along the coastlands towards
Wales.   Thus all along the Roman road we have evidence
of mission stations, which may have been founded or re-
invigorated by him.

We have two roads leading over the old common, from
Ellen*borough* and Ewanrigg and past Kirk*borough* and Hay-
borough, still called Cross*how* loanings, and another from
Craik*how*.   All run to the church, where stood the cross
before the first stone church, and perhaps before either
St. Cuthbert's or St. Kentigern's time.   Another early
mission station stood between Dearham and the sea, at
Cross-Stænanby, now Cross-Canonby, and another at Gilcrux, on the inland side of Dearham.

The Dearham slab, as is well known, was over the north
doorway of the church, whence I took it out.   But, besides
being so badly engraved by Lysons, its Roman and Runic
letterings were unknown.   They were buried under many
coats of whitewash and plaster.   How much we are indebted
to this shielding plaster we cannot say.   Now that the
stone has been taken down, during the repairs, all is
clear. It was intended to be recumbent, not to stand upright,
and is sculptured only on the top and on one long side.
Thus it was originally placed alongside a wall, or in a recess
in a wall, where the further side and ends would not be seen.*
It is of yellowish sandstone, probably from the old quarry near
the junction of Row-beck with the Ellen.   Length, 4 feet 3¼
inches ; least width at foot, 13 inches ; greatest width,
15 inches ; depth 6 inches.   On the top a raised border runs
round the slab, 1 inch in width, but 2 inches at the runic end.

---

* Perhaps placed over relics or *removed remains ?*   For cists holding bodies
removed from other spot of about 3 feet long by 1 foot wide, see tomb of
Warenne and his wife Gundreda, founders of Lewes Priory.   *Archæological
Journal,* vol, XL., No. 161, p. 19.   (Author's note of 1884)

The width of the panel bearing Roman letters is $3\frac{1}{4}$ inches. At the right corner of the upper or broader end a piece has broken away, carrying with it part of the third figure and the beginning of the runic writing. Sufficient remains to show that we have here a representation of the fall and restoration of humanity, in which the seed of the woman shall bruise the serpent's head, though that serpent bruise his heel. (Genesis, iii, 15). Under the runes, seven * revolving bodies whirl above the tabernacle-work of the three round arches, each studded with eight symbolic pellets, under which are *Adam*, in whom all die, hand in hand with the *Woman*, and with *Christ*, in whom all are made alive again. Beneath are two serpents, one biting the foot of a mitred man,† " the shepherd and bishop of your souls " (1 Peter, ii, 25); the other with bruised head, down twisted. Something is left of further sculpture, running up the broken part. Then comes a mysterious quatrefoil, the centre occupied by a revolving body which throws out four tongues of flame or arrows of fire at right angles with each other, whilst each arch of the sign is studded with *raised flat pellets* and *incised points*, arranged alternately, each arch containing four pellets and three points, the whole sign twenty-eight pellets and points in all. Outside the quatrefoil, in three of the angles, again revolve the whirling bodies. What can this be but the sun and moon, the seven days of the week, the four weeks of the month or twenty-eight-days, of which *four* are the great holy days, the Sundays? Then another strange sign, in which thunder-bolts and lightning-arrows take the form of a St. Andrew's cross and a Greek cross. Next, an archway, something of the shape of a horse-shoe, studded with points (only four left), with the revolving sphere again in its centre; beside it, a mitred head under a canopy or halo or arch, studded with eight flat pellets. So comes the emblem of Eternity or of the Ancient of Days, the fret without beginning and without end.—All the sculptures on this upper side or face are in *relief*.

---

* Three of these revolving bodies have been broken away.
† "For ye were as sheep going astray; but are now returned unto the Shepherd and Bishop of your souls.''

The front side has no border, and most of its sculptures are *incised*. Begining on the right, we have the ancient cross sign known as St. Andrew's. Next, I think, the sun in all his glory, or perhaps the earth. Then a straight perpendicular line, with five side-strokes; seemingly, too regular to be chisel-marks, though I dare not give them any meaning. Next a sort of revolving body throwing out rays of light, the six principal being slightly curved, showing *active motion*. This may be the sun. Each figure has six large and six small rays, which I think correspond to twelve hours day and twelve hours night; seven such days being a week, of which four are a month (four Sundays), of which twelve are a year. To the left is an inflected or deflected rod, one end taking the form of a crook. The whole has budded and floriated, and the trefoil is plainly visible amongst the foliations, as also is the arrow-lightning sign. Further left, a four-lobed star, followed by diamond or lozenge work (a bit of the corner knocked off). The (twelve hours' light and twelve night hours, or full) day of active life of our bishop, whose staff has budded and been fruitful among the worshippers of the sun or Thunderer is over. He enters Eternity, with the guiding star before him, which has the shape of the cross.

What is certain is that this Runic slab must be *earlier* than the north doorway of our Norman church, over which it was placed as mere building-stuff.

*   *

The above paper was communicated to Professor George Stephens, and printed by him in *Old Northern Runic Monuments*, part III., with remarks by Professor Stephens, who dates the stone " 850-950 ? " and reads the runes

"(Krist S)U(L) GI-NIÆRA.
May-Christ his-SOUL NÆRE (save, bless)!"

The whole chapter was printed in the *Trans.* of the C. & W. A. & A. S., with a note by the editor (Chancellor Ferguson) on the discovery of hazel wands in tombs; instancing those of the Bishop of Hereford, 1516; St. Richard, Bishop of Chichester, 1253; the 12th century stone coffin at Etran near Dieppe; the Anglian coffins at Selby; and the heathen Alemannic tree coffins at Oberflacht in

Swabia; and comparing the wand carved on a grave-cover at Brigham. Chancellor Ferguson notes Mr. Albert Way's conjecture that
the hazel is the pilgrim's wand, but refers to the importance of this
particular tree in Scandinavian and German mythology, and to the
survival of such beliefs in the superstitions of Christian nations.

Our tracing of the runes differs a little from the copy used
by Stephens. The letters are a trifle over an inch in height;
the Bridekirk runes average ⅜ inch. These have the R very like
the Bridekirk R; and the second letter Λ looks like that which
stands for A at Bridekirk, rather than the usual runic U. The
letter after it is too broken to show more than that it is not an L.
Then follows a stop, and then a word, which Stephens, taking it as
late runes, read HNIÆRM, which has no meaning, he said; therefore he preferred to regard them as *early* runes, and read
GI-NIÆRA.

The ornament of this stone, however, is hardly ninth or tenth
century. The open plait is the same as that which we see on the
Dearham font and other twelfth century work. The revolving
pellets and rosettes recall those of Bridekirk font and various
Norman capitals. The two bunches of ornament beneath the three
figures are alien to Saxon art. We may add that the position of the
slab *over* the Norman door did not conclusively prove that it was
used as material at the *first* building of the church. Walls were
sometimes half pulled down and re-built without touching the lower
arches.

Adam's foot is well into the serpent's mouth in the original;
and his two companions look much more like two female figures
than anything else.

PHOTOGRAPHED FROM A TRACING OF THE DEARHAM RUNES.

DEARHAM.

The Standing Cross.

THE ancient cross still stands near the entrance to the churchyard ; 5 feet 5 inches in height ; having upon its stem the great world-ash Yggdrasil, over which shines the true Sun-God, which, in the teaching of the missionaries, was the Christ.

(*a*) is the continuation of the tree-stem underground. Mr. R. S. Ferguson, F.S.A., in company with myself, uncovered this portion and found that there had not been a socket. A foundation of bricks and cement has now been placed underground for firmness, but the cross was previously in a tottering condition.

*   *   *

The western side also seems to bear out the idea of the tree. A number of strands or stems, interlocked like roots below, rise like a grove, and pierce through an arch, which may be fancied to be *Bifröst*, the rainbow. Above it the boughs interlace again, with quite the effect of tangled foliage,—a very picturesque bit of design. The arch, however, is not a compass-drawn curve, though the artist has shewn in the cross-head that he can draw a much neater line.

The northern edge bears a simple plait like the southern, here shown.

The sculpture has no sharp chiselled outlines ; it seems to be all picked or hacked, but very cleverly handled. The ground is sparingly shown, only between what we have called the ' stems ' and the ' rainbow ' ; and it is far from flat, but picturesquely undulating and rough. This kind of work, so far removed from the hard and tight finish of modern stone-cutting, is very pleasant in its soft and varied surface, and mysterious and suggestive detail. It is like sketching in stone, and implies mastery in the use of tools ; the climax of the craft, midway between the early laboriousness of Bewcastle, and the coarse decadence of Halton.

Mr. Calverley's short account does not bring together his evidence for the theory that this pattern is a conventional rendering of the Tree of Existence ; for which see under Gosforth, Muncaster, and

Two Views of the Standing Cross.

DEARHAM.

(to face p. 124.)

St. Bees. The discovery of the stem, from which the interlace-
ments rise, seem to confirm the theory with regard to these crosses,
whatever use may be made of the pattern in other places.

We may perhaps add here that, according to Mr. Eiríkr
Magnússon, who has written a learned monograph on the subject
(*Odin's Horse Yggdrasill*, 1895), the name Yggdrasil does not properly
apply to the world-ash itself, which ought to be known as "The
Tree of Yggdrasil"; that is to say, "the tree of Odin's horse."
Drasil means "a steed"; *Ygg* is the name of Odin, "the awe-
inspiring"; therefore *Yggdrasil* is literally "Odin's horse." Mr.
Magnússon contends that the myth of Odin's hanging in the tree is
a very late fable, founded on a mis-reading of the Edda poems;
and consequently the Tree of Existence is in no sense the horse of
Odin. But the horse, *Sleipnir*, of Odin the heaven-god, meant
the wind; and the Tree of the Horse was the region in which he
lived and moved, the overshadowing expanse of the material sky
and "middle world."

A. The Face.   B. The Reverse.

"Kenneth" Cross-Shaft.

DEARHAM.

DEARHAM.

The " Kenneth " Cross.

In 1882 we commenced to restore, improve, and enlarge the parish church of Dearham. On clearing off the plaster and colour-wash from the chancel arch, a strip of plait-work, some 4 inches wide, running through the arch on the north side, revealed itself.

The arch itself, of no architectural style, ugly and badly built, proved to have taken the place of an earlier arch whose stones had been re-used, together with pieces of ancient grave-slabs and stones which came handy to the workmen. This arch had to be pulled down; then the narrow strip of plait-work ornament proved to be one edge of a portion of the shaft of an early cross.

The other edge was similarly sculptured with a plait whose strands (in this case) were double. The *edges* of the stone have not been engraved.* The two *faces* have been admirably reproduced (from photographs) by Professor Magnus Petersen of Copenhagen. The engravings are faithful, as may be seen by comparison with the original now in Dearham church, or with the plaster cast, which has been carefully made by Mr. Robinson and placed in the Carlisle museum.

A portion of the lower part of this cross is built into the east end of the vicarage garden wall, churchyard side; on it may be seen the key pattern corresponding to the upper border of the left side of the engraved FACE (see plate). This fragment was discovered amidst the building stuff used as a foundation for an old pulpit which stood alongside the south-east wall of the old church, now the nave. It was built into the churchyard wall, together with pieces of old tombstones,

---

* The patterns of the edges are now given beneath the cross-head, from sketches by the Editor.

part of an early stoup and other relics, for safety, before the part here engraved was discovered.

The *head* of this cross is built into the north wall of the vestry, above a fragment of a Roman altar which fell out of the old wall during the work of pulling down. This fragment is 20 inches in height by 20 inches broad. It was discovered by me near the east end of the church, on information given me by Mr. Bromfield, of Maryport, who remembered seeing it lying about many years ago.

The Rev. Canon Knowles, of St. Bees, assigned it to the times "before the devastations of the Norse heathen." Now that part of its shaft has come to light, let it speak for itself.

(A) Face. In the upper part is a human figure on horseback, carrying or holding something in front on the horse's shoulders. The whole is surrounded by *spiral* work and little bosses; beneath, a bird with long bill and short tail bears a baby or a bundle in its big claws; in front of the bird a deformed man-figure holds forth a vessel in his right hand; above the man's head appears to gape a pair of jaws, which belong to the double-stemmed, many tailed, spiral, worm-like bodies which surround the figures, and curl and twist into every unused space; beneath the bird is twice repeated the ancient symbol of endless existence, the *svastika*, now the cross sign, used in all ages, and passing, as it ought to do, into every faith, because the truth of which it tells is as old as Paradise; and beneath these again the characteristic spirals of British or Celtic or eastern art.

(B) The reverse is very simply and beautifully ornamented with three ribands; the two outer ones being alike, and consisting of two bands folded over and under alternately with a boss in each loop, and the centre one consisting of the easily recognised spiral and key-pattern combined.

Have we not here an illustration of art-work, design and legend belonging to the old British church? I am greatly obliged to Mr. T. W. Jackson, of Worcester College, Oxford, who was kind enough to make extracts from Capgrave, fol. ccv., for the Rev. T. Lees, concerning the Welsh or British Saint Kenet (Kenedus), whose story appears to be told on

HEAD OF THE "KENNETH" CROSS,

WITH (*a* AND *b*) PATTERNS ON THE EDGE OF THE SHAFT.

DEARHAM.

(TO FACE P. 128.)

the face of this cross, and to Mr. Lees for his kind assistance. The real value of these researches lies in the history which may be revealed by them. I merely give a sketch of the story from Capgrave.

Kenedus was son of the daughter of Diochus, a prince in Letaina, Lesser Britain, born a mile from King Arthur's palace, in the province of Soyr; he was lame from birth, "crus femori adherebat." After baptism he was thrown into the river in a coracle and carried to the sea, and by a great storm carried to an island, from which the sea-birds bore him with claws and beaks and placed him on a rock, where they covered him with many layers of feathers, driving *the serpents and worms* from the place. An angel descended, and placed a brazen bell to the mouth of the little one. Each day the bell was replenished with milk from a *deer* or forest doe. A shepherd, who had his house on the sea-shore, found the child in his nest upon the rock, and carried him away from the birds to his own home, but the seagulls gathered in troops, and finally the boy was borne back to his rocky perch. Kynedus grew up—deformed it is true, but a holy hermit, who had learned that of food, the bitterer and sharper and harder—the most pleasing to God, and, like St. David, able to live on roots and herbs. "He lived revered on the storm-beaten rocks of Gower, the associate of seagulls and forest deer."

This sculpture may thus show a connection between South Wales and our Strathclyde at as early a date as St. Kentigern's day; St. Keneth, the hermit, being of the 6th century at the latest.

The rude and weather-beaten sculpture still shows plainly the seagull with its burden in its claws, the figure with the old-shaped "papped" bell in his right hand, and the worm things which the early saints, no less than the seagulls, are credited with having driven away.

＊　　＊

The Rev. T. Lees adds in a note:—
" A Saxon form of this British story is found in life of S. Wilfreda (tenth century). From later legend a child is found in an eagle's nest, taken to the court of Wulfred, King of the West Saxons, and

brought up, being called Nesting, and becoming father of the grandfather of Wilfreda. (Baring Gould's *Lives of the Saints*, Sept 9).

" There are many more modern stories of children being borne
away by birds. The eagle's claw, the badge of the Stanley family, is
noted, and their crest, the Bird and the Bantling.

" Also see ' Pwyll, Prince of Dyved,' in the Mabinogion, and
' Hagen,' part I. of the *Hegeling Legend*, p. 308; *Epics and Romances
of the Middle Ages*, from the German of Wagner, by W. W.
Macdowall and S. W. Anson."

The story is that Hagen, son of King Sigebrand, who lived in the
castle of Balian, in Ireland, was carried off by griffins. One bigger
than the rest seized him from them, to devour him on the top of
a high tree. The branch broke, and they both fell into a thicket,
where Hagen crept away from the griffin, and found a cave in which
were the princess Hilde and her two companions.

Pwyll, and kindred myths, are discussed in lecture IV. of Professor
Rhys's " Hibbert Lectures." We have here an old Aryan myth,
told first of the stealing of the young sun-god by the harpy-clouds ;
then re-told of various deities, heroes and kings, till it is changed
into a legend of a Christian saint, just as the nature-myths of St.
Ursula and St. Dorothy were created.

With regard to the engravings of the shaft, though they are
excellently done, it must be noted that (*B*) the reverse does not
show, to an eye unfamiliar with the original stone, how the two
lines of pattern on the sides are not series of circles with bosses in
the middle of them, but *twists*, like an open cable, or two straps
folded alternately over and under. The pattern on the edge ought
to be particularly noted, especially (*a*) the sham interlacing.

In (*A*) the face of the shaft, the upper figure on horseback is not
a Flight into Egypt. There is no baby on the pommel of the
saddle ; there is only a pellet under the hand of the rider, and this
pellet has no mass joining it with the horse.

The rider has a sword by his side. He is flinging his bridle
loose on the horse's neck, for the uphill climb that seems to be
before them. Is it the ride of the dead, not here to Hel, but up the
rainbow to Heaven ?

THE FONT, DEARHAM.

(TO FACE P. 131.)

DEARHAM.

The Font.

The ancient and curious square stone font is engraved in Lysons' *History of Cumberland*, p. cxciv. It has on one side a winged figure flying through the air; the claws or talons of the monster are curved, and the whole is full of life, motion, and fierceness. This figure may refer to the conquest by the Christian of the "powers of the air," as the figure of the wolfish beast with the almost endless tongue may refer to more earthly powers. It may also hint at the conquest of the leaders of the earlier religion. We know how witchcraft and superstitions generally have credited their leaders with power to raise storms, even until very late times. Need we wonder that a Christian font of early date should be sculptured to teach the subjection of even the powers of the air to the power of the cross of Christ in baptism?

※

We give sketches of the two sides of this fine massive work. The other two sides have a bull-like dragon and a pattern based on the chequer-work of Norman art, being merely rows of small sunk panels of different shapes.

The side upon which the interlaced knot is carved measures 22 inches broad by 23 high from the base. The side with the sea-monster, Cetus, symbolizing the *water* of baptism, is 28 inches broad and 23 high from the base.

The carving is in very low relief, with a very flat surface; highly finished, but not very striking in design, though workmanlike, and far beyond much of the rude work of the twelfth century in this district. The knot shows how the interlacing motive developed; the Cetus shows what became of the Irish-Norse dragon, in the hands of later generations, before the ideas were finally abandoned for the foliage of mediæval work.

DEARHAM.

Two Dials.

Also on either side of the Norman doorway, "on the noble coign-stones, are the traces of dials similar to those at Isel," meaning that from Isel in the plate of dials opposite *Bolton*, and the middle dial in the plate opposite *Isel*. "The porches," Mr. Calverley says, " are additions in every case of a much later date "; which explains why these dials are now so often in places where the sun cannot reach them.

Here, the eastern dial has two rays, one for about 11 a.m. and the other for 3 p.m. Of the dial on the western jamb, only the pinhole is now visible.

Mr. Calverley also notes that there is at Dearham "a fragment of an early holy-water stoup," in his time " recovered from the vicarage garden-wall, and considered by Canon Knowles to be ante-Norman."

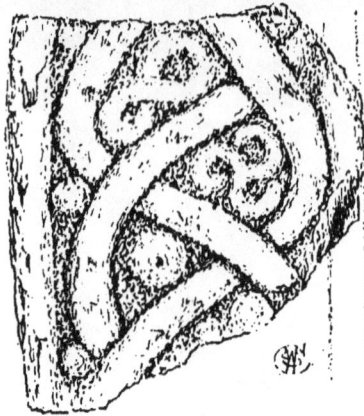

CROSS FRAGMENTS, DISTINGTON.

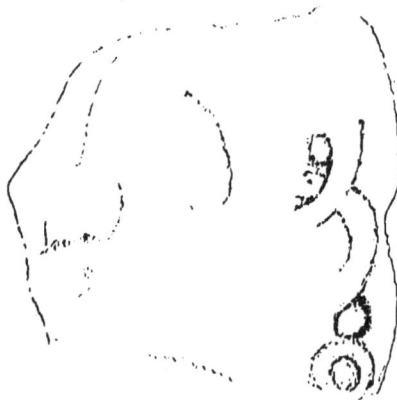

(TO FACE P. 133.)

DISTINGTON.

THREE CROSS-HEADS AND PART OF A SHAFT.

THE plate lettered "Cross Fragments, Distington," shows
the face and reverse of a fragment of a cross-shaft
12 in. by 12 in. by 3½ in. thick, with a smaller fragment of
one of the arms of the same or of a similar cross, 7 in. by
4 in. by 2½ in. thick. Light coloured sandstone. I refer to
the upper drawing as showing the Distington "Triskele
fragment," the sign appearing to the right.

The next plate gives the greater portion of a cross-head
having arms and central boss with raised ring, 16 in. by
14 in. by 5½ in. thick. Also a part of a cross-head, which
has been knocked off square by the builders for walling
purposes, when it was bedded into the old church wall. The
lime-mortar obscures the ancient carving, but the boss, raised
ring, and the meandering spiral-work in relief are sufficiently
clear to fix the type. It is 9 in. by 8½ in. by 5 in. thick.
Light coloured sandstone.

The Distington stones are parts of three cross-heads and
of a shaft. All are of the type having central boss with
rings. One is so much weather worn that no tracing of
older design is found upon it ; it thus resembles the Bromfield
white cross.

Another shows the meandering raised twining work like
that on the Dearham "Kenneth" cross-head, and so well
shown on the Bridekirk white sandstone fragment.

The smallest fragment is the round bossed end of the
projecting central arm within the cross arm, with an S
shaped curve alongside; this may be part of the cross of
which the piece figured with it formed a part, and which is of
later date than the other two heads; its ornament contains
the triskele sign, an 8 shaped figure and a large boss with
central depression within the divisions formed by the broad

bands of a three stranded plait. At the break in the lower portion may have been a svastika within another space. So little remains of the sign that I can only express the opinion.

I think we have here two very early British cross-heads followed by a later but still early cross, of a period when the Saxon "ton" (tún) had become a part of the place-name Distington, through the settlement there of men to whom the symbol with the three curved legs and other signs (as the 8 shaped figure, and the boss with hollow centre) were familiar. The triskele is used here no doubt in place of the well known triquetra form at Gosforth and Aspatria, to signify the Trinity. This sign is cut in relief at Isel and at Plumbland.   *

The spirals of the early crosses arrange themselves in threes and in the S form, as though it were the aim to lead the mind to the Christian doctrines by the use of symbols already recognized.

These fragments were brought to our notice by the Rev. W. G. C. Hodgson, rector, after the rebuilding of the church : they have all been used as building stuff, and the weathering is the work of the centuries before they were imbedded in the old church.

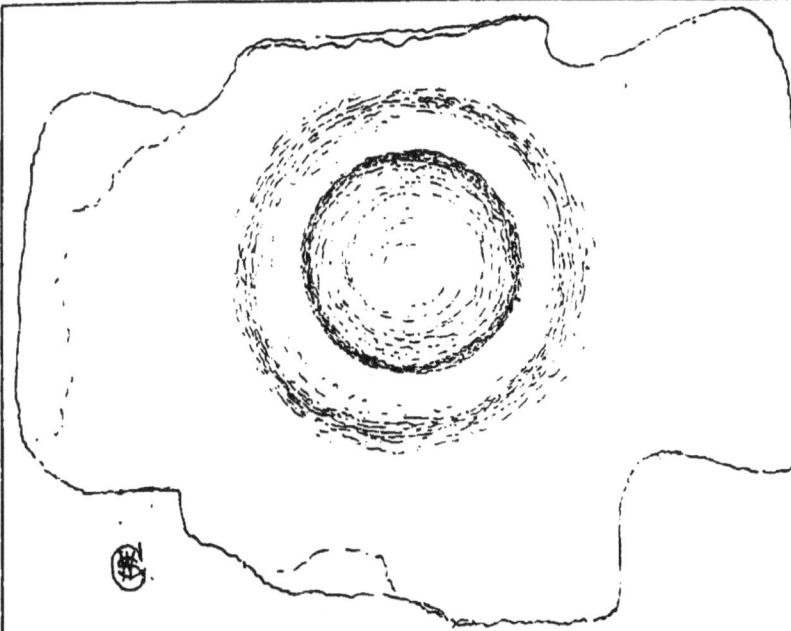

FRAGMENTS of HEADS of CROSSES.
DISTINGTON

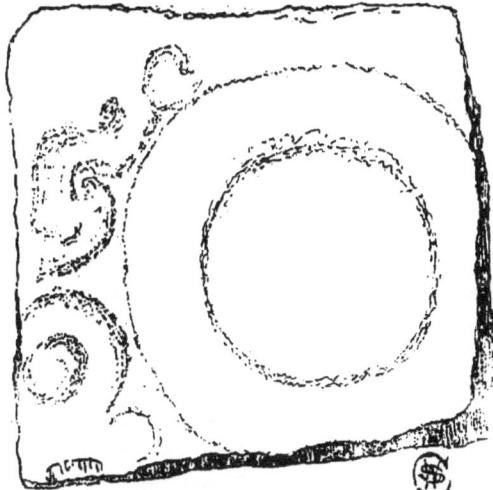

(TO FACE P. 134.)

DOVENBY.

CROSS.

" WHAT was called the Old Cross, formerly stood on the common,
when unenclosed, sixteen or seventeen years ago [before
1859]. A piece of the shaft and base was all that remained. There
used to be a tradition that markets were held there during the
prevalence of the plague. It is still in the same state, and was
removed, on the enclosure of the common, by Mrs. Dykes, as lady of
the manor, into a suitable situation for its security and preservation.
In the Dovenby manor book, date 1690, mention is made of 'the Old
Thorn cross on the moor,' which, no doubt, refers to the cross in
question; the inference being that it was of a religious description,
and either bore, in Roman Catholic times, a representation of the
Crucifixion, or only the appendage of the Passion, a crown of thorns,
inscription, &c." (Whellan, p. 288.)

This cross, or the remnant of it, now stands in the park, in front
of the Hall, surrounded by an iron railing.

It is of red sandstone. The shaft is 23 inches high, and measures
11 by 10½ inches at the base. The edges are chamfered, and the
top has apparently been rudely rounded off, and pierced with a small
socket-hole; as if it had been remodelled at some time or other after
having been broken and reduced from its original height. The
ordnance crowfoot is cut on the top of the shaft, as on the Casterton
cross.

The socket-stone measures 28 by 28 by 12 inches; and has on the
upper surface two curious "heel-marks" about which we have
no legend to relate. They are just like two D's, the larger D
being 2 inches across; and there ought to be some tale of D
diabolic agency attaching.

The cross has been a mediæval one of the type seen at Arthuret,
Cliburn, Kirkland, Lanercost and elsewhere.

GILCRUX.

CROSS-HEAD.

THIS relic is at the church of St. Mary, at Gilcrux, written Gilecruce in the Taxatio of Pope Nicholas (1292) and Gilette, perhaps the " little church " or cella, for the *Gil* must be for *Cil* or *Kil*, and the present church must be the successor of a 7th century foundation, " the cell of the cross." In the time of Henry I. and Henry II. we find Gillecruch and Gillecruz, indicating that the name is of Irish origin, and not taken directly from the Latin.

* * * *

Several years ago workmen engaged in Gilcrux church-yard found the upper part of the Gilcrux circular cross-head. It was broken into two small pieces which they hid in a drain, and afterwards took to Mr. Robinson of Maryport, who made a cast.*

At the alteration of the chancel lately, the Rev. J. C. Pigott, vicar, discovered beneath the altar the lower part of a head, being the boss, the greater part of two of the arms and a quarter of the wheel; on placing the casts and the newly found stone together, more than half the cross-head was revealed. It resembles the Dearham standing cross, but it is much smaller, very roughly worked, and apparently unfinished.

It is or red sandstone ; greatest diameter, 15$\frac{1}{2}$ inches.

This cross has been reproduced as a foot-stone to the grave of the late H. A. Spedding, Esq., of Mirehouse, in Bassenthwaite churchyard, with a copy of the Dearham standing cross as a head-stone.

---

* Formerly in Mr. Calverley's possession, and at his death given to the church at Gilcrux to replace the original, which has been lost.

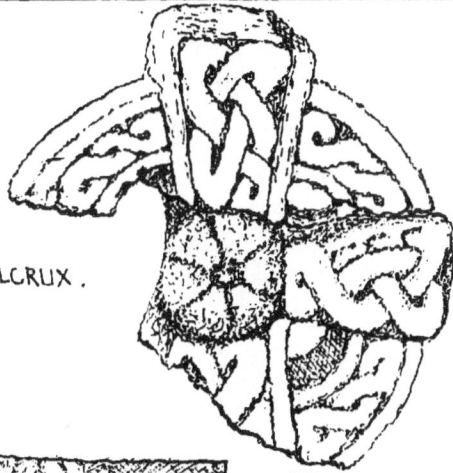

GILCRUX.

PLUMBLAND.

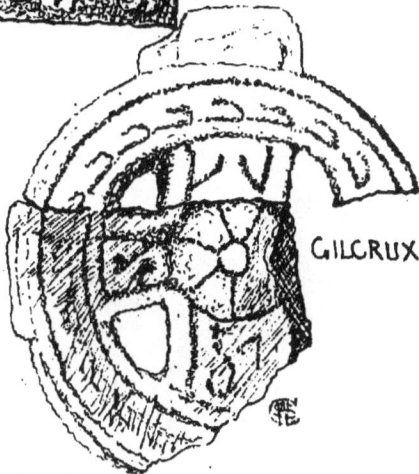

GILCRUX.

(TO FACE P. 136.)

GLASSONBY.

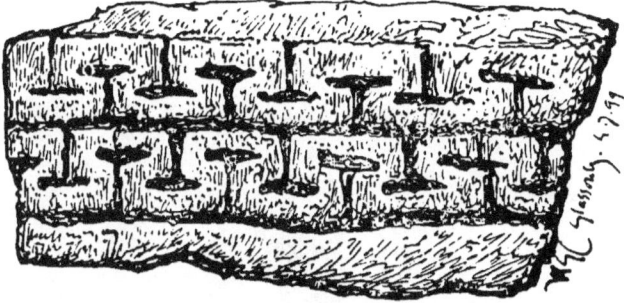

CROSS-FRAGMENT.

ON the right hand of the road, as you go through Glassonby from Kirk-Oswald, there is a large, well-built house (Mr. Rowley's), in the wall of which, at about 4 feet from the ground, the stone figured here was pointed out to the Editor by Canon Thornley.

It is a piece of red sandstone, 18 by 8 inches, bearing a key-pattern which is not common in our district. There can be little doubt that it is a fragment from the shaft of a cross, possibly from the old church of Addingham.

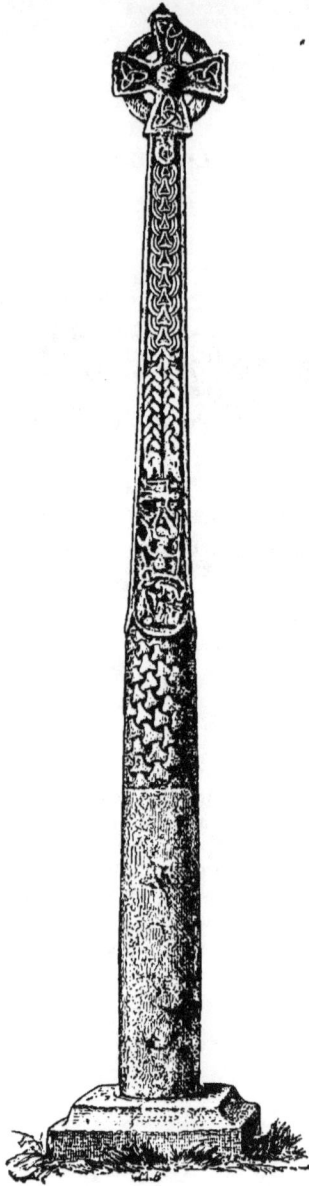

THE STANDING CROSS—WEST SIDE.

GOSFORTH.

GOSFORTH.

THE STANDING CROSS.

GOSFORTH church, village, old hall, and rectory stand on a plateau at the foot of the southern slope of the fell. To the east flows the river Bleng on its way to join the Irt running from Wastwater ; beyond rise the great Cumberland mountains about Styhead Pass, over which the traveller must pass on his way from the coast to Derwentwater and Keswick. The great Roman coast-road lies to the west, with Ravenglass camp and the junction of the inland road over Hardknott to Ambleside and Kendal, less than five miles to the south ; and the camp at Moresby above Whitehaven, twelve miles to the north-west. Hardknott camp is twelve miles away, a little south of east. The sea rolls three miles to the westward, the favoured spot lying sheltered by low dunes from the western winds, and away in the distance rise the peaks of the Isle of Man, Ramsey being thirty miles only from Whitehaven, whilst the point of Ayre is but twenty-eight miles distant and Douglas forty-two.

On the 8th of July, 1881, the Cumberland and Westmorland Archæological and Antiquarian Society inspected the famous cross in Gosforth churchyard. Remarks as to its age and the probable meaning of the figures carved upon it were made by several of the party. Dr. Parker mentioned a tradition of the place that the cross had been erected by Danes who had been converted to Christianity. I expressed the thought that the sculptures on the panel on the west face indicated the binding to a rock of Loki, the Scandinavian Evil One, and that other sculptures represented the Crucified One overcoming Death and Hell.

Further study of the subject, with the help of Dr. Stephens of Copenhagen, and others, has resulted in what a newspaper has called " one of the most important discoveries of recent

years in this district," concerning which the Rev. G. F.
Browne says, in a lecture delivered by him before the
Cambridge Antiquarian Society, Nov. 20th, 1882:—" It is not
too much to say that this year has seen a *revelation* of the
language of these stones which no one had dreamed of before."

Dr. Parker offered his help towards cleaning the stone in
order that photographs might be taken, and " the story of
the cross " made plain, if possible ; and we agreed to work
together to this end. I had thought that I recognized, on the
head of the cross, and in some of its ornamentation, the
symbol of the Holy Trinity and designs similar to those in
the early Irish MSS. besides the sculptures which referred to
the northern or Scandinavian mythology. In this I was not
supported by the members present, and many and strange
were the suggestions offered as to the interpretation of the
figures ; nevertheless, I have a very vivid recollection of
going to Gosforth one dull wet day in the late autumn of
1881, when I thought that the continuous damp and rain of
the previous weeks would have softened the lichens which
had filled every sculptured hollow on the cross-head, and of
standing with Dr. Parker beneath the cross, whilst his
coachman, up aloft, with a dash of a wet brush to the right
and to the left hand scattered the softened mosses, and
revealed—what none had seen clearly perhaps for centuries
—the sign of the everliving Trinity, the triquetra of the
Book of Kells and other MSS. of the early Christian church.

Professor George Stephens of Copenhagen wrote to me
concerning the cross, and I sent him photographs and drawings, with such descriptions as I was able to give and such
opinions as I could form. The result of this correspondence
(which has been of untold pleasure to me), is embodied in the
remarks which follow. The professor made a pilgrimage to
the cross, and pronounced it to be " one of the costliest olden
Roods in Europe "—unique in all his experience, and
" probably of seventh century date."

It is necessary to get a correct idea of the cross *as a whole*
before beginning to study its *details*. This " slim pillar,"
most elegant in design and marvellous in the conception of
its art-stories, is a red sandstone Christian monument, and
it is a monolith. It is not a heathen pillar surmounted by a

cross. The lower part of the shaft is cylindrical, and measures 40 inches round the bottom. The upper part of the shaft is squared off and measures at the top, on the east and west faces, 6 inches, on the north and south faces 5 inches. The head is 20 inches across. The cross is 14½ feet high, and it stands in a rectangular socket of *three** steps, plain, and a foot high. Rather more than the lower half of the rounded surface of the shaft is uncarved ; the upper part (of this circular surface) is ornamented with a design found on the Dearham cross, &c.; curvilinear mouldings divide this round part of the shaft from the four plane surfaces above, which contain the sculptures: above all are the four arms of the cross joined by a circle ornamented with plait-work, and having a boss in the centre projecting more than two inches.

The general appearance of the cross, at a little distance, is that of a gigantic Thor's hammer, the lower part of the shaft being polished. A closer inspection shows the whole to be an elaborately carved Christian cross set in a socket of three Calvary steps. This parallel between northern myths and Christian doctrines, traditions and signs, continues throughout and must be kept well in view, for as the four planes carrying the world-stories taper upwards towards the perfect circle with its centre and Holy Symbols, so the truths displayed thereon—Christian and Heathen—run side by side towards one Infinite Truth.

Some years ago I came to the conclusion that the design carved in relief on the east face of the cross at Dearham represented the World Ash Yggdrasil. Shortly afterwards my attention was drawn by Canon Knowles to a cross socket at Brigham, almost unknown. A study of this socket convinced me that the true meaning of sculptures of this class was to be sought amongst the songs and beliefs of the Anglian or Scandinavian peoples who must have settled here at a very early period. I am now able to prove the truth and value of this conviction, and to this end I ask the reader to refer to my drawings which illustrate the two short papers I have mentioned. The three monsters whose father was Loki, and whose mother was the witch of Jötunheim

---

* The engraving does not show the lowest step.

(the land of Giants), were the Fenris-wolf, Jörmungand, the monster of the universe, also called Midgard's Worm, the huge snake that lay in the great sea coiled round the earth, and a daughter, Hel.

" Now when the gods heard that this kindred was being bred up in Jötunheim, and knowing that from such a stock all evil was to be expected on both father and mother's side, Alfadir bade the children be brought to him, and the worm or snake he cast into the deep sea that lay round all lands, where it grew so that it coiled itself round all the earth and bit its tail with its *teeth*." (Gylfaginning, 34.)

Any one who looks at the huge monster on the top of the Brigham cross-socket, coiled round the hollow (in which at one time was the cross), and biting its tail with its teeth, must at once identify the Midgard's Worm. Now the socket of the Gosforth cross has no carving, but simply *three* steps. Nevertheless from the centre rises up the Mundane tree, the World Ash Yggdrasil, the tree of the universe, of time and of life ; you may see its closely intertwined branches shooting out * from the smooth bole or trunk :—

> " I know an ash standing
> Yggdrasil hight,
> a lofty tree, laved
> with limpid water :
> thence come the dews
> into the dales that fall ;
> ever stands it green
> over Urd's fountain."†

The stag Eikthyrnir browses upon its leaf-buds; its roots below (not seen on this cross) are gnawed by the Hel dragon Nidhögg. Still the ash cannot wither until the last battle shall be fought. Its highest point, Lærad (peace-giver) overshadows Valhöll (Walhalla). There are the twelve halls of the twelve gods, and the plain Idavöll where the champions combat ; in the centre, on the summit, is

* Prof. Magnus Petersen's engraving is in error in marking a line below the pattern and above the plain part of the cylindrical shaft.   Mr. Calverley's drawing, facing page 155 below, is correct in this particular, which is distinctive and characteristic of Gosforth.—Ed.
† The quotations from the Edda are taken from Thorpe's translation, published by Trübner & Co., 1866.

Odin's throne. So you may see the cross-head with its three-fold divisions in the four arms around the central boss, and connected by the circular band—to the followers of Odin typical of the twelve halls of the gods in Walhalla,—to the Christian the sacred symbols of the Trinity, the Triquetra. The great snake does not here lie coiled round the tree; the monster has to take part in the events sculptured above, for the scenes portrayed are from the *Vala's prophecy* (*Völuspá*), and deal with that last battle Ragnarök, the twilight of the gods, when Jörmungand and all Hel's kith and kin are arrayed against the Æsir.

In considering the episodes we have now chiefly to deal with the four plane surfaces on the sides of the cross, and we will begin with the *west* face thereof.

I. The West Face.

From the poem called Œgisdrekka we learn that after Loki had disgusted the gods with his many treacheries and upbraidings, he, in the likeness of a salmon, cast himself into the waterfalls of Fránángr, where the Æsir (the gods) caught him, and bound him with the entrails of his son Nari, according to the words which Skadi, the wife of Njörd, at Œgir's feast, had spoken to the taunting traitor :—

> "Thou art merry, Loki!
> Not long wilt thou
> frisk with an unbound tail;
> For thee, on a rock's point,
> with the entrails of thy ice-cold son,
> the gods will bind."

And the words of Thor who replied to his scoffing :—

> "Silence, thou impure being!
> My mighty hammer Miöllnir,
> shall stop thy prating,
> Hrûngnir's bane
> shall cast thee down to Hel,
> beneath the gratings of the dead."

His other son, Narfi, was changed into a wolf.

"*Skadi* took a venomous serpent and fastened it up over Loki's face. The venom trickled down from it. Sigún, Loki's wife, sat by and held a basin under the venom; and when the basin was full

LOKI PANEL, GOSFORTH.

carried the poison out. Meanwhile the venom dropped on Loki, who shrank from it so violently that the whole earth trembled. This causes what are now called earthquakes."

The scene is thus described in Völuspá :—

> " Bound she saw lying,
> under Hveralund, (the hot spring's grove)
> a monstrous form,
> to Loki like.
> There sits Sigún,
> for her consort's sake,
> not right glad.
> Then the Vala knew
> the fatal bonds were twisting,
> most rigid,
> bonds from entrails made."

Thus the false one lies bound in Hel's dark home, " beneath the gratings of the dead," until Ragnarök. In the very faithful engraving of the panel at the *bottom* of the plain on the *west* face of the cross, here shewn, every particular is clear : the gyves round hands and feet, the bond round the neck, the head of the adder to the left, its body twisted and made fast by a ring above ; Sigún with her woman's hair braided and her long gown, kneeling with poison-cup in hand. But the cup is removed to empty the venom, and the horrid slime eats into the monster's flesh ; he writhes in agony ; every bond is stretched to its utmost strain, the gyves are bent awry ; the last great struggle soon will set the giant free.*

---

* There are known to the world only *two other* representations in stone of Loki bound : one is at Kirkby Stephen Church, Westmorland (see Part i., vol. iv., of the *Trans.* C. & W. A. & A. S. opposite page 187), the other at Vinding Church, Veile Amt, Jutland, Denmark, (published in Professor Stephens' Northern Mythology, page 131). I saw the Kirkby Stephen stone on the visit of the Society to that place, and from it I was led to the discovery of the bound traitor on the Gosforth Cross. Since this discovery the Vinding Loki has been found and communicated to Professor Stephens, who has kindly sent me a woodcut which shows the binding—by the wrists and ankles, and round the neck by a twisted cable—of the giant, but in this case apparently to a horizontal bar which he clutches with his hands. In "Asgard and the Gods" (published by Sonnenschein and Allen, 1880), opposite page 293, the modern artist has pictured Sigún with her poison cup in an attitude much resembling the Gosforth panel. This I had not seen when I first detected the figure kneeling by Loki's side ; I thought the figure might be that of him who fastened the gyves to the rock, and that he held the bolt with his left hand whilst with the other he hammered it home. After the stone had been cleaned, it was plainly seen that the left hand held a hollow bowl and that the figure was that of a woman with abundant hair ; from photographs sent to Professor Stephens he recognized this beautiful story of woman's love and faithfulness before I had again been able to visit the cross. He also at the same time recognized Heimdal with his horn.

HEIMDAL EPISODE. GOSFORTH.

Let us now look at the upper part of this western face of the cross. The first figure beneath the triquetra, (which is on *this* side formed by a *double* band) has its wolfish head upwards, open-mouthed, a single large tooth in either jaw, eye and ear conspicuous; its body consists of ten vertebræ with *double* pairs of ribs :—

" Loki begat the wolf
with Angrboda : "

and his (Fenrir's) children grew into horrible monsters, being fed by the old giantess on the marrow, bones, and blood of murderers and evil-doers, in the last age when the bonds of laws were broken, and the destruction of the world drew near :—

" East sat the crone,
in Járnvidr, (ironwood)
and there reared up
Fenrir's progeny:
of all shall be
one especially
the moon's devourer,
in a troll's semblance.
He is sated with the last breath
of dying men ;
the *gods' seat* he
with red gore defiles."

Here then we see the monster attacking the seat of the gods, ready to gulp down sun or moon ; in the eyes of Christians gaping with wide jaws to swallow the Triquetra.

Beneath are two other of the horrid monster kin parallel to each other, having knotted worm-like bodies and tails, lower jaw to lower jaw, with open mouths, fierce staring eyes, powerful tusk-like teeth (one in either jaw), heads downward, eager to attack the belted, bearded man clad in a tunic, who stands athwart the cross, and calmly with his staff, as tho' with the staff of omnipotence, in his right hand, keeps the Hel worms back. In his left hand the man holds a horn.

The accompanying engraving of this episode must be studied with the engraving of the Loki episode preceding. Thus will be seen (between the man with the staff who holds the horn in his left hand, and the bound fiend), *a man*

mounted on horseback, belted and armed with a javelin or
dart,—man and horse upside down. A few strophes from
the Vala's prophecy makes all plain ; *above,* towards the
top of the cross stem, on this and on the south side, the great
wolves Skjöll and Hati rush up to attack the sun and moon ;
beneath, on this west side, Loki struggles in his final effort to
be free ; *in the midst,* Heimdal,* the warder of Asgard,
restrains the monsters eager for the fray, when all bonds
shall be loosed, he has blown a mighty blast on the Giallar-
horn to awaken the Æsir and Einherjar, and to warn them to
prepare for the last battle. Odin has armed himself and
mounted his horse Sleipnir, and now rides away down
to Mimir's well to consult the fates.

> " Further forward I see,
> much can I say
> of Ragnarök
> and the gods' conflict.
> An axe age, a sword age,
> shields shall be cloven,
> a wind age, a wolf age,
> ere the world sinks.
> Mim's sons dance,
> but the central tree takes fire,
> at the resounding
> Giallar horn.
> Loud blows Heimdal,
> his horn is raised ;
> Odin speaks
> with Mim's head."

Having clearly before us the idea of the impending
Ragnarök, let us pass from the west face of this " column of
the universe," with its Odin and Heimdal, its Loki and the
wolf's progeny, to the south face.

---

* Heimdal was he who brought day to the world, whose path from Asgard to
the outer worlds is by the rainbow or the Milky Way ; he is the watchman who
can hear the faintest sound afar off, even the grass growing on the mountain
tops; who summons the gods by the blast of his horn, kept under the sacred
tree ; in the hour of danger he himself assists the mild ones in their struggle
with the giants. Thus the sculptured planes have the central figure, as it were,
on the top of the rainbow, whose one end joins Valhalla, the other Hel's domain,
and thus on the south side the divine hart from whose horns the dew drops fall
into the rivers which water the dales, stands upon the arch of the bow ; the wolf
bound lying at the *waters' head* towards Asgard ; the howling wolf and hissing
snake below coming up from Hel.

II. The South Face.

The cross is perfect save that a small piece has been chipped off the top towards the south. On the *ends* of the arms are interlaced patterns; round the circle, plait-work.

A belted horseman, armed with javelin, point downwards, in his right hand, and holding the loose bridle in his left, in an attitude of living motion, appears above the coiled body of an adder which separates the home of the living from Näströnd, the strand or shore of corpses:—

> "She saw a hall standing
> far from the sun,
> in Nåströnd;
> entwined is that hall
> with serpents' backs."

Underneath the adder's body is a figure, with limbs interlaced and one great eye.

Odin has sought of coming things the knowledge which lies hid in Mimir's well, (the ocean, the womb of the future, whose sons are the restless billows, the offspring of the past and the present), where the god left his eye in pledge once when he craved a draught of its water, as says the Vala, replying, when Odin enquires concerning the fate of Baldr:—

> "Of what would'st thou ask me?
> Why temptest thou me?
> Odin! I know all,
> where thou thine eye didst sink
> in the pure well of Mim."

Such a ride as is sculptured here is well described in the Lay of Vegtam, which tells us that after the mighty gods, in conference, had consulted "why Baldr had oppressive dreams," and after that "all species swore oaths to spare him," still fearing some coming great calamity:—

> "Up rose Odin
> lord of men,
> and on Sleipnir he
> the saddle laid;
> rode thence down
> to Niflhel.
> A dog he met,
> from Hel coming.

It was blood-stained
on its breast,
on its slaughter-craving throat,
and nether jaw.
It bayed
and widely gaped
at the sire of magic song;
long it howled.
Forth rode Odin—
the ground rattled—
til to Hel's lofty
house he came.
Then rode Ygg
to the eastern gate,
where he knew there was
a Vala's grave.
To the prophetess he began
A magic song to chant, &c.,
until, compelled, she rose."

What questions Odin asked, and what were her answers, will be shown further on; the last words of the prophetess are :—

" Home ride thou Odin !
and exult.
Thus shall never more
man again visit me
until Loki free
from his bonds escapes,
and Ragnarök
all-destroying comes."

Now above the armed horseman (Odin) is the figure of a dog or wolf and the coils of a serpent or knotted bonds (see the engraving) beneath the hart and above the head of the horseman. This engraving does not show the long bushy wolfish tail of the beast, which is plainly to be seen on the stone itself, now that it has been cleaned; * the coils or knots have, in the engraving, much the appearance

---

* In the Facsimiles of Irish MSS. (1874) Part I, illustration viii. on the illuminated Z of Zachariae sacerdoti apparuit Angelus, &c., from St. John's Gospel, I noticed the dog with the red lolling tongue, and action so like to the dog on the south side of our cross, having under his feet lacertine interlacing.

DETAILS OF THE SOUTH FACE. GOSFORTH.

of adders or serpents, the heads spitting venom on him who
rides below, and they are faithful reproductions of the
photograph, though a close inspection of the stone leaves
one in doubt whether they were intended to represent anything else than the loosened bonds, when at the last battle
the wolf breaks loose, the waves of the sea overflow the land,
and the great snake joins in the struggle alongside the wolf:
the wolf howls, and the snake hisses and spits out poison
which fills the air.

Be this as it may :—the chief of the Æsir has made that
last visit to the home " beneath the gratings of the dead."
He has passed the howling dog ; he has looked into the *well
of the future*, and—behold— it is Ragnarök :—

> " Trembles Yggdrasil's
> Ash yet standing ;
> groans that aged tree,
> and the jotün (Loki) is loosed.
> Loud bays Garm (Hel's dog)
> before the Gnupa-cave,
> *his bonds he rends asunder*
> *and the wolf runs.*"

This episode, from the Völuspá, is quite clear; the strophe
(48) follows that in which Heimdal blows the horn, and
"Odin speaks with Mim's head." "The wolf runs" vigorously
enough.

As on the western face the central figure was Heimdal,
"the gods' watchman " at whose right hand (above) we saw
the evil powers restrained, but at whose left (below) were
those powers in the very act of breaking loose, whilst the
ever watchful, the fellow-worker with gods and men, sounded
the alarm, and the all powerful Father himself prepared for
the conflict, so on this southern face the central object is the
hart—the divine hart—the fountain of living waters :—

> " Yggdrasil's Ash
> hardship suffers
> greater than men know of;
> a hart bites it above,
> and in its sides its rots,
> Nidhögg beneath tears it. . .
> Eikthyrnir the hart is called,

that stands o'er Odin's Hall,
and bites from Lærád's branches ;
from his horns fall
drops into Hvergelmir,
whence all waters rise."

Next to the hart, above, that is, at the *spring head*
of the "holy waters" lies a monster, here engraved most
truthfully, much like the uppermost figure on the west face,
consisting of eight vertebræ, and eight pairs of ribs, but these
are single, and the beast is gagged and does not shew
his teeth ; nevertheless the life in his full round eye and in his
jaws, indeed in the whole design, forcibly reminds us that the
wolf is only bound and gagged, not killed, as Frey pictured
him to Loki whom he threatened with a like fate at Œgir's
feast :—

"I the wolf see lying
at the river's mouth,
until the powers are swept away.
So shalt thou be bound."

When the gods had bound the wolf, with a sword they
gagged him, the hilt in the lower, the point in the upper
jaw ; here the iron passes through the lower jaw, round the
cheek bone and behind the ear, then round the front of the
snout and again into the lower jaw. Above, with toothed
mouth * wide open, gaping upwards, is a serpent form knotted
upon itself, the curled tail, such as is also seen on the cross
socket at Brigham ; another form of the old serpent, no
longer "frisking with unbound tail," but still struggling in
his bonds and menacing the Holy powers above.

On the lower part of the plane, beneath the hart who
walks calm and unhurt, we have seen the wolf escaping from
his bonds, and possibly the serpent writhing with a giant's
strength eager for the fray, whilst Odin, armed, rides up
from the sacred well or the Vala's grave, to lead his brave
Æsir in this last and most terrible encounter. The battle
rages : read we the story and its parallels on the eastern
plane of this wonderful cross—a churchyard picture-Bible at
once to the Pagan and to the Christian.

---

* This monster has, like *all the others* on the cross, save the gagged one, *one*
huge tooth in either jaw.

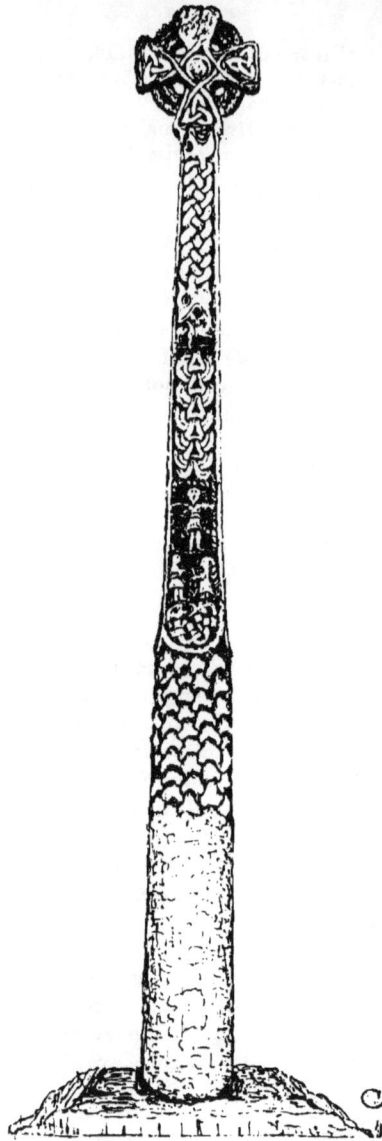

THE STANDING CROSS: EAST FACE.
GOSFORTH.

III. The East Face.

A glance at the outline of this east face will show that the artist is faithful to the plan of his design—a central figure calm and majestic, though below the powers of Hel rage terribly, and above those powers are conquered or brought into subjection.

But who is *this* central figure on the *east side* of the cross? who with stretched-out ·arms grasps the rope-like border of the oblong panel, whose side is pierced with the spear:— It may be that same Odin whom we have already twice seen, for does not Odin's Rune-song say :—

> " I know that I hung,
>   on a wind-rocked tree,
>   nine whole nights,
>   *with a spear wounded,*
>   and to Odin offered,
>   myself to myself;
>   on that tree,
>   of which no one knows
>   from what root it springs."

Or it may be Baldr the beautiful, the peace-giver, the bright son of the Father, who by the treachery of Loki was slain, pierced by a dart sent forth by blind Hödr, and made of the mistletoe which had been overlooked when Frigg, his mother, took vows of all things else that they would not harm her son :—

> " I saw of Baldr,
>   the blood-stained god,
>   Odin's son,
>   the hidden fate.
>   There stood grown up,
>   high on the plain,
>   slender and passing fair,
>   the mistletoe.
>   From that shrub was made,
>   as to me it seemed,
>   a deadly, noxious dart,
>   Hödr shot it forth."

As the Vala had prophesied :—

> " Hödr will hither
>   his glorious brother send,

CRUCIFIXION PANEL. GOSFORTH.

> he of Baldr will
> the slayer be,
> and Odin's son
> of life bereave."

And so the beardless man to the left, holding the spear, may
be blind Höðr, who, with the fatal mistletoe-shaft, has,
unwittingly (for it was false Loki who, unseen, guided the
blind god's aim) done the deadly deed; and the woman to
the right may well be Nanna the wife of Baldr:—"Nanna
sorrowing in earth's deep sanctuaries," as the gods saw her
when Baldr was no more and Nanna had fallen from her high
place, fallen down beneath the tree, and peace had departed
from Valhall;—or it may be Frigg who should grieve a
second time over the death of Odin her beloved.

Whether here, in the panel, we see Odin, or Baldr, or
Heimdal, or all the *three in one*, and so each impersonation or
incarnation of the god confronting his fate in the general
struggle "with the dark followers of the goddess" (Hel), or
Thor himself, the father of victories, the scene as a whole is
the same; it is "The twilight of the gods." Baldr has been
slain : the battle begins : "Odin goes to meet the wolf:" at
the foot of the plane (see the engraving) "The mundane
snake is coiled in jötun rage"; he is the bane of Thor, who, in
the final hurly, shall bruise his head and kill him, though he
himself shall die nine paces off poisoned by the monster's
venom-breath and slime :—

> " Midgard's Véor (Thor) in his rage
> Will slay the worm.
> Nine feet will go
> Mother Earth's son (Thor),
> bowed by the serpent,
> who feared no foe."

Heimdal and Loki fight hand to hand and each the other
slays : and so above the panel lies the headless creature, the
incarnation of all evil, slain. Before the battle, when the
ship fares from the east bringing Múspell's people o'er the
sea and Loki steers :—

> " The monster's kin
> goes all with the wolf."

Against Odin (who rides foremost in the fight, with
quivering spear in hand), comes on the wolf rushing with

gaping mouth ; his upper jaw touches heaven, and his lower
sweeps the earth, as is shewn in the figure at the top of this
east plane of which, one great open mouth, upwards, appears
to attack the holy place and the Triquetra ; the other, downwards, in vain opposes and is opposed by the belted, bearded
man, with staff. Here Odin is not seen, nor his horse, for
the wolf swallows him at one gulp, as Loki fore-threatened
at the Œgisdrekka :—

> " Why dost thou chafe so, Thor?
>   Thou wilt not dare do so,
>   when with the wolf thou hast to fight,
>   and he *the all-powerful Father* swallows whole."

And as the Vala prophesied :—

> " Then arises
>   Hlin's second grief,*
>   when Odin goes
>   with the wolf to fight,
>   and the bright slayer
>   of Beli with Surt.
>   Then will Frigg's
>   beloved fall."

But no sooner has the wolf swallowed Odin, than Vidar,
the silent god, another son of Odin, or another incarnation of
Odin, the avenger, confronts him, and placing his heavy iron
shoe on the nether jaw of the beast, with one hand he seizes
the upper jaw, rends his maw asunder and slays him, as in
the Völuspá :—

> " Then comes the great
>   victor-sire's son,
>   Vidar, to fight
>   with the deadly beast.
>   *   *   *   *   *
>   Then avenges he his father.

And again in the lay of Vafthrúdnir :—

> " The wolf will
>   the father of men devour ;
>   him Vidar will avenge :

---

* Hlin, another name of Frigg, Odin's wife, whose first grief was the death
of Baldr, her son; her second, that of Odin himself when he went to meet the
wolf, and when Frey, the slayer of Beli (the giant), went to fight with Surt and
be slain at Ragnarök.

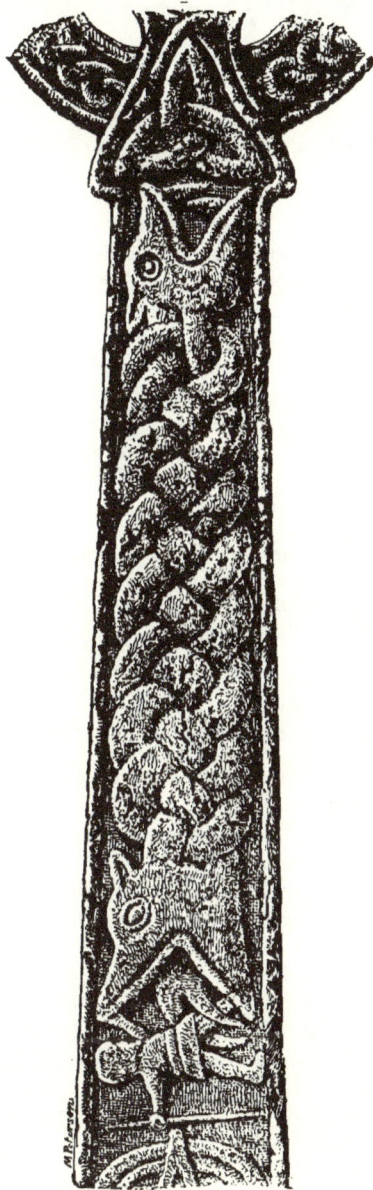

Vidar Episode. GOSFORTH.

He his cold jaws
will cleave,
in conflict with the wolf."

How vigorously this episode is here sculptured, the engraving will show. The attack of the wolf upon the holy
forces, and his punishment are shown by doubling his form ;
his fiendish nature by giving his body the form of a serpent
(each double worm being plaited with the other, making a
fourfold plait), the upper head attacking the triquetra, with
full round living eye, and powerful teeth, and jaws great in
strength ; the lower head, in the very action of defeat and
death, being wrenched open by the mighty Vidar—his left
arm forcing upwards, and his right foot crushing downwards,
as he throws all his weight and god-like energy into the
mortal fight by firmly pressing backwards on his staff which
his hand grasps well up—until the monster's fangs drop
powerless and his eye dims.

" Then shall another come,
yet mightier,
although I dare not
his name declare.
Few may see
further forth
than when Odin
meets the wolf." (Hyndluljod, 42.)

As Prof. J. F. Hodgetts writes in his article in the Antiquary,
Dec. 1882 :—" It would seem as if in all mythology there
were a sort of prophetic perception of what had to be completed in a holier, higher form in the mighty works which
Christianity has taught us to contemplate. Let us not be
accused of irreverence when we fancy that there are such
traces of prophetic truth in these wild poetic teachings ! But
when Odin, in a wondrous weird song, tells his worshippers
that he hung from a cursed tree three times three days, and
saw the bitter evil of man ! When the God-principle (under
another name) descends into Jötunheim to combat the giants,
we are rather awestruck at the evident harmony in some
parts of what we know to be true, and what we have long
ago rejected as false."

Let anyone look upon the Baldr-Odin or Crucifixion scene engraved from our miraculously preserved cross. Is not what the cross says true in every point to the Eddaic stories; and is it not wondrously true also to the very circumstance and event of the great Christian sacrifice?—"But one of the soldiers with a spear pierced His side, and forthwith came thereout blood and water," St. John xix., 34; and as the arms of Jesus are stretched out wide, do we not see that double stream, that sacred fountain for *all* men opened?

There is an old tradition, embodied in the "Lamentations of Mary Magdalene," formerly attributed to Chaucer, and represented in the miracle-plays of Chester, Townley, and Coventry, that the soldier (not centurion) who pierced our Lord's side with his lance (John xix., 34) was a *blind** knight named Longias or Longinus; that

which
> "The purple flood eke from the hartes vain,"

> "Doune railed right fast in most ruful wise,
> with Christal water brought out of Paradise,"

imbrued his hands as it flowed along the shaft of the spear, and that upon accidentally rubbing his eyes his sight was restored. One of the soldiers, fearing to do the deed himself, guided the blind man's hand.

How close a parallel is here seen between Hödr and Longias! If the pagan Northern colonists of this coast saw

---

* See also Chaucer's A.B C.. "La priere de nostre Dame,' x.; also the Townley Mysteries, Surtees Society, 1836, p. 231.
Primus Tortor.—Let oone pryke him with a spere,
And if that it do him no dere
Then is his lyfe nere past
Secundus Tortor.—This blynde knight may best do that.
Longeus.—Gar me not do bot I wote what.
Tercius Tortor.—Not so, but put up fast.
Longeus.—A, Lord, what may this be?
Ere was I blynde, now may I see;
Godes son, hear me, Jesu!
For this trespas on me thou rew.
For, Lord, other men me gart,
That I the stroke unto the hart,
I see thou hynges here on hy
And dyse to fulfylle the prophecy.
There is a representation of Blind Longinus at Naworth Castle, in the oratory. The same painting shews, amongst other figures of those present at the crucifixion, Mary Magdalene with long hair flowing down, and in front of her, with lid open, the box of precious ointment. (Note by the Rev. T. Lees).

the *blind* god piercing unwittingly with fatal spear their hero's side, no less clearly did the native British Christian see that he whose spear opened the fountain in the side of their Christ was a *Roman soldier* * with shaven face who knew not what he did.

If the heathen saw Nanna weeping for her beloved, or the mother of Baldr holding forth the mistletoe branch on which she collected the tear drops of all who lamented her dear son, and fain would have him return from the halls of Hel to gladden the hearts of men, the Christian might see Mary Magdalene, with her wealth of hair, standing by her dead lord sorrowing, holding in her hand the Alabastron † filled with precious ointment for his burial, waiting till the body shall be taken down from the cross and the last sad honours done to Him she so much loved. St. Mark xv., 47; St. Luke xxiii., 55; St. Matthew xxvii., 61.

If *one* saw beneath this death scene the great serpent coiled which Thor should slay and be by its venom slain, the *other* saw that the Seed of the woman should *bruise the serpent's head*, though that serpent should bruise his heel; if the jaws of the great wolf swallowed Odin, the sepulchre was opened for Jesus and he entered the jaws of Hel; if Vidar wrenched asunder the maw of the monster and overcame him, God the Son, after the "harrowinge of Helle," after he had visited the spirits in prison, rose again victorious over death and the

---

* The face of the soldier is the only one on the cross which is shaven, after the fashion of the Romans between B.C. 300 and the time of Hadrian. Heimdal, all the horsemen, the Christ, Vidar, each one has a pointed beard distinctly seen. "The censors compelled Marcus Livius, who had been banished, on his restoration to the city, to be shaved before he came to the senate." (Smith's Gk. and Rn. Antiquities).

† The Alabastron was a vessel used for containing perfumes or ointments; it was usually made of the Onyx Alabaster, which was considered to be better adapted than any other stone for the preservation of perfumes. (Plin. xiii., 3.) Hence the name. "These vessels were of a tapering shape, and very often had a long narrow neck, which was sealed; so that when Mary, the sister of Lazarus, is said by St. Mark (xiv. 3) to break the alabaster-box of ointment for the purpose of anointing our Saviour, it appears probable that she only broke the extremity of the neck which was thus closed." (Smith's Gk. and Rn. Antiquities.) The figure of Mary Magdalene holding this tapering Alabastron in her left hand is very faithfully engraved. I took a rubbing of the whole cross, after the South Kensington moulds had been taken, and when the stone was most free from lichens, and from this rubbing and the photographs Prof. Petersen has been able to give us absolutely correct representations of this and the Heimdal, Vidar, and gagged wolf episodes.

grave, heralding a new era, a new kingdom of brightness and beauty, purity and love.

> " There shall the righteous
> people dwell
> and for evermore
> happiness enjoy."

So says the Völuspá, so teaches the Christian.

IV. THE NORTH SIDE.

And now we come to the last, the north side of the cross. There is again a central figure, in this case a horseman armed with a spear, as we saw the horseman on the south side ; *beneath* him is a like armed horseman upside down, as we saw on the west side ; above him is a strange uncommon figure taking up fully half the sculptured space ; its head is downwards having mighty teeth and fiery eye ; * above its tail is the sign of the Blessed Trinity ; its body has eight pairs of wings attached to it by eight rings, the rings passing alternately over the wing bone and under the vertebræ, and under the wing bone and over the vertebræ, the lowest ring passing under the wing. †

---

* In examining the Fac-similes of Irish MSS., Part I. (published by command of Her Majesty, 1874) I was struck by the similarity of one figure in illustration xi. to the head of the winged creature on the north side of this cross. The illuminated page is from the Book of Kells, St. Matthew xxvii., 38, "Tunc crucifixerunt X R I cum eo duos latrones," and the figure is to the left of the page ; it is a monster, head downwards, with full eye, dilated nostril and fierce teeth, one in either jaw, trying to swallow the Holy Shamrock, whose stem below buds out into palm fronds which curve upwards and inwards around the sacred symbol's stem, like flames of fire. Around the neck of the creature, and behind his up-pricked ears, is a sort of ornamental collar at the throat having the Triquetra, in shape like those upon our cross, not the shamrock.

† My first formed opinion (expressed at our Egremont meeting) concerning the horsemen was that the upper one represented the triumphant Christ, or the Christian Faith. The lower one, the heathen faith, or death, overcome. Odin with his spear of death, man and horse upside down, may well by some be taken to be death on the pale horse carrying his dart, here overthrown and conquered— cast down to his final perdition by the entrance into the world, the life, the death and the resurrection of Christ. Still, I think that the horseman is always the same—twice doubly shown, even as Odin's horse Sleipnir had eight legs—*once* seen (west side) going down to the place where Utgard Loki lay bound, and (the same figure turned round on south side) coming back from the tomb of prophecy to the world's battle :—*again* seen (North side, lower horseman) coming up from Hel, and (upper horseman) riding in majesty, the conqueror ; for Heimdal, and Baldr, and Odin, are the same god-principle in three persons.

Surt has come from the south :—

> "On the wings of tempest riding
> Surtur spreads his fiery spell " :—

and he and his warriors have cast their flames over all the
earth ; the dynasty of Odin is overthrown ; but there is to
arise from the conflagration a new heaven and a new earth
purified by fire ; hither Baldr shall return from Hel:—

> " Unsown shall
> the fields bring forth,
> all evil be amended ;
> Baldr shall come ;
> Hödr and Baldr,
> the heavenly gods,
> Hropt's glorious dwellings shall inhabit."

So the eight winged orbs, (like the eight petitions of the
Lord's prayer), the perfect number in one creature, rushing
down over all things, restrained or held in order by the
" three in one," and so the Baldr-Christ returning from Hel
and riding up the rainbow in majesty after Æstra has opened
the gate at the glorious resurrection.

Thus we may either see in the central figure Surt riding at
the head of the fiery flying sons of Muspell (the personification of fire), whilst the horseman beneath tells of the fall of
Odin and the power taken from Gungnir, the death-spear, in
Odin's hand, or (which is better, for the lower horseman is
in active motion, not overthrown, and is exactly like the
upper one in every detail and even attitude), we may see in
the lower horseman, on this plane, another representation of
that Odin who, on the west side, rode down to Hel's dark
home, and who as Baldr, and Odin, and Thor, each, and all
in one, was fated to go thither at the last battle ; and in the
central figure, the upper horseman, we may see the same
personification of the Deity, riding back in majesty to
rule and dwell in peace in Gimill,—

> " With gold bedecked,
> than the sun brighter."

The same figure being doubled and two positions shewn on
the same plane, as is often the case in ancient art, Pagan and
Christian. Below the horseman is the eternal endless knot,
the last home from which none return until Christ or Baldr
leads the way.

As on the Ruthwell cross the song of Cædmon was written in runes, so on the Gosforth cross is "The Vala's Prophecy," and much of the god-lore gathered together in Sæmund's Edda carved in stone, sculptured in relief. Parallels are drawn and contrasts shewn between the heathen and the Christian faiths :—Ragnarök, "the twilight of the Gods," is graven in stone,—a miracle of art,—and the new heaven and new earth are shewn to be those in which Christ takes the place of Odin, and Thor, and Heimdal, and Vidar, and Baldr, and even of the great Surt himself.

Much more might be written. Many deep truths lie hid in this " sermon stone."

These episodes have never before been recognized, and I rejoice that I have thus been made an humble pioneer in a cause worthy of the efforts of the more learned. How successfully *pure heathendom* is used on this monument as a means of teaching the gospel may be clearly seen by comparing it, beginning at the west, the Loki side, with the prayer of the priest and people in the baptismal service when the child is grafted into Christ's body—" that he may have power and strength to have victory and to triumph against *the devil, the world, and the flesh.*"

On the west face we have a *central Heimdal-Christ,* the incarnation of the Deity, holding at bay the dread offspring of Satan, while Loki himself lies bound beneath, and Odin the father approaches the future. The *devil* overcome.

On the south side we have a *central divine Hart* triumphantly walking through the world unhurt by the slime and venom of the great worm of the middle earth, or by the howling dog ; the Christ, the fountain of living waters, the incarnation of the deity who below rides armed, to battle with and to " overcome the *world.*"

On the east side we have a *central Thor, Odin, or Baldr-Christ* who fights the last great battle and overcomes the *flesh* which is crucified and pierced with the spear ; who, though the jaws of Hel gape wide and swallow him, in another personification—Vidar the Silent—he who opened not his mouth before his foes—rends asunder those very gates, victorious over death and the grave, and as we see on the north side rides on, the everlasting conqueror through His glorious resurrection.

The Rev. H. D. Rawnsley allows me to reproduce his sonnet, composed after hearing the paper read at Carlisle, and the remarks of Dr. Stephens : —

We are not wiser than the seers of old,
    Our fathers—they twelve hundred years agone
    Hewed from its silent place this prophet stone,
And bade the sacred Yggdrasil uphold
A Baldr-Christ whose triumphs should be told
    In Pagan picture,—here the battle won
    By Horn's blast,—there the Horse with Death thereon
Cast down for years whose coil is endless rolled,
Preacher of Christ, stone-lipped, and not in vain,
    Preacher of Woman's love to help her Lord
        By faithful tendance, yea, though earth should quake ;
    For lo ! her feet upon the bruised snake,
    Here Mary stands beside the Christ in pain !
There Loki's queen prevents with cup the poison pour'd !

And again :—

When I bethought me of the woes and cries
    Now hushed for aye within each grassy door,
    The sorrows of the uncomplaining poor,
The pain—where now at rest each labourer lies,
I said, for these what prospect did arise
    To bid them, ere they turned to dust, endure,—
    What tree of healing could their anguish cure ?
When lo, this cross rose up before mine eyes ;
Then knew I how above each opening grave,
    For those who toiled through generations long,
    Since first our Father carved with holy craft
    His saga signs upon the rosy shaft,
A preacher stood and told the weary throng
Of One who suffered silently to save.

                                   H.D.R., Oct. 6, 1891.

*   *   *   *

A cast of the cross has been taken for the South Kensington Museum, and the cross itself has been protected by an iron railing.

A copy of this cross was carved by the Rev. W. S. Calverley and Christopher Dickinson, and set up in the Aspatria churchyard, 1887.

The above is Mr. Calverley's paper of 1883, with some alterations made by himself in his own copy. To bring it up to date would destroy its documentary interest; and the student, while noting points for criticism, will recognize the value of an essay which it is not too much to call epoch-making.

What may be the exact value of each figure and symbol must be open to dispute. It is curious, if Mr. Calverley's interpretation is correct at all points, that the spectator is required to go round the cross *withershins*. It is still more curious, if every part has both a heathen and a Christian significance, as expounded by Dr. Parker in his monograph on " The Ancient Crosses at Gosforth, Cumberland."

With regard to the technique of this cross, it may be noted that the work is chiselled, and very beautifully chiselled—not merely sketched with the pick, like so much of the Scandinavian work which seems to be connected with it by style and subject. In one place, the bit of interlacing of double strands on the north side, the drill has been used as in the stone at St. John's, Beckermet. This is the only bit of plain interlacing—simple rope, not considered as a dragon's tail or other zoomorphic form—in the cross, by which it differs greatly from the early Anglian designs of Bewcastle and Irton, and this piece of simple interlacing is forced out with the drill, as if to heighten the interest; a sign of a late period in the school. The rest of the work is deeply cut, but the emphatic points are chiselled, not drilled.

The " Saint's " hogback is similarly handled, with chisel and drill; the drill sparingly used. The " Warrior's " tomb is much flatter.

The art of these Gosforth remains makes it hardly possible to regard them as Anglian. They connect in every way with Irish-Viking thought and work. Mr. Magnússon has given good reasons in his book, elsewhere quoted, for doubting that the " Hanged Odin " myth was known earlier than the end of the tenth century (" Odin's Horse," pp. 41-45.) It is just possible that the idea was brought to this coast, frequented by vikings, at an early time in the eleventh century: and it is farther possible that this very cross may have been the means of spreading the idea of Odin=the Hanged One= Christ. At least it is comprehensible that half-christianized folk,— of whom we have so many examples,—carved a cross with a crucifix on the Irish model, and added Pagan ornament, like the Sigurd at Halton, without all the *arrière pensée* or deep comparative philosophy of religion which we may be tempted to read into their work. Poetic artists, like Botticelli or Turner or Burne-Jones, while quite aware of the meaning in the symbols they use, deal in hints, not in arguments. Our Gosforth viking was like them; and we must not expect a very elaborate system in his dream of the old gods and the new.

GOSFORTH.

The " Fishing " Stone.

The fragment (probably of another cross) has the divine hart trampling on the worm above the plaited body of the adder, and—beneath—what Dr. Stephens recognizes as the fishing scene thus represented in the lay of Hymir :—

> The mighty Hymir drew,
> he alone,
> two whales up
> with his hook ;
> but at the stern abaft
> Véor (Thor) cunningly
> made him a line.
> Fixed on the hook
> the shield of men,
> the serpent's slayer,
> the ox's head.
> Gaped at the bait
> the foe of gods,
> the encircler beneath
> of every land.
> Drew up boldly
> the mighty Thor
> the worm with venom glistening,
> up to the side ;
> with his hammer struck,
> on his foul head's summit
> like a rock towering,
> the wolf's own brother.
> The icebergs resounded,
> the caverns howled,
> the old earth
> shrank together :
> At length the fish
> back into ocean sank.*

---

* In the prose Edda the giant took out his knife and cut Thor's line.

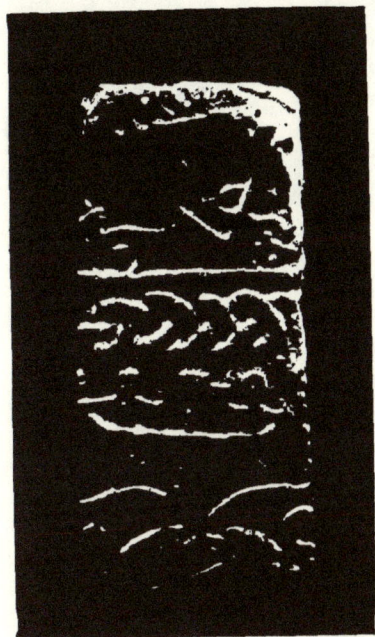

The Fishing Stone.

GOSFORTH.

(TO FACE P. 168.)

The fishing stone was discovered in 1882 by Dr. Parker, and is now built into the chancel wall. It is of red sandstone, measuring 27 by 13 inches, chiselled very clearly and rather deeply. Being more than double the width of the panels of the great cross, it cannot have belonged to any similar monument. It may be part of a low broad cross as at Dacre or Muncaster.

For the sake of the object lesson in treatment of interlacing, it is worth while, after looking at this, to compare the capitals of the Norman chancel-arch, and then to come back to our next item. Nothing but such comparison of originals will really explain the difference between the Norman and the pre-Norman feeling, though we have tried to illustrate it in this volume.

The Snake Fragment.

A little bit of carving found in 1894 and figured by Dr. Parker, now built into the wall close to the Fishing Stone, seems similar to it in style and age. It is of red sandstone, measuring 8 by 9 by 4½ inches; and has on one side a serpent's head, and on the other a very curly serpent's tail, interwoven. This also would be, in its complete form, too large to be a fragment of a cross like the standing cross.

The Sundial Shaft and Socket.

Dr. Parker, in his book above mentioned, quotes from *The Gentleman's Magazine* for 1799 an article signed "Carbo," saying that seven feet from the great cross another used to stand, which was cut down for a sundial,—perhaps, adds Dr. Parker, in 1789, when the church was altered. The same article says that between the two crosses was a flat stone with a sword sculptured on it. This, Dr. Parker notes, is now reported to be in use as a lintel at Gosforth Gate, with the carved side cut away or hidden in masonry; and as he remarks, it seems by the description to have been post-Norman.

The dial in the churchyard stands upon an octagonal pillar of red sandstone, like the stone of the standing cross. This pillar is not quite three feet high from the base, 32 inches in girth at the upper end and 29 in girth below. It is fixed in a socket stone, 33 by 30½ inches in size, and rising 15 inches out of the ground. The hole is square and too large for the pillar standing in it, though much too small for a shaft of which the fishing stone would be part.

Socket.

With this, another socket should be noticed; it was pointed out to us by the Rev. Rees Keene, built into the churchyard wall, on the east side. Red sandstone, measuring 37 by 24 inches, less than a foot in thickness. The hole would admit a shaft of about 8 inches square at the opening, and 6 inches square at 8 inches depth.

GOSFORTH.

THE CROSS-HEAD *A*.

In November, 1897, a part of a cross-head was found in the churchyard, and proves to belong to one of the fragments already preserved in the church, completing the head of what Dr. Parker believes to have been the cross destroyed in 1789 (Jefferson's *History*) and whose stump was then made into a style for a sun dial. This cross-head is said (*Gentleman's Magazine*) to have been kept in the parson's garden in 1799; it is now fixed in the wall of the church, for which let us be thankful.

      ✻   ✻   ✻

It is to be looked for above the Fishing Stone and Hog-backs, over an arch. It measures 23 by 17 inches. Some have supposed that it was a finial, because its neck seems to have been cut to fit into a socket on the ridging of the gable; but it is obvious that it was originally the head of a pre-Norman high cross; and it would fit in with the general indications suggested by the sun-dial shaft.

THE CROSS-HEAD B.

This cross-head was found in 1843 built into the north chancel doorway; and is now fixed in the wall alongside the cross-head A.

B 1 and B 2 are the two sides, from photographs taken before it was fixed in its present position.

It is of red-sandstone, measuring 21 by 14 inches; and from its style and size might have served as head to the cross of which the Fishing Stone was part.

THE CROSS-HEAD C.

This is of light-coloured freestone, measuring 11 by 9 in., coarsely chiselled: at present walled into the porch. This, says Dr. Parker, "though later than the others, is considered by Professor Stephens to be very ancient." We have no difficulty in recognizing it as one of our series of mediæval resting crosses or churchyard crosses. It is extremely like the cross-head at Cumwhitton already described.

B¹   B²   C

Its shaft would have been nearly square in section, 7 or 8 inches thick—and without ornament, except a chamfer or notches. It would have fitted the socket stone which is built into the churchyard wall.

We have therefore at Gosforth:

—this late cross, head and socket :

—the Fishing stone, Snake stone and head B, making up a low broad cross of Scandinavian type and subject:

—the sun-dial stem and socket, with the head A :

—and the standing cross.

So we have four Gosforth crosses in all ; of which two, the standing cross and the sun-dial cross stood together, until 1787, in singular resemblance to the two Penrith crosses of the Giant's Grave: not necessarily forming one grave, but more likely a pair of graves. At Penrith there are the hogbacks ; at Gosforth there was only a mediæval slab between the two, but the hogbacks, though hidden, were not far away.

GOSFORTH.

THE HOGBACKS.

In the month of June, 1896, when the north wall of the church was taken down in order that an aisle might be added, a large stone was found embedded in the foundations at the north-west corner. The illustrations* show two sides and one end of this stone. It is of the red sandstone of the neighbourhood, and is 5 feet 6 inches long, 1 foot thick at the base, tapering upwards to the ridge, and 2 feet 3 inches high in the centre, being slightly curved along the top so that the ends are only about 22 inches high. It is much weathered, and was broken into two by the blasting of the foundations at the taking down of the wall.

The stone is shrine-shaped, having the appearance of a house with almost perpendicular sides and a tiled roof, the tiles being cut away to a width of about 1 inch at the lower ends. On the sides of the shrine or walls of the house, beneath the tegulated roof, and on the ends, are sculptures. On one side (A) is depicted a truce-making between two parties of warriors. To the left is seen the conquering force with circular shields, and spears pointed upwards, their leader with outstretched arm accepting surrender or dictating terms to the weaker force, who, smaller men with smaller circular shields and with spears downpointed, the butt ends appearing behind their shoulders, attend their leader bearing the flag. One may count fifteen men and shields to the left and ten to the right; there have been more on both sides, the perishing and breaking of the stone having almost

---

* All the illustrations are printed from most admirable photographs taken by W. L. Fletcher, Esq., of Stoneleigh, Workington, who very kindly accompanied me on several occasions, and for whose assistance in the matter of photographs and rubbings, I am grateful. Our thanks and gratitude for help and hospitality are also due and are heartily tendered to the Rev. Rees Keene, M.A., the Rector of Gosforth, whose reverent care for all the relics in and around the church is so apparent.

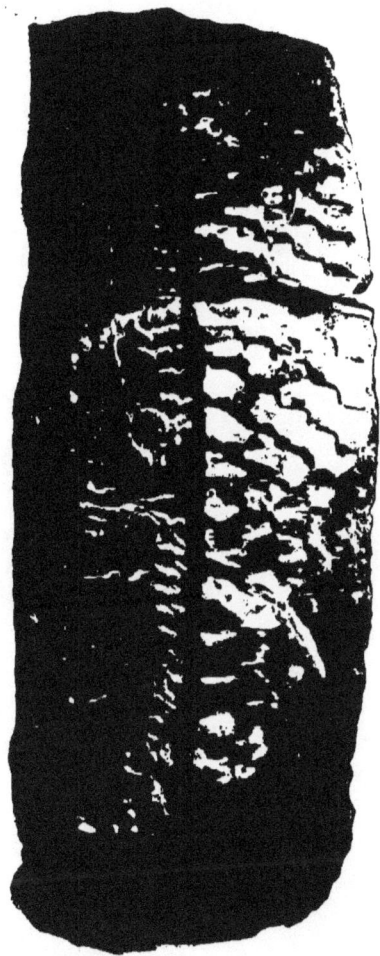

THE "WARRIOR'S TOMB," GOSFORTH. (A.)

(TO FACE P. 172.)

THE "WARRIOR'S TOMB." GOSFORTH. (B.)

(TO FACE P. 173.)

obliterated the traces of them. The points of the spears of the men to the left hand reach nearly to the eaves, whilst the butts of those to the right are a greater distance below. The flag-bearer holds the flagstaff in his right hand : the flag floats out in triangular shape towards the opposing company : the shield is on the left forearm, whereas the shields of the opposite party are carried on the right arm : thus the legs of the men are not seen, the shields overlapping each other and completing the lower part of the design throughout.

On the other side (B) five interlaced rings are seen to the left ; a single ring is seen to the right, with a small boss within the centre of a triquetrous form, which, on meeting the ring, at each of the three places of contact, divides and passes under it, folding back over the circle on either side and joining again beneath the arm of the triquetra. Between these two designs appears knot-work, amongst which is a serpent form with great head near the five rings, and in the lower part nearer the single ring a fine specimen of ring and band-work, apparently complete in itself, and only marred by the break in the stone done in the blasting of the wall at its taking down.

On one end of the stone is the figure of a man (C), possibly the chieftain, champion, or warrior who was buried beneath the stone. He is bareheaded, bearded, clothed in a short tunic, and belted, and may carry in the left hand a spear or battle-axe, the shaft of which seems to appear below, but the ends of the stone are much weathered and broken away ; beneath the left arm are traces of ornament. On the other gable, in spite of the weathering, &c., are also traces of interlaced ornament.

This is a most interesting example of this class of monument ; of which a dozen are known to exist in the diocese of Carlisle, and very few in the more southern dioceses. The curious patterns of rings interlacing and interpenetrating, and worked in with interlacing bands, may have been intended to represent the great wealth and munificence of the buried dead, "the bestower of rings," "the ring-scatterer," as the chieftain, according to the speech of the day, might be called; whilst the central part of the design, so weather worn that it cannot all be made out, represents the great dragon sprawling

over and guarding the treasure, the evil power which
must always be overcome before any good can be attained.
The Svastika may be seen at the intersections of the rings
and the symbol of the Holy Trinity within the circle and
amongst the knotwork, as if to draw the mind away from
temporal things to thoughts of the eternal treasure-house,
and the abode of the blessed. The question may be asked
'what great warrior leader lies buried here.' The same
question may be asked at many a place between Duddon and
Derwent. The land between the mountains and the sea-
board is full of the fragments of the memorials of our early
fathers and their faith, and the saints of the old British
church ; often almost the only record left to us of the doings
of that time.

A second shrine-shaped tombstone (see D. E. F.), of which
we give illustrations of two sides and one end, was found in
1897 under the north-east corner of the nave, as the warrior's
shrine was found beneath the north-west corner. This second
find we shall call the Saint's Shrine. Both stones had been
placed under the foundations of what we believe the architect,
Mr. C. J. Ferguson, F.S.A., considers to be a twelfth century
wall. The wall between the north aisle and the organ
chamber was being taken down in order to provide a recess
in which to place the warrior's tomb and other sculptured
stones found during the work of restoration, when this second
marvel was revealed and finally removed. It is 5 feet 1 inch
in length, 2 feet 10½ inches high, and a little less than a foot
thick in the thickest part. It is house-shaped or shrine-
shaped, and broken into three pieces by the weight of the wall
built above it. A large piece had been broken away from
one of the upper ends long before the tombstone was made
use of as a foundation stone—the chief corner-stone—for the
new part of the church built (possibly) in the twelfth century,
and when the tomb stood in the Kirk-garth, bedded in the
turf and surrounded by a rank growth of grass and herbage,
which had so protected the lower part of it that the marks of
the inch-wide chisel which the masons or sculptors of
those early pre-Norman times used upon the flat surface,
are quite clearly visible now, though plainly the upper
parts have suffered by the weathering of centuries. The

The "Warrior's Tomb." GOSFORTH. (C.)

(TO FACE P. 174.)

THE "SAINT'S TOMB. GOSFORTH. (D.)

(TO FACE P. 175.)

flat top of this broken part has been used by the natives
of those days as a whetstone on which to sharpen their
weapons, and besides the smooth surface so caused, appear
narrow grooves, made by the sharpening of some very
small and pointed weapons, such as arrow heads of fine
steel. The warrior's tomb has a rounded or bulged-out
roof, as well as the somewhat circular or 'hog-backed'
form of its ridging. The newer find, the saint's tomb, has a
steep, straight, high pitched roof, though the ridging is
slightly curved. The earlier find appears to follow more
closely the lines of the ordinary builder of the time; the new
find appears more nearly to approach the rigid lines of
the artist who would design an ornamental shrine. The main
idea is the same, no doubt, in both; but in the new
discovery we have the more ornamental roof, with its varied
designs, its ornamental gabled ends, and its characteristic
treatment of the ridge. The ridge is slightly curved and
sinks down at either end (one end being now broken away)
into the huge toothed jaws of the monster—death or hell.
Along this curve, on either side of the ridge, lies a wreathed
serpent form, apparently moving swiftly with open mouth
towards the great toothed maw awaiting it with hook or
hooked tongue protruding, suggesting the thought, "Canst
thou draw out leviathan with a hook or his tongue with a cord
which thou lettest down?" *Job* xli., 1. Up each side of the
roof, along either edge, appears a serpent form, whose head
upwards disappears beneath the throat of the monster jaws
forming the ends or corners of the ridge.

The roof,—it may be intended to represent one of beaten
gold, or of bronze, or of silver, and may once have been
made brilliant with colour,—is a highly decorated one, with
lozenge-shaped designs, and takes our thoughts at once
to the patterns seen in the illuminated MSS. of the Celtic
period. Indeed there is nothing on this stone which might
not have been wrought, though perhaps rudely done, after
the designs seen in these MSS. It would be difficult to
believe that the designer had not seen some such MS.

Beneath the eaves, on the sides of the stone, are serpent
forms plaited, with great heads and eyes, and with jaws
prolonging themselves and intertwining with their bodies, and

evolving other heads of themselves, so that the whole serpentine design reveals a conception of the several incarnations
of the evil power treated as a whole; and amidst it all,
at one end on the one side of the sculpture, and at either end
on the other, the human form appears naked in combat with
the beast. "Naked came I out of my mother's womb and
naked shall I return thither. The Lord gave and the Lord
hath taken away; blessed be the name of the Lord." *Job* i., 21.

In each lower corner of the side on which appear two
human figures pushing back the wreathing monster, seems to
be a human head.

On either gable and each end of the shrine, the crucified
and risen Saviour of mankind appears with arms outstretched;
clothed, and girded beneath a double arch on the one end,
—and ungirded beneath a triple arch on the other end.
Above the arches is the great symbol of the Holy Trinity.

Man's home is here for a time beneath the arch of heaven.
The Holy Ones dwell in the higher heavens. All the powers
below trend towards the great battle. Even mighty Thor
himself must some day go forth "to meet the wolf." But
there is an incarnation of the Holy One who will slay the
monster and overcome death and open the jaws of hell; and
through Him, His children, even the faithful dead shall
conquer, and the righteous with Him "for ever dwell in
Gimil gold-bedecked:" and so each end of the shrine shows
forth the Lord Christ beneath the arches, and above is the
great double triquetra issuing from a single upper angle, to
set forth for ever the great doctrine of the ever glorious
Trinity and the revelation of God unto man, even as the
purpose of every temple or church, or indeed the shrine of
man's heart, should be to set forth the Lord's death until He
come.

At Aspatria the triquetra appears in each alternate division
of the highly ornamented roof; and the design in this respect,
and also as to the ornament along the eaves, is nearly
identical with that of the representation of the temple
(Jerusalem) in the book of Kells, saving that the ornament
which runs up the edges of the ends of the roofing of the
temple, lies along the eaves at Aspatria. Beneath the eaves
in the representation of the temple runs interlaced work, and

THE "SAINT'S TOMB." GOSFORTH. (E.)

(TO FACE P. 176.)

THE "SAINT'S TOMB." GOSFORTH. (F.)

(TO FACE P. 177.)

in the very centre of this, the narrower bands are made to form a knot (a small triquetra-like knot) in exactly the same manner as is done in this Gosforth sculpture, where a similar knot has been broken away by the cracking through of the stone. The piece is safely kept and was shown to me by the clerk, and may be affixed. There are no human figures in this Kells band of interlacing. Two great heads stand up above the upper corners, their jaws interlacing and forming a square sided knot or fret.

At Plumbland, the very ornamental triquetra is seen on the gabled ends, and the sides are composed of intertwined serpent forms.

The Penrith "hogbacks" resemble the warrior's tomb.

At Heysham, Lancashire, the very remarkable "hog-back" has huge heads at either end over the upper corners, and the four legs of the beast, made small but quite appreciable, appear on either side of the ends of the stone.

At Cross-Canonby the "hogback" is all roof and the ends are raised as though intended to represent the great heads.

There is a very rich later specimen of the shrine-shaped coped stone (the so-called tomb of Abbot Hedda) in Peterborough Cathedral, with full-length figures of the Apostles, and by some believed to be the tomb of St. Kineburga.

At Lowther there is, lying in the churchyard, a portion of a coped tombstone, with figures rudely carved and much weathered, and the only fragment of such work in this diocese known to me.

At Bongate, (Appleby), Cross-Canonby, and Bromfield, the late Norman workmen placed the coped tombstones of the former lords of the land as lintels over their doorways.

Speaking of the burial of St. Chad in the seventh century, the Venerable Bede says : " The place of the sepulchre is a wooden monument, made like a little house, covered, having a hole in the wall, through which those that go thither for devotion usually put in their hand and take out some of the dust."

GREAT SALKELD.

T HE church of St. Cuthbert is remarkable for its massive peel
tower, like Burgh-on-Sands, Dearham, and Newton Arlosh ;
also for its fine doorway, which was cleared of plaster in 1898, and is
now for the first time illustrated.

DIAL.

On the east jamb of the door is a dial like those at Bolton,
Milburn, etc., which are figured in the plate opposite *Bolton*.
This one has no circle, but a large hole for the gnomon and
four rays, indicating perhaps Nones, Sext (a short line), and
Tierce, with another marking some point of time a little after
one p.m.

INTERLACED CAPITALS.

On the right hand of the same door are the three capitals,
most curious and interesting, drawn opposite. That to the right
has a bird with wings outstretched, holding a fish in one claw
and pecking at its head ; underneath is what may be meant for a
lamb, and on the inner side of the capital is a curly snake with
a quaint calf-like head. The middle capital has a couple of snakes
twisted together and biting each other ; underneath them a head,
or perhaps rather a skull. This device reminds one of the abode of
Hel as described above in Mr. Calverley's quotations ; and the
innermost capital seems to be literally honey-combed with little
hexagonal cells, in each of which is what appears to be meant for
a skull. Above is a long band of irregular and angular interlace-
ment, here and there ending in an abortive spiral. This recalls the
spiral, cellular, and irregularly interlaced work as the series of
crosses which we have remarked as somewhat like the Rowler

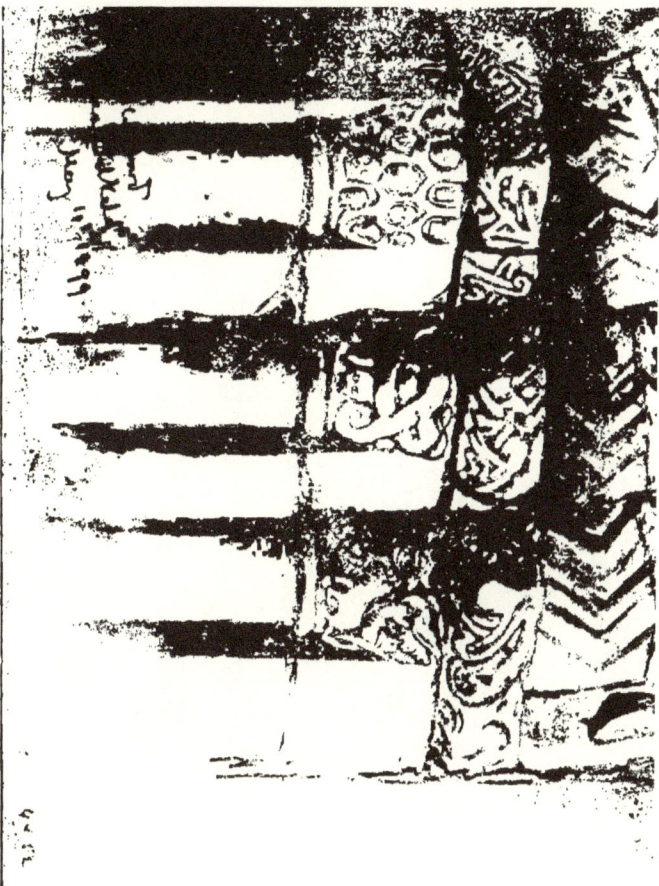

CAPITALS OF THE DOORWAY; EAST SIDE;

GREAT SALKELD.

(TO FACE P. 178.)

CAPITAL OF THE DOORWAY, WEST SIDE.

GREAT SALKELD.

(TO FACE P. 179.)

cross at Maughold, Isle of Man, and may be some help for comparison ; though the degeneracy of the pristine classical scroll and
plait has here gone to great lengths.

The other sketch shows the middle capital on the west side
of the doorway. It is more floral in character and without animal
forms.

At the head of the Norman arch are grotesque faces, in two sets
of three each, not figured here.

HAILE.

THE church was appropriated to Conishead priory in 1345; the manor is mentioned in early Norman times; but there must have been a church here long before, and a settlement before that, for into the wall of the vestry is built a small Roman altar, found on the site.

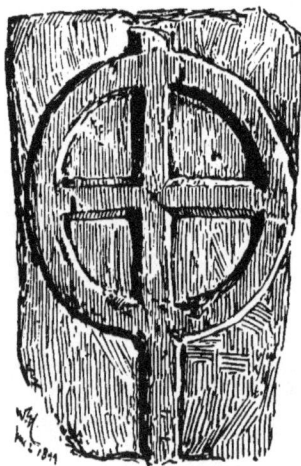

RING-CROSS.

Built into the vestry, with the Roman altar, at the restoration of 1883, is the Roman-looking ring-cross figured opposite. It is of red sandstone, 10 by 6½ inches in size, and chiselled in relief; part probably of a mediæval grave-slab.

In *Trans. C. & W. A. & A. S.*, vol. III., part I., 1877, Canon Knowles gave drawings of fragments " which are, I think," he says, " six in number, but have all suffered much from weather and ill-usage . . . they show what I call an ear-shaped guilloche, occurring also on the front of Irton Cross." He attributed them to the eleventh century. The drawings are here copied with Canon Knowles' permission. The size of A is not given ; B is about 3 feet 1¼ inches ; C, 3 feet 7¼ inches, and D, 2 feet 7¼ inches. These fragments have disappeared.

THE LOST FRAGMENTS.

HAILE.

HAILE.

SPIRAL FRAGMENT.

Outside the church is built into a corner of the church wall, on the south, a fragment from a cross-shaft of the ' spiral ' type, like that at St. John's (Beckermet), St. Bees, and elsewhere. It is of white sandstone, 20 inches broad (taking the true breadth of the shaft, for the stone has been laid on its side to build it into the wall). The length of as much as is visible is 18 inches, and the thickness 7½. All that can now be seen of its ornament is given in our drawing.

HALTON.

HALTON is not in the diocese of Carlisle; it is a little way over the border; but Mr. Calverley's paper can hardly be omitted, for two reasons : for the share he had in recovering and restoring the two crosses as they now stand, and for the analogy of the Scandinavian subject with those at Gosforth and elsewhere in the Cumbrian series. To these reasons may be added the justice due to an original investigator; for Mr. Calverley seems to have been the first to point out the Sigurd legend at Halton, in his papers read before the Lancaster Philosophical Society on February 26th, 1891; and before the Royal Archæological Institute in the autumn of the same year. Bishop Browne had already shown the Sigurd legend on the Leeds cross in 1885; but Halton was still misinterpreted.

The story of the restoration of the fragments is told in Mr. Calverley's own words. Writing on August 4th, 1891, he said :—

A very interesting work has just been successfully accomplished by the rector of Halton, Lancaster, the Rev. S. Hastings. This is no less than the putting together of about a dozen pieces of sculptured stones, fragments of very ancient crosses, which were mostly found in the walls of the old church and in the churchyard, and surmounted by a sun-dial placed there [in 1635] when the old cross was cut down.

This shaft was carved on one side with a cross. St. Mary and St. John stand on either hand, with other figures, and one above; and on the other sides are adapted and Christianized saga-scenes. Canon Browne and Mr. Romilly Allen have both been interested in this cross-shaft and in the other fragment which had been built into the wall of the porch, and both have written papers thereon full of interest.

It was, however, in the summer of 1890 that the Cumberland and Westmorland Antiquarian and Archæological Society were invited by the Lancaster Philosophical

Society to visit the neighbourhood. The Halton cross and
the remains of known fragments were examined, and some
remarks were made on them by the present writer. A desire
was expressed that an attempt should be made to preserve,
and, if possible, to replace the sculptures, as had been done
in the case of the great Leeds cross. The Rector, it was
found, was entirely of the same mind, and he soon had the
carved stones taken from the walls. After a good deal
of work they have been built up nearly as they were before
the crosses were broken down.

At his kind invitation I stayed at the Rectory a few days,
arranging, and making drawings. It soon appeared that
the fragments belonged to at least three, and possibly to four
different crosses, all of pre-Conquest date. The churchyard
dial-stone with the top of the shaft bearing the Evangelists,
which had been lying long in the churchyard, having
been brought from Caton, to which place it had at some
time been carried away, together with a small portion of
a panel found in the churchyard wall (which the mason has
unfortunately fixed a little too high) gave the height and
proportion of the cross. The upper arm of the cross-head,
found in the staircase leading to the room over the porch,
gave the design of the whole head ; and although the mason
has not carved the new head in such relief as the old work
showed, and has not quite followed the drawing, but has
made both sides of the central design the same, which should
not have been ; yet the new work gives a satisfactory idea of
the old cross, and draws attention to the losses sustained in
the iconoclastic period. It will surely teach beholders the
need there is of treasuring the art relics which still remain
to us from that interesting age when Christian thought was
gradually leavening the minds of our Northern ancestors.
The Rector must always deserve thoughts of gratitude for
saving these treasures from destruction ; treasures which
may be the means of teaching many generations chapters of
the history of their country, which could never have been
written had not such old-time picture books been rescued
from the destroying hands of the careless and indifferent, and
of those who continually cry, " Give us some new thing, and
disperse the old."

It was disappointing at first to find that many of the fragments would not fit together so as to prove themselves part
of the cross standing outside the church, but as some new
discoveries were made, and the edges,—in one case a part of
the back,—of another cross were revealed, I was able to
decide with certainty the measurement of the width, and
thickness of the lower part of a second cross, and also the
full size of one of the upper panels of the same cross, and to
arrange several of the intermediate panels. This was built
up against the north jamb of the lower arch inside the
church, and will be of lasting interest, as it bears some
hitherto unknown carvings. This, with the churchyard cross,
is to be the subject of a paper to be read before the
Royal Archæological Institute in Edinburgh, this autumn.
Fragments of one or two other crosses have been built into
the tower.

(From the paper just mentioned we omit a few prefatory pages,
dealing with the Cumbrian crosses in general, and proceed) :—

The cross to which I now draw your attention is surmounted
by a head almost all new. This I have drawn out from data
furnished by a fragment which was lately found built into the
wall of the church-porch. The shaft was cut down in the
17th century and surmounted by a flat metal sun-dial of the
ordinary type. The fragments were dispersed ; all but three
pieces are lost. The upper piece of the cross-head, carved
in every part, shows what the original was. The upper part
of the shaft bears on its four sides the emblems of the four
Evangelists, the symbolic beasts: St. Matthew, with the face
of a man ; St. Mark, the lion ; St. Luke, with the head of a
calf ; St. John, the eagle. This fragment was spirited away
to a house at Caton, a neighbouring village, but was brought
home again, and lay a long time in the churchyard. A
smaller fragment we found in the churchyard wall facing the
street, and we were enabled to fit it into its proper place in
the cross.

The lower part of the cross-shaft, standing in a massive
socket-stone of three steps, with those of the other fragments

which were then known, have been described by Canon
Browne, Disney Professor of Archæology at Cambridge, and
Mr. J. Romilly Allen, F.S.A. Scot.*

The south face is covered with conventional foliage and
interlaced work in panels. A cable moulding runs up each
of the four angles of the shaft. .

The west face, in the bottom compartment, which (as in
the case of the other divisions) is marked by an arch
springing from a square corbel upon jambs slightly sloping,
shows a tall Latin cross with the figures of SS. Mary and
John on either side, and beneath the figures two chalices of
the old type. The compartment above contains a seated
figure, without nimbus, having an orb or boss above his left
shoulder, and two small figures seated at his feet upon the
floor. Small round pellets adorn the band above the arch.

The stone has come from the quarry much as it now is,
and the work has been done on the unsquared surface.

The north side shows strips of knot-work partially surrounding square or oblong spaces which appear to have been
left for inscriptions, or other purpose. A small panel contains
a well-shaped and spirited horse, and, above, two beasts
intertwined ; the head and tail of another pair appear above.

The east face in the lower compartment contains the figure
of a smith with uplifted hammer in hand, seated on a chair,
near a forge. Beneath the forge a veritable pair of black-
smith's bellows, with the central round aperture and the projecting hand-piece, is in use. Above lies a pair of pincers;
above the pincers and intervening mass a hammer is seen ;
above the hammer a man's body without his head, which
may be lying in the corner above the hammerhead. On the
man's right hand side a huge pair of pincers and a short
sword are seen ; and above the shoulders of the man a piece
of iron in the form of a knot and ring.

In a square compartment above this remarkable scene
stands to the left a man holding something which lies along
horizontally above four bands which are interlaced below,

---

* Mr. J. Romilly Allen's paper was read before the British Archæological
Association on the 17th February, 1886, *British Archæological Journal*, vol.
xlii., p. 328; and Canon Browne, now Bishop of Bristol, treated of Halton in
his address on the pre-Norman Sculptured Stones in Lancashire, read to the
Lancashire and Cheshire Antiquarian Society, November 2nd, 1886. (ED.)

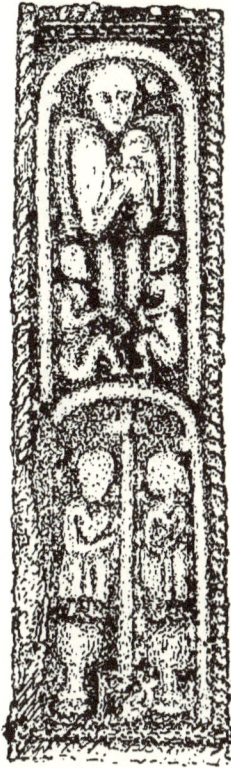

East Face.   West Face.   North Face.

THE "SIGURD" CROSS.

HALTON.

and placing the thumb of the other hand in his open mouth. Above, in an arched space, is a tree or foliage work, with two birds seated on the upper branches, and what has appeared to some of us as a man standing to the left. This figure is very indistinct, though parts seem clear enough in some lights.

The other cross consists of fragments which the rector, the Rev. S. Hastings, caused to be taken out of the porch wall last year; they had been placed there by him on the rebuilding of the church.

The lower niche, arched like the compartments of the first cross, contains a standing figure, apparently within a second circular-headed space or canopy. This is not a halo or nimbus, as the continuation passes round the shoulders and down towards the feet. The ecclesiastic holds in his hands and in front of him a large rectangular figure, much larger than the ordinary book of the Gospels, filling the whole width of the panel and covering the greater part of the body; his hands appear on the under edge. At his feet kneels, making obeisance, or kissing the hem of his garment, or receiving some grant or honour, a small human figure apparently naked.

Above is another compartment, with a seated ecclesiastic holding in his right hand a cross, and in his left a book of the gospels or missal. Above is a blank space, and then, above again, is a fragment containing the upper part of an arched panel holding three figures, each with a book; and above this another arched niche holding a tall standing figure facing to the left, and engaged with his hands on what seems to be an animal sitting on its haunches. If it were on mediæval work we should suggest David and the lion ; if upon Scandinavian work, Tyr and the wolf: possibly here it may be a Christianized form of Vidar, the silent one, an incarnation of Deity, wrenching open the jaws of hell after those jaws have swallowed the Holy One, as we see in another portrayal on the great cross at Gosforth.

On the edge of this panel there is what has never before been seen since this cross was broken up for building material in the old church, many centuries ago : a figure of the archer * with his bow, shooting upwards towards the

---

* Compare the kneeling archer on the Ruthwell cross.

cross-head, the emblem of the Christ (and perhaps in this case bearing the Christ). This, I think, must be taken as Hödr with his mistletoe shaft, under the instigation of the deceiver, aiming the death-shot at the Divine one.

This fragment should, I think, be turned round; the arches and the subjects are a little different from the rest of the face of the stone. But if turned round it would be built up against the tower wall of the church and never be seen; so we thought it best to place it where it is, and make the explanation.

The topmost fragment is again of the full thickness of the original cross. The carvings at the back are worn away; the edges have interlaced patterns; the face bears the head and bust of a lady with an ornament around her neck, within an arched panel and surrounded by the usual canopy.

There are fragments of two other crosses. One shows scroll-work; the other scroll and foliage, with interlacing and knot-work. One is fixed in the tower and the other will be placed with the rest for security.*

Now what is to be said about the subjects carved on these crosses and about the date of the work? One of the subjects is most remarkable, and gives a special interest to this cross; for here on the west face and north we have the story of Sigurd Fafnir's bane; here is his sword and the forging of it; his horse Grani which bore away the treasure; the roasting of the dragon's heart; the listening to the voice of the birds, and the killing of Regin the Smith.

The story, so far as it relates to our subject, is this:—We all know that the love of money is the root of all evil. Now there were two brothers, Fafnir and Regin; Fafnir held all the wealth, and became a huge monster dragon, keeping watch over his underground treasure-house. Regin, his brother, had all skill in smith's work, but no courage. He it was forged the sword wherewith the hero Sigurd went forth to kill the dragon and take the treasure. This he did with the help of his wonderful horse Grani, who, when the heavy boxes of treasure were placed on his back, would not move until his master had mounted, but then went off merrily

---

* As is now done.—(ED.)

enough. This story, Anglicized and Christianized, is the
story of our English patron saint, St. George the horse-rider
and the dragon-slayer.*

We know the ancient belief that the strength of every
enemy slain passes into the body of the conqueror. Men
thought that in order to obtain the courage and powers of
beasts and other creatures it was necessary to eat of their
flesh. Thus when Sigurd had killed the dragon, Regin asked
for some of the flesh which Sigurd was about to give, and
was even roasting it for him when, happening to burn his
fingers, he put his throbbing thumb into his mouth, as anyone else might do. Upon the first taste of the heart's blood
of the serpent, the voices of all animate things were made
plain to him, and he heard a little bird telling him that Regin
was a cunning deceiver and would cheat him ; and another
little bird said he had better acquire the wisdom of the
serpent for himself, rather than give it to his enemy ; and
another told him to slay the evil one for his own safety, and
so forth. The which Sigurd did, and was ever afterwards
the emblem of all that was noble and courageous amongst
men.

Well, here is his story, written in stone. It is also shown
in a drawing given by Mr. du Chaillu in his book on " The
Viking Age," (vol. i., p. 187) representing the Ramsund rock,
Söderland, Sweden. This is a grave-memorial, bearing an
inscription not relating to the subject of the sculpture, which
is taken from the Sigurd story as told in the earlier Edda and
in the Völsunga-saga. Perhaps the Sigurd and Holmger
commemorated on the stone thought they were descended
from the famous Sigurd (as Professor Säve, the discoverer,
remarked, to account for the introduction of the subject.)

There is another stone at Gœk in the same province, with
a similar treatment of the legend, but " above the horse
Grani is a Christian cross."

There are door-jambs at Hyllestad church, Sætersdal (Du
Chaillu, *Viking Age*, vol. ii., p. 267), with seven episodes from
the Völsunga-saga ; also at Lardals church, Jarsberg (the

---

* The parallelism of the next part of the story of Sigurd and one of Finn-mac-
Coul is noticed in an amusing passage of " The Romany Rye " (chap. 44) by
George Borrow. [ED.]

same, p. 269), and at Versas church, Vestergötland (the same,
p. 248): Also in the Isle of Man [at Kirk Andreas, Jurby,
and Malew, the Sigurd legend is carved on monumental
crosses.]   In King Olaf's time ladies embroidered such
subjects. A poet being asked to make a song upon the
hangings of the hall "looked and saw that Sigurd slaying
Fafnir was embroidered on them " (the same, p. 248.)

Now as to the date. The work seems to show a mixture
of ideas and a transition state, generally. I can only give
what I should think must be the latest time at which it could
have been executed, the time of Tosti, Earl of Northumbria.

Tosti was brother of Harold Godwinson, King of England.
He fell at the battle of Stamford Bridge, two nights before
Michaelmas, 1066, after Harold Sigurdson had been slain.
This Harold, son of Sigurd, is known as Hardrada.

Tosti was lord of the manor of Halton.   Halton had been
given by Athelstan, who reigned 925-940, " to God, St. Peter,
and the church at York," during the prelacy of Bishop
Wulfstan. The site of a Saxon castle, which may have been
the seat of Earl Tosti's barony, is to be seen near the church.

Tosti was sent to Rome * by Edward the Confessor
to obtain privileges from the Pope for the new abbey
of Westminster. Aldred, then Archbishop of York, just
translated from Worcester, with the King's two chaplains
and Gurth, the King's brother-in-law, and Guy, kinsmen to
the Confessor and companion of Tosti, joined the company.
The Archbishop of York wanted to receive the pall as
Archbishop from the Pope, and a dispensation to retain
Worcester as well, which was refused; and Tosti was furious
at the refusal. Some of the party made pilgrimages to
the graves of the apostles ; and upon one expedition robbers
attacked them and stripped even the Archbishop naked.
Tosti returned to Rome with threats that he would expose
the weakness of a pope who could not protect his people
from bandits. He obtained the suit of the Archbishop and
the privileges for Westminster Abbey ; and Edward the
Confessor made Tosti Earl of Northumbria.

---

* In 1061 ; see the story in detail, Freeman's *Norman Conquest*, vol. II., pp.
462-466.—(ED.)

May it not be that these crosses commemorate some of those historic events ?

There is a painting of St. Dunstan (who was a smith also, A.D. 988) where he is shown kneeling prostrate at the feet of the Saviour. The kneeling figure at the foot of the robed figure on one of these fragments has reminded Mr. Romilly Allen of this painting.

The northern expedition of Athelstan, the first real king of all England ; the expedition against Malcolm (1031) whose territory at one time extended to the boundary of the parish of Kendal ; and the erection of the Earldom of Northumbria are amongst the events which remind us of the active part which this district must have taken in making the history of the times immediately preceding the Conquest. The position of the castle-hill, near the church ; and the finding of the great treasure near Halton,—coins of the date 1014-1036, all of Canute,—would suggest that the lord of Halton was in league with Malcolm.*

Again, Harald Hardrada was Harald Sigurdson. He was wise beyond other men. He never fled from battle. His forces, if combined with those of our English king Harold Godwinson, would have proved very formidable, and might have been too strong for Norman William. But the brothers Harold and Tosti quarrelled ; for though Tosti had been made chief over the late King's host, and was the defender of the land, and ruler over all the other earls when Edward began to grow old, his brother Harold (Godwinson) was nearest attendant on the King, and had charge over all his money. Thus, when the king was about to die, he called those around him to witness that he gave his kingship to Harold. Tosti did not like to be Harold's under-man † ; he went to Flanders ; tried to raise a host and allies in order to seize the kingdom, but did not succeed. Then he went to Norway (so the saga tradition says) to Harold Hardrada

---

* Malcolm raided Tosti's earldom in 1061, during the Roman pilgrimage, but in 1066 they were "sworn brothers."—Freeman, vol. III., p. 346.—(ED.)

† The quarrel between Tosti and Harold is full of difficulties. Freeman thought that it really arose out of the revolt of Northumberland (*Norman Conquest*, vol. II., p. 676) and quotes what is more interesting in this connection, Peter Langtoft's repeated title for him, "Tostus of Cumbirland."—(ED.)

(Sigurdson), and the result was the landing in England, the fight at Scarborough, and the final overthrow at Stamford Bridge, where Tosti and Hardrada both fell.

His followers may have carried his body from the battle of Stamford Bridge, where he was slain, to be buried in St. Wilfrid's churchyard, near his hall of Halton. I have heard it said that he was buried at Trondhjem Cathedral, * but the bishop's secretary has not been able to confirm such opinion, and his place of burial is really unknown. His followers, at any rate, may have raised a cross in Halton churchyard to his memory, and carved upon it the story, popular in that time, of the treasure and the strife for it between the brothers, and of Sigurd the dragon-slayer.

Godred Crovan, who came from Iceland to help Tosti in the battle, may have seen this stone. He fled westward from Stamford Bridge, and on the way to Ireland called at the Isle of Man. He afterwards returned and became king of Man [where Sigurd crosses yet exist.]

On this cross we see the figure of the Pope seated, and a little naked figure bowed down at his feet, receiving a charter. This, I believe, shows the Pope granting the charter for the building of Westminster Abbey.

We all know that in cases of difficulty or of greatness a woman bears a prominent part. Further research may tell us who is the lady in this case, shown in the uppermost panel but one, on the cross-fragments now put up in the church tower, or may in some way reveal more of the history of these most interesting relics.

I would mention that the tree, figured on the stone at Ramsund rock, is almost identical (without the birds) with a tree figured in one of the illustrations, supposed to have been done about the year 1000, to Cædmon's paraphrase. This MS. would be a kind of authorised version of the Holy Scriptures at the time of which we speak, and would be the means of spreading its art motives wherever men connected with the English Christianity of the time might journey.

---

* The Liber de Hyde says that the body of Hardrada was taken to Norway. Snorri Sturluson tells us that Tosti's sons went to Norway and settled there; but William of Malmesbury says that Tosti was buried at York.—See Freeman's *Norman Conquest*, vol. III., pp. 374, 375.—(ED.)

The above is Mr. Calverley's lecture from the manuscript, illustrated with a drawing of his, hitherto unpublished.

It seems a 'far cry' from Halton in Lonsdale to Ramsund in
Sweden ; but the relations between England and Scandinavia, before
the Norman Conquest, were very intimate. Danish arms invaded
England ; but English arts invaded Denmark and Norway and
Sweden. Norway was christianized from England ; English com-
merce penetrated the North, even to Iceland, in the tenth and
eleventh centuries ; and the languages were not so differentiated
at that time as to put a bar to intercourse. The closing chapter of
Olaf Tryggvason's Saga tells how Edward the Confessor used to
read the story of King Olaf to his nobles and guardsmen every
Easter: " Orm Thorliotsson, a wise and truthful man, who lived at
Dryness in the Orkneys, declared that he heard King Edward read
the Saga out of the very book that Olaf himself had sent to King
Ethelred from Jerusalem : "—a book in Old Norse.

It is no wonder, then, that similar art-motives should be found
in places so widely apart ; and even the far-away Sigurd legend has
a demonstrable connection with Tosti and his family. Mr. Calverley
mentions Professor Säve's remark to the effect that some claim of
descent from Sigurd Fafnir's-bane may have suggested the commemoration of the Ramsund dead by sculptures representing the
the Völsung story. Now, curiously enough, Tosti might have
claimed a similar pedigree ; which we have drawn out below,
following the saga of Olaf Tryggvason (c. 61) for the ancestors
of King Gorm of Denmark, and Heimskringla (Harald Fairhair,
c. 29, and Harald Greyfell, c. 11) for the ancestry of Styrbjörn,
which shows how the name of Tosti came into the family. The
word is said to mean ' Frog,'—perhaps a bit of archaic totemism.
The g at the end of the Anglo-Saxon form Tostig is like the g in
the English Swegen for Danish Svein, and must have been
pronounced as y. The name was not uncommon in Scandinavian
families, as in Kormak's saga ; for Sköglar-Tosti was a great
Viking, surnamed "of Skögul " the Valkyrie.

Earl Tosti was evidently proud of his Viking blood and connections.
His father, Earl Godwine the Englishman, was a ' self-made man ';
but his mother was a great lady of high Danish and Swedish
lineage. Throughout he seems to have ' taken after ' his mother
and her kin ; his sons, to whom he gave Norse names, settled in
Norway and founded families there. His grandfather Thorgils came
on the father's side from the Swede-kings, and on the mother's from
the Dane kings and Sigurd ; and was called Sprakaleggr, meaning
" Dandylegs," no doubt from his tight and smart hose. In Eyrbyggja-
saga (c. 45), the servant of Snorri the priest says to the wounded

man whose thigh—as he did not observe in undressing him—was
pinned through by a broken shaft:—"It's no lie they tell of you
Thorbrandssons, when they call you dandies; your breeches are so
tight, they will never come off!"

Of course, Sigurd Fafnir's-bane was more or less of a mythical
personage, as was Ragnar Lodbrok; but in the belief of Tosti's age
the pedigree would stand somewhat in this manner :—

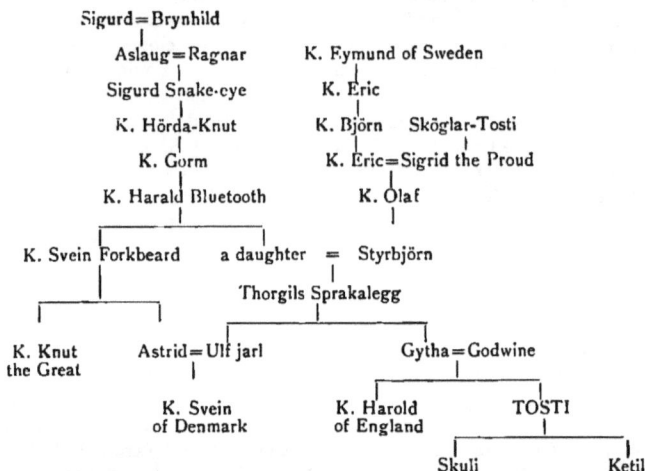

```
Sigurd = Brynhild
       |
   Aslaug = Ragnar          K. Eymund of Sweden
       |                          |
  Sigurd Snake-eye             K. Eric
       |                          |
   K. Hörda-Knut             K. Björn    Sköglar-Tosti
       |                          |            |
     K. Gorm                   K. Eric = Sigrid the Proud
       |                          |
  K. Harald Bluetooth          K. Olaf
       |                          |
   ┌────────┴────────┐
K. Svein Forkbeard   a daughter   =   Styrbjörn
       |                    |
                      Thorgils Sprakalegg
   ┌───────┴──────┐              |
                         ┌───────┴────────────────┐
K. Knut      Astrid = Ulf jarl          Gytha = Godwine
the Great            |                       |
               K. Svein          ┌──────────┴─────────┐
              of Denmark      K. Harold          TOSTI
                             of England            |
                                           ┌───────┴───────┐
                                         Skuli           Ketil
```

Mr. Calverley's drawing gives the standing cross in the churchyard. It is deeply cut, though the weathering makes it doubtful
what tool has been used. The design is very puzzling and curious,
for though the general resemblance to Bewcastle and Ruthwell is
obvious, the difference is decided. It has similar panels of fruit
and flowers, but the feeling with which these are executed is
totally different; the curves are not strongly struck, but weakly
drawn and feebly composed; the interlacing is vague, stringy and
asymmetrical, resembling the interlacing of the latest periods, not
that of the fine Anglian time; the cable-edging is petty and poor.
The figures under arches are also like but unlike the other
great crosses; they are very badly drawn, with none of the classic
proportion and dignity which must strike even the least critical
visitor to Bewcastle or Ruthwell. The Mary and John are practically the same as at Burton, and over the Sigurd scenes there is a
double conventional pattern recalling the designs of the Burton
shaft. The horse is very spirited; as good a bit of animal drawing

as the stag at Dacre; and over the horse is a vague pattern like the spiral in Aspatria vestry wall. These characteristics connect the Sigurd cross with a series of sculptures quite different in style from those which its general form recalls. In a word, it gives the impression of being a late imitation of Bewcastle.

The fragments in the church are similar in style; deep cut, ill-drawn figures in niches, much weathered, but still showing plainly their design, or want of it, as compared with the classic examples in the north of our district.

There are preserved in the tower the two fragments mentioned above; a bit of a large cross with " blobby " interlacing on it, very weathered, but apparently resembling Gosforth cross in style; also a fragment of a smaller shaft with very neat spiral scrolls on a zig-zag stem, well designed and well carved, with a good ring-plait in panels up the side. This looks like Anglian work, and of the best kind. It is like the shaft at Heysham, but like nothing in our district.

In the porch are two fine Norman capitals with deeply-cut spirals or volutes for ornament, and cable mouldings ; showing the outcome of this kind of art in the twelfth century; for art did not by any means ' turn over a new leaf' when the Normans came in. It was influenced, but not revolutionized.

HEVERSHAM.

ANGLIAN CROSS-SHAFT.

HEVERSHAM, a parish some eight miles long and three wide, and containing several townships, is mentioned in Domesday by the name of Eversham, Euer being possibly the name of an early owner whose patronymic, we are told, was not extinct in the district in 1777.

The church stands near to the Roman road from Chester to Carlisle, and between Lancaster (where all the western traffic which was not destined to follow the tedious roads around and across the æstuaries of Morecambe and Duddon must strike northwards) and Kendal, at which place the road to the head of Windermere,—the camp at Ambleside,— into the very heart of the mountains, and over Hardknott into the Coupland district to Ravenglass and Whitehaven, turned a little to the westward.

About a mile to the north-east of the church and within the parish is the village of Hincaster. The name seems to point to a Roman camp or fort. Whether there are traces of a Roman colony or settlement here I have not ascertained, but that a considerable degree of Christian culture had been attained in the immediately succeeding centuries appears to be attested by the existence of the cross at Heversham, and by records written in the early days after the Norman conquest. Unfortunately the dedication of the original church of Heversham is not known, and there has been some confusion of the names of St. Mary and St. Peter. A well 200 yards north-west of the church is known as St. Mary's Well, and may have led to the supposition that the ancient dedication was to St. Mary. On the other hand, the names of St. Peter and St. Mary may have been allowed to supplant as far as possible the name of the patron saint of the original church of the British period, or of the time when the Teutonic settlers had embraced the faith, and after the first Norman baron of Kendal, Ivo de Talebois, had granted the church to the Abbey of St. Mary at York, which grant was confirmed to the abbey by the name of the church of Eversheim by Gilbert, son of Roger Fitz-Reinfred, in the reign of Richard I.

The *manor* of Heversham was formerly held by Tosti, Earl of Northumbria, who fell fighting against his brother Harold Godwinson, the English king, at Stamford Bridge, where also fell Harold Hardrada (Harold Sigurdson) on the eve, as it were, of the battle of Hastings. Something of the story of Tosti is told, I believe, on the crosses at Halton, at which place he probably had a residence, and concerning which I had the honour of reading a paper before the Royal Archæological Institute at their meeting at Edinburgh two years ago. Domesday book states that Earl Tosti had held, amongst other lands, two carucates at Hennecastre, two at Evreshaim, two at Levens, &c., which lands are now held for purposes of taxation by Roger of Poictou and a certain priest under him. " In Biedun habuit comes Tosti sex carucatas terræ ad geldum; Nunc habet Rogerus Pictaviensis et Ernuin presbyter sub eo. In Jalant 4 car., Fareltun 4 car., Prestun 3 car., Berewic 2 car,, Hennecastre 2 car., Evreshaim 2 car., Lefuenes 2 car." (Domesday). The manor, as well as the church, passed through the hands of the barons of Kendal into those of the Abbey of St. Mary at York, and was after the dissolution of the monasteries granted to different persons, one of whom, Richard Bowskell (whose arms 1601 were in the east window of the south aisle of the church), bought out several of the others, excepting certain tenements in *Rowell, Leesgill, Woodhouse, Aughtinwaite, Milnthorpe,* and *Eversham,* names which serve to remind one of the antiquity and comparative independence of the holdings, as does the clause in the inquisition reserving to the owner a right to " all the works of the tenants of the said manor called *bond days*," if any such appertain thereto.

Heversham presents a fair specimen of the history of parochial and church property from early times. Seized by the Conqueror and given to his friends, by the year 1459 it had been appropriated to the Abbey of St. Mary, the Archbishop reserving a portion for a vicar. This portion was set out next year as one third of the mill at *Milnthorpe*, anciently belonging to the church, tithes of demesne lands, one quarter of the tithes of the people, &c. The vicar was to find bread, wax, wine for the church, pay 106s. 8d. to the abbot and convent, repair the chancel and bear Archiepiscopal and Archidiaconal charges. The residue was alienated from the parish to be eventually swallowed by the Crown at the dissolution. There are two chapelries within the parish which deserve attention, Crosscrake and Crossthwaite. Whether crosses ever stood at either place is not known, but *Stainton*, one the townships of Crosscrake, is older than the conquest, being named in Domesday as belonging to Gile-Michel, and its chapel was endowed by Anselm de Furness, son of the first Michel le Fleming, about the time of Richard I. The name of the " tun " appears to point to some stone pillar or cross of much earlier date than Domesday, whilst the name of the other township of the chapelry, *Sedge-wick*, leads us back to a like period. Crossthwaite chapel, five miles north-west from the parish church, stands upon an ancient foundation, though it had been allowed to fall into decay before 1556, when the Bishop of Chester, on petition of the inhabitants, granted a licence that Mass should be said, the canonical hours rehearsed, the sacraments administered by a priest approved by the vicar of Heversham without prejudice to the mother church. This license was to be produced every three years by the chaplain and read in the parish church on the second day after Pentecost.

In 1580 an award was made on certain disputes between the inhabitants of the chapelry and other inhabitants, which award was destroyed when the parish church was burnt down in 1601, whereupon a reproduction was made as nearly as possible from memory, setting forth that the inhabitants, by their churchwardens and sworn men, should yearly, upon New Year's Eve, make their accounts and reckonings at Heversham church and pay what fell due ; also that they should pay a certain share of the stipend of the parish clerk ; also 3s. 4d. for every corpse buried above the quire wall in Crossthwaite church ; also one fourth share of repairs, &c., of the parish church ; also they should appoint two men to serve as churchwardens at Heversham church from their hamlet, and six others, to be sworn men, as assistants, to make up the number of twenty-four sworn men, the said churchwardens and sworn men to join with the other church-wardens and sworn men in all things needful and necessary to the said church, and always to be appointed on New Year's Eve, and to take their oaths on the 5th day of January, being the twelfth even, at the church of Heversham according as hath been accustomed. It seems to me that we have here an indication of a reversion to the *Mark* or *Mearc-Mot*, an institution which, as Mr. Kemble says,* lay at the basis of Teutonic society. "The Mark contained within itself the means of doing right between man and man; it had its principal officer or judge, and its priest and place of religious observance." At the great religious rites thrice in the year the markmen assembled unbidden. On emergencies summonses were issued to a bidden "Thing." "The Mark was a voluntary association of free men, who laid down for themselves and strictly maintained a system of cultivation by which the produce of the land on which they settled might be fairly and equally secured for their service and support; and from participation in which they jealously excluded all who were not born or adopted into the associa-tion. It was a union for the purpose of administering justice, or supplying a mutual guarantee of peace, security, and freedom for the inhabitants of the district."

The use of the lands, the woods, and the waters was made dependent upon the general will of the settlers, and could only be enjoyed under general regulations made by all for the benefit of all. The principle was retained and acted upon in the relations of the hamlets towards each other and towards the parish church.

It is peculiarly interesting to find the remains of a very beautiful piece of sculpture of pre-Norman date upon the very site upon which it was first set up, amidst so many evidences of the state of the country about the time of its erection, and in the neighbourhood of dedications to St. Oswald and St. Wilfrid, and of such varied work as may be seen at Heysham, Lancaster, Halton, Melling, and other churches at no great distance.

---

* " The Saxons in England."

The fragment now standing in the porch of Heversham church is of a coarse-grained sandstone, 56 inches high, 11 inches wide and 9 inches thick at the bottom, and 11 wide by 7¾ inches thick at the top. Portions have been broken away and a considerable part of one edge knocked off, so that it is difficult to ascertain what may have been the exact measurement of the original block. There is a sun dial of the same kind of stone fixed in the solid socket-stone of two steps placed upon slabs of limestone in the churchyard, which appears to be a part of the original cross. The stem of the dial has been cut away from the thickness of 9¾ inches to 6 inches, and from a width of 13½ inches to 7½ inches at the bottom, so that all carving has disappeared from this portion of the cross, if such it were. At Halton, the date of the cutting down is known, and we learn that a monument, the like of which does not exist, and one bearing upon an important factor in our national history, after weathering the storms of six hundred years, fell before the infatuation of the seventeenth century. The Heversham dial is dated 1690. The carving upon the fragment in the porch is of that kind which appears on the crosses of Ruthwell and Bewcastle, having spirals, fruit-clusters and foliage, with animals, but this stone is not so massive as either of the two mentioned, and two fruit and leaf-bearing stems rise and gracefully inter-twine upon the broader face of the stone, whereas one main stem only appears on those parts of the Bewcastle and Ruth-well crosses which show animals and birds amidst the foliage.

The effect of this double vine-stem, with its tendrils, clusters and leaves, and with the bodies and limbs of the animals curving and interlacing with the more delicate work of the design, must have been very beautiful in its original inception. Enough of it remains to arouse our interest in the search for other works of the kind which may lie hidden in walls and buildings near our ancient churches or in the foundations of the churches themselves, and which may be exposed during the progress of repairs or alterations. A couple of years ago the foundation of St. Andrew's Church (Scotland) revealed the stems of two great crosses, possibly of the time of Benedict Biscop, whose influence over Christian art may

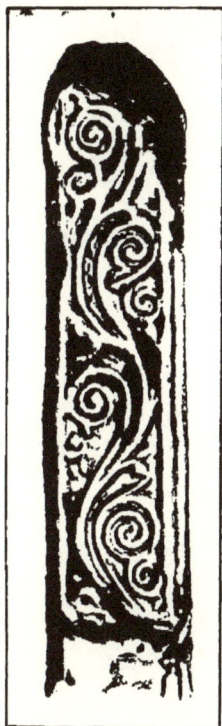

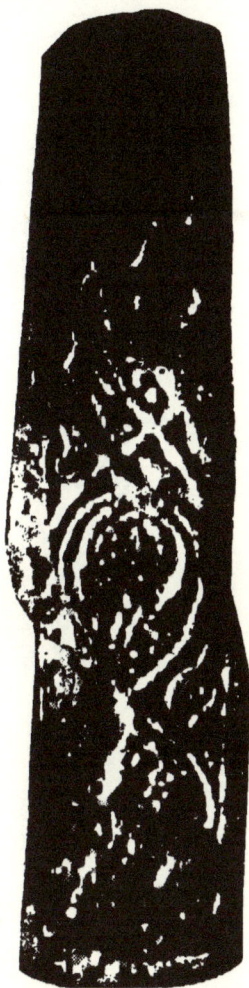

EDGE.   FACE.

ANGLIAN CROSS-SHAFT.

HEVERSHAM.

(TO FACE P. 202.)

have been felt through the more eastern coasts in some such manner as we believe that of St. Wilfrid to have been exercised here. What may have been carved upon the parts of the cross now lost we need not conjecture, but I do not know of any design so pure, so free apparently from the possibility of any admixture of legend amongst any of our recent discoveries. I should expect to find only Scripture subjects at most as the complement of this rich portrayal of the vine of life, if indeed the whole cross-shaft were not covered with similar work, varied by elaborate interlacing patterns on one of the faces.

An examination of the outside walls of the church was rewarded with the discovery of a fragment of one arm of the cross showing that the head of the cross itself was adorned with the leaves and tendrils of the all-pervading Christ vine.

I am indebted to Canon Cooper and his son, Mr. Edward Cooper, for valuable drawings and photographs, the procuring of which cost both of these gentlemen a considerable amount of trouble.

*   *   *

Our plate gives the front of the shaft from a photograph, and the side from a sketch. The back is much defaced ; a big flower or leaf can just be traced, with stalk wound round it three times in a great spiral ; and underneath, perhaps a bird.

The edge nearest the church door is also defaced, except the lower part, which has a scroll much the same as that on the edge given in the plate.

This edge is interesting from its neat conventional adaptation of the vine which is more freely treated on the face. The curves are squarely drawn and masterly, with plenty of spring and flow. The surfaces are quiet, but by no means flat ; the tendrils rise and sink perceptibly, but not violently, It is a very gentle and refined art ; one does not feel the want of more undulation, such as gives interest to the half barbarous reliefs of the Viking and Norman age; nor is it the least degree weak or ineffective like what may be imitations of this style. It is a fine example of the classic Anglian school,— closely related to the Hexham school,—though it is not necesssary to suppose that the monument was brought from Northumbria.

The fragment mentioned at the close of Mr. Calverley's paper is about 6 by 3 inches in size, and to be seen below the window next the porch to the east, to the right-hand side.

HUTTON-IN-THE-FOREST.

Cross-Fragment.

I N one of his note-books Mr. Calverley writes :—

Hutton-in-the-Forest was visited by me on December 15th, 1888, with the Rev. T. Lees. Snow on ground. I went to the church, though Lees said I should find nothing, as it was an entirely new church, though on an old foundation.

However, there was the dial stem, a cut-down cross, just within the gate. The dial is not original.

I found a coarse gritty red sandstone cross fragment, 18 inches by 6 inches, showing rings and bands interlacing, built the north side of the church, west of the westernmost window, and below it. East of this, and beneath the window, is a questionable trace of the north door. I believe the fragment was one part of the cross which had been cut down to make into a dial stem.

*   *   *   *

" The church is dedicated to St. James and was anciently called the chapel of Hutton in the Forest, but for several ages it has been reputed a rectory. The present church was built about 1714. Robert de Vaux gave this church and one carucate of land at

Hutton to the priory of Carlisle, whose grant was confirmed by King Henry II., and afterwards by King Edward II." (Nicolson and Burn).

The dial in the churchyard has been a fine one, with a number of different gnomons on different sides of a cube; but it is rusting away, like a similar dial at Lazonby.

The shaft on which it is set looks extremely like an old pillar trimmed down for the purpose. The lower part of the shaft is about 45 inches in circumference, and is an irregularly shaped and much weathered cylinder. It fits into the socket of a base with three steps; but a few inches above the base, the old shaft is whittled down, and trimmed into a neat and slender cylinder for the dial: so slender that it has broken, and is clamped together again. This would have been done in the dial-making period, say the 18th century; and at the same time the base would have been restored.

The fragment in the wall is picked or hacked work, rather deeply cut, 18 inches by 6; the original breadth would have been about 7 inches. It looks like the edge of a slab, of which the breadth is hidden in the wall. It tapers a little, like the neck, or carved and panelled part, of the crosses at the Giant's Grave of Penrith. Indeed from the shaft of the dial and this fragment we might almost venture to reconstruct a cross at Hutton of the Penrith type; which would not be improbable, considering how often these types are found in groups.

IREBY.

Mediæval Crosses.

THE Ordnance Map marks "Crosses," in the Gothic type which denotes antiquities, at the old church called Ireby chapel, between Torpenhow and Ireby. These, however, are mediæval grave slabs.

Whellan (p. 245) says, "The ancient market cross, after lying in ruins for nearly a century, was restored some years ago," that is, before 1859, " by Henry Grainger, Esq., who is the owner of the old building, once the Moot Hall of the town."

This cross is now to be seen in the steep and picturesque street; the upper part is modern, the base and lower part of the shaft date from the middle ages.

IRTON.

THE STANDING CROSS.

THIS monument has been made known to the world by a cast in
South Kensington Museum; and indeed, taking size and preservation together into account, it may rank next to Gosforth Cross
in general interest, though Bewcastle is far the finer art.

It is carved from a single block of red sandstone, head and shaft
in one piece, 10 feet high from the base. The shaft is 90 inches in
length, 19 by 9½ at the base, and 15 by 7 inches at the upper part,
before the width and thickness contract to form the neck.

The socket-stone measures 39 by 32 inches, rising 7 inches out of
the stone platform surrounding it; like the cross, of red sandstone
brought perhaps from Gosforth, where is the nearest quarry. The
carving has been all done with the chisel, without drill or pick, and
is smooth, highly finished work, very varied in depth. The parts
where the pattern runs closely together are kept shallow and flattish;
here and there a few emphatic points are deeply hollowed, giving
strong touches of shade, and throwing the flatter parts into breadth
and delicacy. What the drill-holes at St. John's, Beckermet, did
rather mechanically, and what the ground spaces of Bridekirk Font
did rather violently, is here done moderately and with judgment. It
is interesting to note these evidences of artistic intention, and to
observe in how many ways a pattern may be treated: for after all it
is the treatment that is the most important thing in all works of art.

A very finely engraved plate is given of the Irton cross in Lysons'
Cumberland, but it is an architect's rectified and restored plan,
rather than a representation of the stone as it is, or even as it was
a century ago. Some weathering, no doubt, it has undergone
of recent years. Few stones go through the ordeal of casting
without direct, or at least indirect, harm; for if nothing is chipped,
the patina is more or less injured, and the surface laid open to
weathering which shows after a while.

In 1863 Father Haigh made a mould of the runes on this cross,
and sent them to Professor Stephens, who read

+ GEBIDÆTH FORÆ
" Pray for............."
(*Old Northern Runic Monuments*, II., p. 469).

West   South   East

THREE VIEWS OF THE STANDING CROSS.

IRTON.

(TO FACE P. 206.)

These have now entirely gone; only the lines remain which divide the space they occupied into three panels for the three rows of rune-staves. But it shows that this, like Bewcastle, is an Anglo-Saxon work of art.

On the west side, where the runes were, there is a curious double-cord interlacing in the lower panel, very troublesome to sketch, and showing no small ingenuity on the part of the sculptor. The upper panel has a tendency to free design in plait-work, which suggests a somewhat later date than the earlier Anglian crosses.

The south side bears a very fine Anglo-classic scroll, with varied spandrils, some filled with the triquetra, and some with pretty knops and leaves. On the edge of the cross-arm above is an incised web, unique in our district.

The east side is again of a type very unusual with us. It has two panels of a diagonal key-pattern, and two of a circular geometrical design; and the remaining panel is filled with chequers, as at Bewcastle, only these are not squares but little sunk " St. Andrew's " crosses. Much of this ornament can be found in the Lindisfarne gospels, and taken with the Anglo-Saxon runes, marks the cross as Anglian.

The north side we have not drawn, as it is very nearly the same with the scroll on the south.

ISEL.

DIALS.

THREE dials on the jamb of the south window of the chancel, and one on the doorway.

These dials were revealed to me upon the removal of the whitewash after the restoration of the church by the exertions of the vicar, the Rev. W. H. Sharpe, and under the directions of C. J. Ferguson, Esq., F.S.A., of Carlisle, both of whom have taken pious care of the old details of this most interesting and most ancient little church, whose wonderful history has yet to be written.

No. 1, the uppermost in the jamb, cut in red sandstone, has *twenty-four* division marks; the letter N is clearly cut, apparently done at the time of the cutting of the dial; on the right, and beneath it, another N partially obliterated; the whole has been most carefully worked.

I think this dial may have been used as a horizontal dial before being placed in its present position. The N may have marked some special shadow or limit in the sun's course, and the stone may have been built into this jamb the wrong way about, in which case the two N's might mark the divisions indicated on the left of the similar dial engraved in the Rev. Daniel Haigh's paper on Yorkshire dials ("The Bottesford Dial," *Yorkshire Archæological Journal*, vol. v., p. 210).

This dial is 4¾ inches in diameter.

No. 2. I offer no opinion as to the mark across the upper part of the circle, or the nearly obliterated N to the left and opposite the ray which would mark about 9 a.m.

5 inches in diameter.

No. 3, the lowest in the plate opposite. Where the circle is broken by a dark hole, an iron nail has been driven into it. The rays appear to mark from 6 a.m. to 3 p.m. and 6 p.m.

6½ inches diameter.

SOUTH WINDOW OF THE CHANCEL WITH DIALS.

ISEL.

(TO FACE P. 208.)

The above have been carefully redrawn on the spot, to replace Mr. Calverley's lithograph, which no longer exists. We have been obliged, however, to omit his arrow-heads, marking shadow at certain times and dates, for which see his paper on Dials, Trans. C. & W.A. & A.S., 1885.

This last example is figured on our plate opposite *Bolton*. It has six rays and is 6¾ inches in diameter.

* * * *

No. 4 is cut on the east jamb of the west doorway. Part of the circle is not visible, and some of the rays are scarcely traceable. They appear to have marked the hours between 9 a.m. and 3 p.m. A porch has been built over this doorway.

I take these three last-named dials to have been used to mark canonical hours.

THUNDERBOLT.

THE TRISKELE.

FRAGMENT AT ISEL CHURCH.

THE SVASTIKA.

ISEL.

"Triskele" Fragment.

The stone is a small pyramid without its apex, of light coloured Permian sandstone from the neighbouring district : height 10½ inches ; width at wider end, 6 inches ; at narrower end, 4½ inches. Its form suggests the uppermost part of the shaft of a cross, but no trace exists of the place from which the arms should spring. In the upper end of the stone a cup-shaped hollow has been formed, and the smooth or worn edges may seem to indicate that the stone is complete in itself. Tradition finds this stone amongst the building material of the ancient bridge over the Derwent, near the little Norman church and the vicarage of Isel, at the time of the building of the present bridge in the early days of the last generation.

The four faces of the stone are sculptured in relief, in the manner of the earlier crosses, bearing marks of a pointed tool, such as a drill or a pick, and not of broad or narrow chisels. Each face has an upper and lower panel bearing a single design, the design in the upper panels varying, that in the lower one being always the same, namely an ∽ shaped design. (The " sun-snake " sign).

The sign in one of the upper panels is the " svastika " or "fylfot," its arms turning in this case to the left or from the sun, instead of to the right or with the sun.

So far as I know this is the first example of work of this kind bearing this sacred symbol, with the exception of the Dearham shaft, which has yet been revealed.

Many remains Roman, Trojan, Buddhistic, Scandinavian, bear the sign incised in stone or engraved in metal on coins and ornaments, but none but these at Dearham and Isel, and a few sculptures belonging to the same era, and known to me here in old Strathclyde, have these devices worked in relief; at least my attention has not been drawn to any such.

In two of the other upper panels is the " triskele " sign, with this peculiarity that the curve of the two lower limbs of one of these symbols takes the opposite direction from the curve of the upper limb instead of all the three limbs turning round in the same direction—towards the right—with the sun. This figure is here shown with a part of the "sun-snake" sign in the mutilated panel beneath.

It is to be noted that on the other face, which has not been figured, the " triskele " whirls round to the right, every limb moving in the same direction. This sign, in which one may discern the origin of the three legs of the Isle of Man, is also found engraved on Danish ornaments in metal, and on Scandinavian coins, and even knives and hatchets of the later bronze age which also bear the "sun-snake" and the "sun-ship," but this is (so far as I am aware) the first example of the same sign sculptured in stone in relief.

The fourth symbol is, I believe, either a form of Thor's sign, the thunderbolt, or Odin's sign. It is here shown. All these signs appear to me to belong in this case to the Norse faith, and a wonderful interest attaches to the sculpture which bears the fylfot, svastika or Thor's hammer—the triskele, the thunderbolt, and the ↭ shaped sun-snake, altogether on one stone, carved in relief in panels and in the very style and fashion of the work of the early Christian monuments.

This sculpture is in the best style of the very early work, it being wrought in regular panels, whereas many of the other designs known to me have been traced irregularly by a free hand over the face of the stone used.

If the three symbols are Pagan and Scandinavian they may be the signs of Thor, Odin, and Frey, placed in an unlucky manner, the svastika turning from the sun instead of towards it, and the limbs of the other two signs turning in different directions, whilst the perfect triskele on the fourth side, not engraved here, shows the true Trinity of Christian faith steadfast amidst all changes even as the sun himself.

The engravings are by Prof. Magnus Petersen, of Copen-hagen, from photographs of great beauty very kindly taken for me by the Rev. A. Watmore, of Maryport.

The fourth side, not figured, resembles the middle design, the triskele. The work is not chiselled but picked out. There are large round socket holes at top and bottom of the stone.

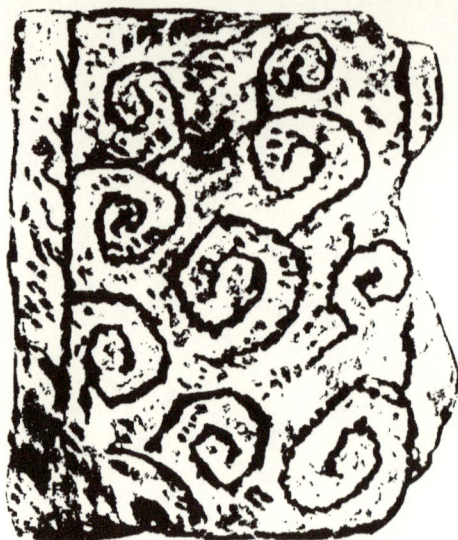

SPIRAL FRAGMENT

IN THE WEST WALL OF THE PORCH

ISEL.

(TO FACE P. 213.)

ISEL.

SPIRAL CROSS-FRAGMENTS.

On the plate illustrating the Cross-head at Bridekirk are figured the two sides of a fragment with rather rough and flat spiral-like design at Isel. White sandstone. 18 inches by 16½ inches by 6½ inches thick.

The spirals on both sides of the Isel stone are very noticeable. The work is unfinished, being picked out rather than worked in relief. A piece of the same cross has been built by the vicar, the Rev. W. H. Sharpe, into the west wall of the porch, within. At the bottom of the drawing to the left hand will be seen a broad arrow, point downward; this would be the sacred emblem of Woden. In Gautrek's saga, the sacrificer marks the victim's breast with a spear-point, and devotes him to Woden, while the halter is round his neck, after which he is hanged. The ceremony of marking to Woden is noticed both in Ynglinga and elsewhere by Ari. The spear is as characteristic of Woden as the hammer is of Thor. The cross itself is the gallows on which the victim is hanged. The tree, the ash Yggdrasil, is the horse of the hanged one—the gallows. The cross of Christ and the ash Yggdrasil of the northern tribes bore a like meaning, at a certain time, to the mixed peoples on this coast.

*   *   *   *

The fragment mentioned as built into the west wall of the porch is here given. It measures 19 by 14½ inches. The surface is roughly "scabbled," and the pattern hacked out with the pick.

KIRK-BAMPTON.

TYMPANUM.

THE church of St. Peter " is an ancient structure, the great arch and doorway of which are in the Saxon style. Within the latter there is a rudely sculptured bas-relief representing two animals, and what seems to have been designed for an abbot." (Whellan, *Hist. of Cumberland*, p. 173).

The animals seem to have been intentionally defaced, to judge from the tool-marks which cross and re-cross them at right angles. The edge of the back of some lion-like or dragonesque beast is part of the original sculpture, for the old surface with its diagonal tooling appears on both sides of it. But the lines somewhat resembling lions' heads are only fractures where the stone has flaked off.

The figure has been called an abbot, from the crozier-like staff he holds. But in his other hand he carries something which looks like David's sling; and possibly the subject was the shepherd David with his crook and sling attacking the lion and the bear. Mr. J. Romilly Allen in his lectures on *Christian Symbolism* (pp. 203-208) has collected a number of early instances of this favourite symbol of Christ's conflict with evil.

The tympanum is very rude; it has been broken up and reset; but at any time the work must have been of the roughest. The two stones with zig-zags hardly seem to belong to their place.

Within the church the Norman capitals of the chancel-arch on the north side bear a very barbaric demon's head with the tongue sticking out; and volutes and chequers, like Torpenhow.

There is a small Roman inscribed stone built into the south side of the chancel-wall, and two or more stones with cross-broaching have been used as building material. A mediæval grave-slab is in the churchyard.

THE BOUND DEVIL.

KIRKBY STEPHEN.

KIRKBY STEPHEN.

The Bound Devil.

THE fragments were described and figured by the Rev. J. F. Hodgson in a paper read to the Cumberland and Westmorland Antiquarian and Archæological Society on September 13, 1871, and published in their *Transactions* for 1879. He dated the Norman church 1170-80, and contended that the dedication did not give its name to the town, which he considered a corruption of Kirkby-o'-t'-Eden; that is to say, "Kirkby" localised, like Kirkby Kendal, Kirkby Lonsdale; for it is not "Kirk-Stephen," which would have been analogous with Kirk-Bride, Kirk-Andrews, etc.

The late Canon Simpson gave 1220 as the date of the church; but in any case there must have been a religious foundation here long before Norman days.

We have re-drawn and newly described the fragments ; and as to the name and antiquity of the church, we might remark that Kirkby Stephen seems to be be parallel with Preston Patrick, Crosby Garret (Gerard), and perhaps Kirkby Thore (for Thored ; certainly not directly referring to the god Thor). The compound name denotes the place by some famous owner. Stephen was probably the pre-Norman lord of the place, which was *already* in his time known as a Kirkju-bær, an estate belonging to a church. We have the name Stephen connected with pre-Norman place-names at Stephengarths in Furness (a word known in the time of King John) and Stavenerge, that is, Stephen's sæter or dairy farm in West Cumberland, known by that Norse name in the time of Henry II. The name Stephen was used in the Viking age ; Earl Stephen (sometimes written Stefnir) of Bretland (Wales) was father-in-law to Palnatoki, the chief of the Jomsburg Vikings, and lived during the middle part of the tenth century. Another, Stephen Thorgilsson of Iceland, met King Olaf Tryggvason in Britain in 995 (*O.T. Saga*, ch. 139).

We may therefore infer that there was a Danish tenth or eleventh century lord of this place, which, from a previously established Anglian church, was known as the Kirk-by of Stephen. And further, the Scandinavian settlers were not heathen, for they did not sweep away the church, but continued to call the place Church-farm. These indications of an Anglian church and a subsequent Scandinavian one harmonise with what we learn from the fragments themselves.

The famous " Bound Devil" discovered in 1870, is now set up in the church close to the font. It is of yellowish-white sandstone, measuring 25 by 13½ by 8 inches. The carving is roughly but effectively done with the pick, leaving the contours square and the surfaces flat. The sculpture is very well preserved, though the back has been defaced.

One edge shows the ordinary three-strand plait; and the other has a twist of two strands.

The figure on the face has been the subject of a monograph by Professor George Stephens in " Studies on Northern Mythology," reprinted in *Trans.* C. & W. A. & A. S. The Rev. J. F. Hodgson had said that the subject was *Satan Bound* ; Stephens tried to show that a bound Satan was not familiar to southern Christianity, but borrowed from the *bound Loki* (see Gosforth) of northern Paganism. He thinks that in this figure we have an instance of overlap—the adoption of a heathen idea into Christian thought; and he dates the stone about 700, believing that the Angles were acquainted with the Eddaic account of Baldr and Loki; a belief which he justifies by Cædmon's reference to Satan as bound.

We cannot help feeling that the passage in Revelation xx., 1-3 was well known throughout Christendom : " I saw an angel come down from Heaven, having the key of the bottomless pit and a great chain in his hand. And he laid hold on the dragon, that old serpent, which is the Devil, and Satan, and bound him a thousand years, and cast him into the bottomless pit," etc. *When* this should be, and *how* it should happen, was a mystery ; but the promise was one to which every Christian looked, and the symbol was one which any Christian might use. To a Northern mind, no doubt, it would appeal with double force.

The workmanship and design suggest a rather late date and Scandinavian influence. A horned, round-shouldered figure, much like this, is in the Durham Cathedral Library from Gainford, on the Tees, just to the other side of the Stainmoor pass.

The Semi-Cylindrical Shaft.

Of contemporary type, and still more curious in its unfamiliar form, is the semi-cylindrical fragment; the neck of a cross from which the head and the lower part of the shaft have been broken.

This piece is of a yellowish-white sandstone, 24 inches long, 10 broad, and 5 thick (broken across). The carving is done with a pick, like the ' Bound Devil ' ; the drawing in both is remarkable for its squareness; and in both the designer has used pellets to

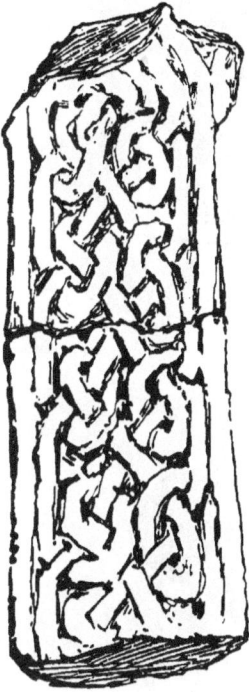

b   *a*

SEMI-CYLINDRICAL SHAFT.

KIRKBY STEPHEN.

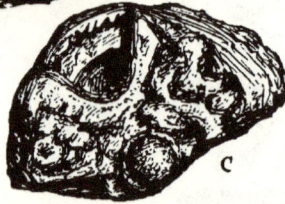

HOGBACK AND CROSS-HEADS.

KIRKBY STEPHEN.

fill spaces accidentally left by the pattern; this is the Northern love of filled-up composition, showing no ground.

The fragment is partly spiral and partly interlaced. Down the middle of the round or semi-cylindrical side (*a*) runs a plait of three, irregularly becoming a plait of four; this is a characteristic of eleventh and twelfth century interlacing, as opposed to the studied regularity of early Anglian plaits and knots. On each side of this plait is a spiral scroll-band, without flowers. On the back (*b*) is a knotted plait of eight.

This is not part of the Bound Devil cross, but seems to be of the same hand, or at any rate of the same school. We have no parallel to the form of this shaft. The patterns are of an Anglo-Danish type.

HOGBACK AND CROSS-HEADS.

In the next plate, *A* is a hogback of white sandstone, measuring 31½ by 15 by 7 inches; the carving done with the pick. There are three rows of triangular tegulæ on the roof of the shrine-tomb, and remains of interwoven pattern at one side; nothing at the other side, or on the ends.

C is a cross-head of yellow sandstone; the fragment measures 17 by 11 by 5 inches; the radius from the centre of the boss to the end of the arms is 10 inches, so that originally the cross-head was 20 inches high. It is roughly picked with an interlacing pattern, not easy now to follow.

The above pieces, cross-head, fragments of two shafts, and hogback are all of light-coloured stone, with picked work, and seem to belong to the later period of pre-Norman art.

B is a later cross-head; red sandstone, 18½ inches across the arms, 6 inches thick, chiselled very neatly; a plain flat Maltese cross, superimposed upon a wheel; the four holes sunk, not pierced; in the centre a flattish boss, in a sunk circle. This is the head of a tall mediæval cross, like the churchyard cross at Arthuret, Kirkland, &c.; or the resting crosses at St. Bees and Rheda.

There are also fragments, one with a boss and ring, which may belong to another early cross; and among the mediæval effigies and slabs there are some interesting bits of Norman and later sculpture, of which one or two, in their broken condition, might be taken for Anglian work.

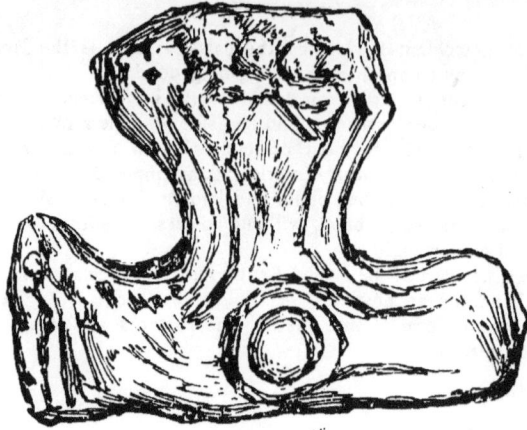

CROSS-HEAD.

KIRKBY STEPHEN.

KIRKBY STEPHEN.

One more cross-head we illustrate, as no doubt pre-Norman. Mr. Hodgson, in the paper above mentioned, pointed out its resemblance to a series of Anglian cross-heads, and especially to St. Cuthbert's pectoral cross.

It is of yellow sandstone, 19 inches across the arms, 12 from the centre of the boss to the top, and 6 inches thick. The pattern is now obscured by the weathering-out of hard bands in the stone, but it seems to have been skilfully and deeply carved in the Anglian or mediæval fashion ; not merely chipped in the manner of the Scandinavian period. It is to be compared on the one hand with the series of light sandstone crosses in which the central boss is connected by spines with small bosses on the arms ; and on the other hand it somewhat resembles the red sandstone head at Bromfield, which seems to be post-Norman, and imitated from this type.

KIRKLAND.

CROSS.

A T a site on the Maiden Way, between "The Hanging Gardens of Mark Antony" and a Roman Camp, is the church of St. Lawrence, rebuilt 1768, and twice since then restored. "There is a stone cross with steps in the churchyard," says Whellan (p. 566.)

This is a tall red-sandstone monument of the class of Resting crosses, or the churchyard cross of Arthuret, etc.

The shaft and head together are 98 inches high. The shaft is 14½ inches broad at the base, tapering to 11 inches at the neck; and 7½ inches thick. It is without ornament, but chamfered; the chamfer not running quite to the base nor quite to the head.

The head is crumbling away, but has been a free-armed cross, without any wheel, but with round holes between the arms, and a . diamond-shaped hole pierced through the centre.

The socket stone is of red sandstone, measuring 28 by 24 by 15 inches, and set on a platform 54 by 53 in. This has a still larger and lower base, now sunk into the ground and overgrown with grass; but formerly there were three distinct steps, the three Calvary steps, leading up to the cross.

KIRK-OSWALD.

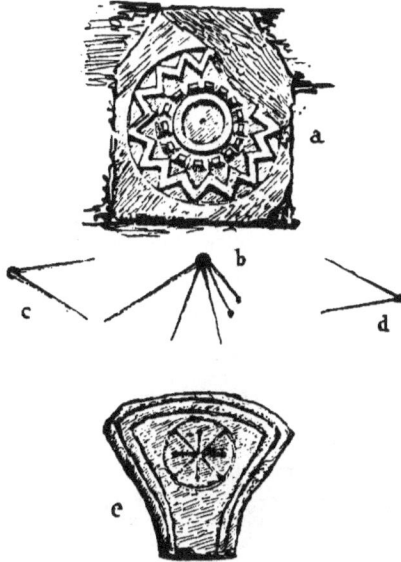

TWO FRAGMENTS AND A DIAL.

THE bit of sculpture figured at *a* was found buried in the wall of the north aisle of Kirkoswald church, 1879. It is a stone of 4 inches thick, 10½ inches broad, and 15½ inches high. The number of divisions, fifteen, seem to preclude the idea of its having been intended to represent a dial : if there had been sixteen such divisions the resemblance would have been very striking between it and the representation of the construction on the Mull mountain in the parish of Rushen, Isle of Man, figured p. 159 of Mr. Haigh's " Yorkshire dials," and in which the sixteen divisions of "day-night" are marked by parallelograms of four stones each, similar to the parallelograms round the centre of this, and in which only the Maypole as a gnomon is required in the centre. If this were thus divided into sixteenths, the zig-zag border would subdivide the circle again into thirty-two parts, and we should have another testimony to the use of the octaval system of time division at *Kirkoswald*. But the stone may be a memorial slab. It is worth careful preservation in any case.

❊   ❊   ❊

The stone *a* is now dressed down to 12 inches in height, and built into the wall behind the church. It is red sandstone, neatly carved, and not pre-Norman, nor a dial.

Of the rude dial *b* is a good example. It is carved upon the west capital of the south doorway. It has five rays, marking perhaps 9 and 11 a.m., 1, 2, and 3 p.m., but the wall faces a little east of south, so that the 1 p.m. ray might mark noon.

Inside the west jamb of the same door are two little incised figures like pairs of compasses, side by side. Inside the east jamb of the same door are two similar figures, one over the other. On the south-east buttress is a similar figure, *c*, turned on its side: and on the north-east corner of the church is another, *d*, turned the opposite way. These are evidently not dials, but mason's marks.

There is the arm of a cross-head, *e*, built into the wall near *d*. It is of red sandstone, and measures 11 by 10 inches. This recalls the head at Brigham, having a little cross on the upper arm; also the Standing Cross at Addingham, with the crosslet on the boss. But its neatly chiselled work looks rather like the remains of a mediæval high cross.

"*Ecclesia sancto Oswaldo sacra* is the name of the town and parish there; and of a very ancient time it hath been so termed," says John Denton, in 1610. "A triangular Saxon ornament of silver (engraved in Lysons's *Cumberland*) enriched with red paste, was found some years since at Kirkoswald . , . now in the British Museum." (Jefferson, *Leath Ward*, p. 296.) But though we should expect Anglo-Saxon stones here, rather than anywhere else, none seem to be forthcoming. The place, however, is rich in Norman and mediæval remains.

LAMPLUGH.

Lost Cross.

IT is worth noticing, in the hope of some fragment or information forthcoming, that "an ancient cross which, until lately, remained in the parish, has shared the same fate as the old hall, and has been wantonly destroyed" (Whellan, writing 1859, p. 399).

LANERCOST.

Cross.

ON the green there are the remains of a high cross of the mediæval type, all of red sandstone.

The socket-stone measures 27½ by 23½ by 17 inches, and has the edges of its upper face bevelled.

It stands on a broken platform of four steps. In the corner of the upper step is a small round hole, as if intended to hold something; compare the stone cup, socketed into a similar position in the mediæval cross-base of Bromfield churchyard.

The stump of the shaft measures 13 by 7½ inches, and is 20 inches high. It is chamfered like Cross Lacon, Kirkland cross, etc., but further ornamented with notches cut in the chamfer, about 4 inches apart from centre of notch to centre of notch.

LAZONBY.

Cross.

ANOTHER of these late high crosses remains at the church of St. Nicholas, Lazonby, which was given by Sir Hugh Morville to the priory of Lanercost, and in 1272 was appropriated to that house. (Whellan, p. 576).

The cross is on the south side of the church, as at Cliburn, Newbiggin, Kirkland, etc., and is of red sandstone, unornamented.

The shaft is 74 inches in height, and 14 by 13 in thickness; it is chamfered like the Kirkland shaft, but has no head.

The socket-stone measures 29 by 27 by 13 inches. It stands on a larger stone, 41 by 32 by 8 inches in size; and this in its turn rests on a platform, like that supporting the socket-stone at Lanercost.

An old dismounted cube dial, like that at Hutton-in-the-Forest, may be mentioned as lying in the churchyard. The slab ornamented with two crosses, at the east end of the yard, noticed by Whellan forty years ago, is not there now.

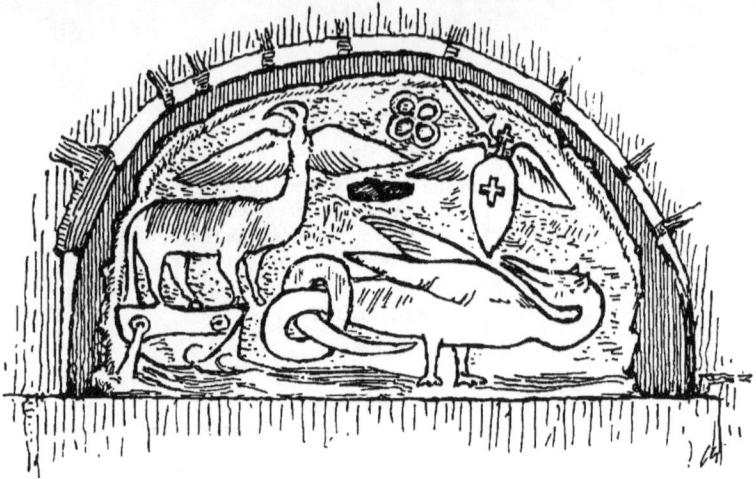

SOUTH DOOR.

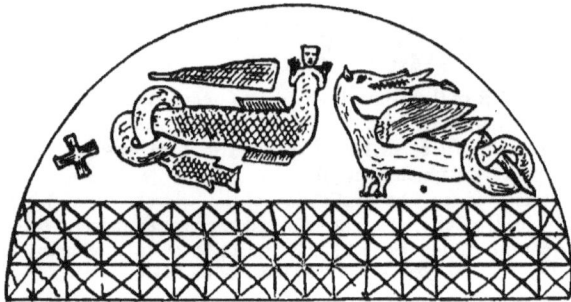

WEST DOOR.

THE TYMPANA.

LONG MARTON,

LONG MARTON.

IN a paper communicated to the C. & W. A. & A. S. at Penrith,
January 19, 1881, the late Rev. Thomas Lees described the two
Norman tympana of Long Marton church, with sketches by Mr.
J. A. Cory. He said that the dedication to SS. Margaret and James
was unique in England, and that the church was too old to be
dedicated to St. Margaret of Scotland; but he found in the
dove over the dragon, and in the winged figure emerging from
the other dragon (of the south door) the emblems of St. Margaret of
Antioch. This last dragon, he said, is escaping from the brazen
vessel in which it was imprisoned by Solomon, according to
the legend. The double M, like a four petalled flower, he recognized
as the monogram of Margaret Martyr. On the west door he found
the club of St. James, the dragon of St. Margaret, and a mermaid,—
called in the Norse [Icelandic] *Speculum Regale* of the twelfth
century *Margygr*, the Gaelic *Mairgreg*, that is, Margaret; who is
also Marina and Pelagia, the Christianized Aphrodite, Atergatis or
Derceto. Mr. Lees concluded that this work was Scandinavian.

We give the south tympanum from a new sketch, and the west
from Mr. Cory's, as published in the Society's *Transactions*.

The tympanum of the south door, set above a lintel like that at
Cliburn, is about 47 inches long, carved in very flat relief, with
clean contours neatly chiselled, and the ground roughly tooled into
flatness. The "dove" looks to us more like a winged shield,
charged with a cross, and having a little cross above it. Between
the last and the monogram is a sword. The oblong shape below the
monogram is a hole, made in later times for affixing something
over the door. The winged figure emerging from a dragon above a
brazen vessel, we should have described as an ox (?) whose neck and
head are replaced by a bird; the object on which it stands
resembles the conventional ship of art; and there seem to be waves
of the sea beneath it. Round the field of the tympanum are
remains of a ridge or cable-moulding, as at Kirk-Bampton.

The other tympanum with dragon, mermaid, club and cross, is
remarkable for its chequers, like the tympanum at Bromfield. The
"mermaid" may perhaps be a variant of the figure of St. Margaret

emerging from the dragon, which, according to the legend, had
swallowed her, but burst asunder and let her go free. There are
two representations of this, illustrated by Mr. J. Romilly Allen
in *Early Christian Symbolism*, pp. 316, 317, which are as early and
even more grotesque ; in them her head and arms are coming out
of a hole in the dragon's back, while her feet and skirt are still
between its teeth. On the other hand there is a siren or mermaid
not unlike this on a tympanum at Stow Longa, Huntingdonshire,
figured by Mr. Romilly Allen, p. 360 ; other instances of sirens are
given by him at p. 368; and on p. 366 the treatment of the monsters
in the tympanum of Ault Hucknall, Derbyshire, resembles ours.
In short, twelfth century sculpture, as Bridekirk font shows, is
largely fanciful, though not without allusions to recognized symbolism ; and these tympana seem to be works of an artist or school
whose hand is seen also in the Midlands : not especially Scandinavian.

TWO VIEWS OF THE HOGBACK.

LOWTHER.

(TO FACE P. 231.)

.

LOWTHER.

HOGBACK.

THE accompanying plate represents the two sides of a coped tomb found by me at Lowther, Oct. 1st, 1886. Red sandstone—length 2 ft. 8 in.; height 1 ft. 6 in.; thickness 1 ft. Coping of tiles, partly broken away. The walls are decorated with human figures. A long serpent form coils and stretches along the lower portion as though a survival of pagan belief. Sacred symbols (key pattern—or interlocking S shaped pattern) appear, notably on either side of what seems to be the central figure of B.

In the dexter corner of each side will be seen a figure with folded hands as in prayer. The figure to the right in A reclines on his right elbow, and appears to hold a ring. The designer has been content to give one arm and one long curled lock to each of the three figures accompanying the one who prays. Each hand is pressed to the breast. In B the central figure, between the sacred signs, has full flowing locks curling over the shoulder; each figure has *both* arms and hands, which the artist has made out of all proportion in order to accommodate his space and drawing. I think there may have been a fifth figure. Is it the descent of our Lord into Hell?

The chief figure in B has an eastern look. The limbs of the figures are very rudely and falsely drawn, but the faces have been good and true. The stone is so worn by time and exposure that much which might have explained the intention is lost. I hope that Mr. Lees who was present at the finding of this fragment and assisted me to take rubbings of the figures will be able to identify the scene portrayed.

*　　*　　*　　*

Mr. Lees accordingly wrote a paper suggesting that this house of the dead was taken by its makers to represent the Hades or Limbus, where the souls of the departed await their final judgment; and that

these figures are meant for the patriarchs in Limbo. He described
the early exposition of this doctrine in the Apocryphal Gospel of
Nicodemus, and showed that the constant connection of the church
in Cumbria with that in Italy made it possible, at an early age, for
the "household stories of Christian dwellers on the Mediterranean
shores to penetrate to this remote corner of the Islands of the
West."

* * * *

Mr. Calverley wrote further in the *Aspatria Parish Magazine* a
little article which we think well worth reprinting. It shows how he
found "sermons in stones" and it shows, also, how he taught his
rural neighbours to respect the monuments they had disdained.
With a lithograph of this hogback he wrote:—

Look at the pictures which I have drawn in front. I dare-
say you will think that they are queer looking things and that
you can make nothing of them. They are the two sides of a
tomb made like a little house. In each picture there are
two rows of tiles on the roof, and there has been a thin ridge
standing up above; you can see a bit of this ridge on the
right, at the top of the upper drawing (A).

The stone is perhaps more than a thousand years old, and
has been a good deal knocked about. I found it lying in
Lowther churchyard grown over with moss which had hidden
its carvings; the ridge has been broken off and one end has
been broken away, but there is enough left to teach us something worth remembering.

It was once the tomb of a great Christian Briton or
Englishman, before the Norman conquest; and you may still
see four other "hog-backed Saxon" uncarved tombstones in
Lowther churchyard, marking the graves of the noble of that
day. When a stone church was built, our sculptured shrine
was built into the walls of the church, and some of the
mortar still sticks to the red sandstone. When this old
church was pulled down to give place to a new one, this
same stone, covered with lime and unsightly, was left lying
about, to be found by me after the frosts and rains of many

winters had once more revealed the forms carved upon it by decomposing the builders' mortar without entirely destroying the face of the stone.

You will see something twisted and coiled along the bottom of each drawing beneath the figures, and you will see some strange designs (they are sacred symbols used long ago) on either side of one of the heads in the lower picture; but what will strike you most will be the long curls of hair, and the hands pressed to the breast or folded and pressed together as if in prayer; and above all you will notice that all these people seem to be asleep—their eyes are closed and their hands folded or pressed to their breast, and they all look as if they were either asleep or praying, or very peaceful and at perfect rest. These people are not dead—look at their faces and mark generally the attitudes of repose.

Now let us find something worth remembering about all this.

The tombstone is made like a little house to represent the *home* of the dead. But at the time I am speaking of, the people believed that only those who died bravely fighting would have a life of happiness afterwards; other people who were not wicked people at all—but all who died of sickness or old age—went to the cold dark world ruled over by a goddess called Hel, who was the daughter of the Evil one. " Such is the origin of our word Hell, the name of a goddess applied to a locality. Her domains were very great and her yard-walls very high. Hunger is her dish, starvation her knife, care is her bed, a beetling cliff is the threshold of her hall, which is hung with grief." All, except the warriors who died fighting, however good, went to her domain. It might be thought that to be with such a goddess after death was bad enough, but there was a worse place. For the wicked another place of torture was prepared, a great hall and a bad; its doors looked northward. It was altogether wrought of adders' backs wattled together, and the heads of the adders all turned inwards, and spit venom, so that rivers of venom ran along the hall, and in those rivers the wicked people must wade for ever.

Now you will see that the side of the Plumbland tomb is

actually carved with adders or serpents twisted or wattled together. On one side of the cross at Dearham the same thing is shewn. The Christian wished to shew that this terrible idea of man's future state was to give way to something better through the *Lord of Life*, our Lord Jesus Christ; and so at Aspatria and Plumbland and Dearham and Cross-Canonby, and many another place, they set up crosses and carved the sacred triquetra, the sign of the ever blessed Trinity, on their sculptured tombs, to teach the people to believe no longer in gods and goddesses of darkness, but to look to the one God, the Father, Son, and Holy Spirit, to drive away all Evil Spirits from their homes and all evil thoughts from their hearts, and to give them a quiet time and a perfect end. Was there any wonder that years afterwards, when the bright light which shone forth from the cross of Christ had for ever dispersed the dark clouds of paganism, men said that holy men such as Patrick and Kentigern and Cuthbert had driven all poisonous snakes out of the land?

In my picture the twisted and coiling thing beneath the figures is no doubt the old serpent, the worm that never dieth; but it is overcome and harmless to these people resting quietly in the tomb, and only served to shew to onlookers that *the place of rest* was attainable by those even who had held the old ideas of Hel's dark domain and the place of venomous things, as the only hope of the dying who had not the luck to fall in battle. The teaching is that of our burial service: " *Blessed* are the dead which die in the Lord, for they *rest* from their labours." The Lord of Life still lives. He went down into Hell, but He does not remain imprisoned there. He is the Light of the World. Blessed are the dead which die in the Lord.

*   *

This fragment shows the rudest kind of chipped or hacked work, but it is evidently of the same type as the Penrith hog-backs. The size and style of the stone in general, the forms of the tegulation, the curves of the serpents, all indicate this; but the figures betray an overbold ambition on the artist's part.

This valuable relic still remains in the churchyard, exposed to the weather and thickly grown over with moss. In the paper last quoted, Mr. Calverley mentions "four other hog-backed Saxon uncarved tombstones in the churchyard"; but in another paper he notes :—

, At Lowther there are two hog-backs *in situ*, six feet and five feet long, probably not sculptured, cope about eight inches deep, no ridge-tiles or enlarged ends; otherwise of the Cross-Canonby type.

These are to be seen close to the Lowther mausoleum on a little hill or mound in the turf. It looks as though there had been four, as at the Giant's Grave, Penrith, and as though alternate hog-backs had been removed. They are of red sandstone, one rather more than 4 feet long by 9 inches thick; and the other about 62 inches, by 10 thick. Being deeply embedded in the turf, their height is unknown. By pulling aside the grass it is possible to see inter-lacing or serpentine coils on the side of one stone. Both have coped and tegulated roofs.

Around them are six parts of slabs set in the turf, two of which have mediæval lettering and ornament upon them.

Mr. Calverley further mentioned in a note :—

On the south side of Lowther church, in a solid cross-socket of two steps above ground (split), stands the shaft of a cross cut into a sun-dial stem ; sides chamfered.

This adds another to our Arthuret, Cliburn, Kirkland, Lanercost, Lazonby, etc., series of late high crosses.

MELMERBY.

Lost Cross.

WHELLAN'S *Cumberland*, published in 1860, says that in the churchyard of the old church of St. John the Baptist, " on the south side, are the remains of an old cross which was broken up some years ago." And as visitors occasionally enquire for these remains, it may be as well to state, on the authority of Mr. John Armstrong, the sexton, who speaks from personal knowledge, that the fragments are those of a finial cross taken down from the church-roof about forty years ago, and left in the churchyard, where it was broken by sheep which were put in to keep down the grass.

There seems also to have been an old cross on the triangular grass-plot before the churchyard gate, but this has entirely disappeared.

MILBURN.

DIALS.

TWO dials are built into the west jamb of the west doorway of Milburn church. One is a very early dial *upside
down*, its alternate rays being more deeply cut and longer
than the intermediate rays, as though the greater time
divisions had here once been sub-divided. The stone was a
good one, and the mason made use of it when he inserted
this transitional Norman doorway, as he also used the carved
diaper work, and no doubt any other useful stones which
came to hand. Luckily the quiet sculptures on these stones
did not protrude sufficiently to excite his wrath, and so they
got built in face outwards; whereas a thousand others have
been scabbled past recognition, or built with their faces
inwards, bedded in lime, and buried alive. Below is another
removed dial, for it is too low to allow us to think that this was
its original place. Right side up, much like the upper one,
its rays vary in depth; the one which should probably mark
about one o'clock, appears to have crossed the circle, but as
this stone has been re-cut to form the second coign from the
foundation of the jamb, we cannot be certain that this ray
now marks the hours it was first intended to mark, nor
indeed that the mark beyond the circle is in this case a part
of the dial at all.

These dials are re-drawn on the spot and given in the plate
opposite *Bolton*.

CROSS-SOCKET.

At the gate leading from the main road to the church, which is in
an isolated position, away from the village of Milburn, there is a
broken red-sandstone cross-socket, measuring 24 by 24 by 17 inches,
of the type already mentioned as belonging to the mediæval high
crosses. A stone post is loosely placed in the socket-hole.

MUNCASTER.

CROSS, CROSS-HEAD, AND SOCKET.

THE church, dedicated to St. Michael, was given by Benedict de Pennington to the hospital of Conishead in the time of King John.

On the south side of it, in the churchyard, stands the cross, of red sandstone, 54 inches high from the modern socket in which it has been re-erected (this would be its whole original height, less the head); 16 inches in breadth at the base, tapering to 10½ at the top; 7 inches, tapering to 4½, in thickness.

It was first figured by the Lysons' in their *History of Cumberland*, 1806; also by Canon Knowles in the *Trans. C. & W. A. & A.S.*, 1877. He thought that the triquetra (which appears just at the top, in our photograph) showed Irish work, and that the chain-interlacing, underneath it, resembled the Scandinavian crosses at Kirkmichael and Ballaugh, Isle of Man. He compared it with the cross at Irton and with Dearham and Gosforth standing crosses, which he thought later.

Mr. Calverley saw in this Scandinavian chain-interlacing the tree of Yggdrasil; for in the Dearham cross he discovered the stem or trunk from which these branches spring.

The other face is ornamented with a simple plait of four, made out of plain ribbons nearly 2 inches broad, and treated very flatly. The edges of the cross are alike, and both have a simple twist of two broad ribbons: the whole twist being rounded at the top and square at the bottom.

Under the main design of both front and back is a simple step-pattern. The whole cross has a tendency to run into square draw-ing, like others in which we find evidences of Irish-Viking influence.

In front of it, on the same base, is now affixed a wheel cross-head of red sandstone, 18 inches across the arms, 15 high, and 4½ thick. It is possible that this may be the head of our shaft.

More recently an old and much damaged socket-stone has been placed beside the cross, of red sandstone, 23 by 23 by 13 inches; the hole measuring 14½ by 4½ inches, too small to admit the base of our shaft; and 6 inches deep.

THE STANDING CROSS.

MUNCASTER.

(TO FACE P. 235.)

NEWBIGGIN (on Eden).

Dial and Cross-base.

IN the plate of sun-dials (opposite *Bolton*) is figured the dial on the western buttress of the south side of Newbiggin church, remark-able for its resemblance to the dial on Bewcastle cross. The block on which it is cut is red sandstone, a little under 14 inches in length.

In the churchyard is a standing sun-dial which is *not* on the old cross-base, which remains on the south side of the church. The stump of the shaft is 14 inches thick, 9 broad and 11 high, unornamented; the socket stone measures 29 by 24 by 10 inches, and stands upon a platform about 4 feet square and one foot high; all of red sandstone. It seems to represent another of the later high crosses.

NEWTON ARLOSH.

Dial.

Mr. Calverley says in his notes on dials :—

At Newton Arlosh, where is no porch, traces of the dial are found on a stone in the east jamb of the west doorway. Worked freestone.

There is a circle 8¾ inches in diameter with a large hole for the gnomon, and two rays, one marking noon and the other about one p.m. This we have not thought necessary to illustrate.

If there is anything in the tradition that a church was built here by St. Ninian, this must be the oldest Christian site in our district; but there are no pre-Norman remains. Bishop Halton, by a charter dated Linstock, April 11th, 1303, granted a license to the abbot and convent of Holme Cultram to built a chapel or church within their territory of Arlosh. Early in the nineteenth century the fourteenth century church and its massive peel tower, like those at Burgh, Great Salkeld and Dearham, were in ruins. In 1844 it was restored, and has been since enlarged.

PENRITH.

The Giant's Grave and the Giant's Thumb.

THE venerable Bede speaks of a monastery existing in his time near the river Dacore (Eamont), and William of Malmesbury names Dacor as the place where Constantine, king of Scots, and Eugenius (Owain) king of the Cumbrians put themselves and their kingdom under the protection of the English king, Athelstan (A.D. 926). The monastery of Dacre no longer stands, nor does it appear by any records to have been standing since the Conquest. There is, however, a fragment of an early sculptured stone which may bear upon the Convention of the kings: the sculptures and symbols differ from those on the Penrith crosses and shrine-shaped tombstones.

Leland (*temp*. Henry VIII.) says :—" In the forest of Inglewood a six miles from Carlil, appear ruines of a castel cawled Castel Lewen " or Ewain ; and that Ewaine, king of Cumberland, joined with the Scots and Welsh against Athelstan before the congress at Mayborough or Dacre, and that the tradition seems to give strength to what is told of the tomb at Penrith said to belong to Ewaine Cæsarius.

In Bishop Gibson's Camden the monuments are described with this setting of the tradition :—" It is said they were set in memory of Sir Eweine Cæsarius, Knight, in old time, a famous warrior of great strength and stature who lived in these parts and killed wild boars in the forest of Englewood. He was buried here, they say, and was of such prodigious stature as to reach from one pillar to the other ; and they tell you that the rude figures of bears which are in stone, and erected two on each side of his grave between the pillars are in memory of his great exploits upon these creatures,"

E. Bellasis, Esq., *Lancaster Herald*, very kindly sent me a rough tracing of Dugdale's drawing preserved in the College of Arms, c. 39, Westmorland Visitation (1664-5), in which

Two Views of the Giant's Grave.
PENRITH.

(TO FACE P. 240.)

the pillars and side stones are shown as they appear to-day;
the different sculptures, serpent, men, scroll and ring-and-
band work, with the coping tiles of the side stones, and the
cross in relief, and the lamb of the upright pillar crosses—
quite plain, though mutilated as we see them now. These
are Dugdale's words :—" In cimiterio de Penrith ex parte
Boreali extat Monumentum vetustissimum; ob quam causam,
vel cujus memoriæ erectum, minime constat; Forma vero
istius tale est. The height 11½ feet. The diameter of the
basis, 3 feet. The diameter of the shaft 1½ feet. The
distance betwixt them 15 feet. The middle stones in height
2½ feet. The length of each stone 6 feet."

Sandford, in his account of Cumberland, written about
1675, says he was told by Mr. Page, who was schoolmaster
at Penrith (1581-1591), that a stranger gentleman coming to
see the antiquities of the place, invited Mr. Page and some
of the considerable inhabitants to sup with him : and after
supper said that one Sir Hugh Cesario had an hermitage
called Isey Perlis somewhere thereabouts " in a disert place
in a Rocke ; a marshall man : like a knight errant : killing
monster, man and beast : and he was buried in the North
side of the Curch ith green feild." Sandford says that when
he was at school at Penrith this place was opened by William
Turner,* who found "the great Long Shank bones and other
bones of a man and a broad sword."

Stukeley (1692) says, on the authority of Roger Gale, that
there were four square pillars: but unless remains of the
other pillars be found I think we must assume that the monuments are now pretty much as they were 300 years ago. All
that time the place has been regarded as the tomb of some
eminent personage of remote antiquity—Owen, Ewain or
Hugh—king or knight, or " Cæsarius."

Bishop Nicolson (1703) being parson and patron, had, as

---

* Mr. George Watson, in preparing the foundation for the resetting of the
stones (in 1888) had occasion to excavate beneath them. He found a few
shattered human bones, but the soil was a recent mixture of brick, freestone and
broken cobbles in the mould, with a bit of blue willow pattern pot at the depth
of 7 feet, below which was the undisturbed boulder clay. So that whether the
grave was left in this state by William Turner, or whether the stones have been
moved from their original position, as Mr. Watson believes, there is nothing to
be learned by digging beneath the monument.

he said, frequent opportunities of observing every particular
in and about this church, but having described the monument
he dismisses it with the relation of the Ewain and wild boar
tradition, and the queer statement that he takes " the whole
to have been erected on no other design than for an ornament
(such as it is) to the porch."

Mr. Pennant, in his tour (1769) retains the idea of the
boars, but also notices " two figures like men at the bottom "
of the north-west side stone ; and " work like that on Danish
obelisks in Scotland presented itself to his imagination." In
the 5th edition (1790) he mentions the cross in relief at the
top of the pillar, the figure of an animal beneath, and human
figures beneath this.   Pennant, like Lyttleton, fails to see
the cross in the Giant's Thumb, which he says is in no part
mutilated; whereas the engraving he publishes shows the
thumb as it now is, with the upper part of the cross and
circle broken away.

Dr. Todd, vicar of Penrith (1699-1728), had made a
curious drawing of the two crosses and the four side stones,
in which he showed the crosses squared from bottom to top,
and two of the side stones embellished with two realistic
boars, having snout, tusks, and all complete.   Dr. Todd's
account, quoted by Pennant and illustrated with the
drawings, repeated the tradition of Owen Cæsarius "fourteen
hundred years ago," with a reference to his prodigious
stature and to the "boars which had the honour to be killed by
this wonderful giant."   Dr. Todd's " imagination " did even
allow him to see the sculptures which Pennant himself saw,
and which are plain enough even now ; and he gets rid of
the whole concern as being " the erection in the form of
a cross, long after Christianity was introduced, at the north
or death's door of the church, in order to rest the bodies of
the dead upon them, and to pray for their souls as manner
was."   In the end Dr. Todd makes the four side stones
to be four bears, and the broken crosses to be ragged staffs :
the bears and ragged staffs of the Earls of Warwick, whose
arms they were, and who held Penrith and the castle, and
might have done the work.   Finally, seeing the heads of the
human figures on the columns, he says that they may have
been cut in memory of some petty tyrants of the neighbour-

hood whom "this Mr. Cæsarius," the knight errant, who cleared the country of monsters, had demolished.

There may be some humour, though not much useful testimony, in all this. Pennant, later on, was "convinced that Dr. Todd's drawings were entirely fictitious."

Bishop Lyttleton visited the place (1755) and in his account, published by the Society of Antiquaries and illustrated by an engraving, he says that the stones had never been engraved before, nor accurately described by any author ; that the story of the side stones representing boars is an idle tale, and that, so far from this, it requires a pretty strong imagination to discover any regular figure in the rude sculpture which remains upon them." Maybe the stones were then covered with moss or lichen. He says : "This work is too rude to be Roman " ; he knows of no monument of the kind which was attributed to the Saxons, and that it must be either British or Danish. He remarks that the Britons maintained their ground in these parts long after the Saxons were in possession of the rest of England, and gave British names to this country and this place. "Arthur's round table, the barrow at Ormstead hill, and Long Meg and her daughters are all (or at least the two last) undoubted remains of the Britons here ; but if our monument be British, it is later than either the stone circle or the Druid temple, being probably erected to the memory of some British prince or chief, after Christianity was established amongst them." But after all, he thinks it may be Danish, though the name Giant's Grave strengthens the opinion that it is British, as "both in England and Ireland the vulgar ascribe every stupendous and very ancient work of their ancestors to giants."

As to the rudeness of the sculptures, Mr. George Watson, the architect, found, on reproducing the designs on the circular-headed cross known as the Giant's Thumb, from my rubbings, that every curve had been originally drawn correctly and geometrically true by the same method which would be used by a skilled draughtsman in preparing such a design now. The same designs appear on the side stones of the Giant's Grave, and are, I believe, equally well drawn.

Mr. Gough, then director of the Society of Antiquaries,

says, shrewdly enough : " Perhaps this grave might contain several bodies, and a memorial of some battle lost in the darkness of history."

Hutchinson, in his *Excursion to the Lakes* (1774) says " the side stones do not at present show any any marks of the sculptor." " The pillars are of one piece and formed like ancient spears." He inclines to the belief that the whole is a monument to some British hero, and remarks that in the time of Richard I. the bones of Arthur, King of Britain, were said to be found at Glastonbury in just such a sepulchre ; that perhaps Penrith was a royal residence and this the tomb of Ewain, King of Cumberland, who was a party in the congress at Dacre and Mayborough.

The connection of Arthur with the subject is as old as the ballad of " The Marriage of Sir Gawaine " (Percy's *Reliques*, III., 2), which localises the story told by Chaucer's Wife of Bath in this neighbourhood. " King Arthur lives in merry Carleile," and a Carlish knight of Tearne-Wadling (which is Castle Hewen) overcomes the king, spares him, and afterwards becomes his friend.

Mr. Hodgson, in Britton and Bayley's *Beauties of England and Wales*, ascribes the monument to the British king, but says : " Recurring to early British writers we find the latter part of this traditionary tale false ; for Owen was not king of Cumberland at the time of Athelstan * but in that of Ida, whom the Britons assert he slew in battle." That this Ewain was the chieftain actually buried at Penrith appears in the highest degree probable from the verses of "the Graves of British warriors," written about the close of the sixth century, which notice his sepulchre in words meaning " The grave of Ewain, son of Urien, is in the space enclosed by four curved ridges, beneath the soil of the church of Morvael." The principal ground on which this statement can be contested is the difficulty of identifying the church of

---

* *i.e.* the Owen here buried. It may be worth noting that Owein ab Urien, partly historical, partly a Celtic mythological hero, was fixed by the Welsh bards and English balladmongers as a Knight of Arthur : he was a giant slayer, hero of castle adventures, tamer of the lion, " Llew." A real person, Owein (early Welsh Eugein, Latinized Eugenius) was king of the Cumbrians 934 (Simeon of Durham, Hist. de Dunelm. Eccl.) [ED.]

Morvael with that of Penrith, but as we know that Morvael was a British saint, it seems probable that Penrith church, when originally built (probably a wattle-built church standing to the north of the monument), "was dedicated to St. Morvael, though afterwards it found a new patron in St. Andrew." "The hypothesis derives a new support from an elegy on Ewain in the Welsh language, which mentions him as chief of the splendid Llewins, words which can only be referred to Castle Llewin, constantly asserted to have been possessed by King Ewain."

In 1816 we come to the Lysons' account, which mentions the ornament on the upper part of the crosses, and the evident remains of some rudely sculptured figures in bas-relief, one especially that of a large serpent and two human figures on the curved stones.

In Whellan's *History* (1860) we have the statement that the grave is a family burial ground, and that it belongs to the Dano-Celtic period which preceded the breaking up of the state of society and laws which followed the Roman occupation, and that the fabulous antiquity Ewain, the proprietor if not the founder of Castle Ewein, a name found at Eamont, Tarn Wadling, and Ewanrigg, near the Roman station in the Manor of Ellenborough (Maryport), and only six miles from Derwent mouth (Workington), the southern boundary at one time of the kingdom of Strathclyde—is a strong proof of the existence of such a person, who seems to have claimed, by his name Cæsarius, Roman extraction, and was probably the King Arthur of the North, who made himself a terror to the invading Angles and Danes. Whellan rightly adds : "The grave identifies itself with the early history of Christianity in these counties."

Mr. Walker in his *History of Penrith* says that the name Giant's Grave is identical with the Kemp's graves and the Kemp howe of other parts of these counties, commonly applied to Danish burial grounds, made to contain a number of bodies, simply on account of their extraordinary size.

I find in the Terrier of Kirkland (Bishop Nicolson) "one little close nigh the churchyard called Kempgarth ; " and on enquiring whether any site near Penrith church bore the name "kemp," I was told that the brow and road leading out of Penrith towards Eamont was known as Kemp-ley.

This place-name appears to give a key to the term Giant's Grave. The word "Kemp" does not originally mean a "giant," but it is the Anglo-saxon *cempa* (Icelandic, *kempa*), "a soldier, a champion." Kemp-lea, the name of the high ground standing over the Round Table, is expressive enough; and this grave and monument are the monument and grave-dwelling of a champion or champions.

Whether the Kemp here buried were an "Arthur of the North" or a prince of the peoples who were destined to follow the Celtic race as rulers, we may remember that the struggle before the final breaking-up of the old British kingdom was continuous throughout many generations; and that Celt and Angle, Dane and Pict, were pressed to make strange alliances one with another for temporary safety. One thing at least is certain, that in the blackness of the storm which raged, the sun shone forth from the cross and pierced the heathen darkness; our Lord Christ appeared as the Champion of Right, the Conqueror of Evil; whilst the deceiver Loki was fast bound with links of iron.

The two crosses mark the grave or graves of a warrior or warriors. They were erected at a time when the old mythology was giving way before the true faith. To quote Professor Stephens:—"That religion of the past had some cardinal doctrines and features in harmony with the steadily advancing ' Religion of the future; ' a circumstance which made the translation from heathendom to Christendom much easier than it else would have been. In general the northern system led up to a manly, loyal, active and useful life. It taught that law must build up the land, that principle is before passion. It looked on this life as a school for the next, life itself being compared as nothing to each Kemp's battle task to work together with the Father of the Gods in fighting against everything false and foul, all trolls and giants and earth-snakes; so that we may take our seat victorious in his shining home (Walhall) eventually aiding Him in the regeneration of creation."

Our monument marks the grave of a giant-killer, a mortal warrior. It also, in a figurative way, marks the grave of

heathendom, done at a time when heathendom had made
itself felt as a giant in the land formerly regenerated by such
men as St. Ninian and St. Kentigern.

One may well imagine the presence of the holy Kentigern
here. He was of royal blood, and Castle Ewain bore the
very name of his reputed father. He may even have caused
to be planted the cross on Crossfell, and driven forth the
fiends which gave it the name of Fiendsfell. At all events,
tradition still sees, as you look eastward from the heights
beyond Keswick, with the mountain country all around you
and the plain along the Solway at your back, peopled
with the old races,—Blencathara lying like a warrior armed,
between the British homes and the region eastward beyond
Crossfell, from whence the hordes of the heathen came,—
and as the sun shines on Blencathara's peak, they say that
the good King Arthur lies there waiting till the bugle shall
sound and awake the warriors to the final battle on these
plains, when Arthur shall lead the faithful, and the Fiend,
again unbound, will rush to the shock.

The symbolism of the eastern cross is complete.

At the top is a cross in relief; the arms of the main cross
have been broken off. Beneath this raised figure of a cross,
and at the uppermost part of the shaft is a lamb, the sign of the
Crucified One, and beneath this figure is the evil one, bound
hand and foot, with the serpent over his head,—the northern
demon Loki,—and Sigun his wife is at his side just as on the
Gosforth cross, which indeed seems to be the type from which
this one has been worked, though less skilfully.

These lines from Cædmon, who died 680, illustrate in some
way the idea of a bound fiend, as here shown :-—

> " But bands of iron
> over me circle,
> fetter's link holdeth
> a *fugitive kingdomless*,
> Hell-gyves hasp me
> hard in their grip
> in fastest prison.
> Fire here playeth
> above and under,
> not ever saw I

landscape more loathly ;
low ne'er dieth,
hot over Hell.
Heavy ring-clasps
a merciless manacle,
mock my weakness,
foil the struggles
of Feet sore bounden
Hands tied helpless.
Hell-doors those yonder
for others an out-gang,
idly hang I
limb-shackled here.
Lie around me
of hardest iron
heat-forged deftly,
grindles greatest ;
God's dread lock-fence
close nipping my neck."

Above the bound fiend walks freely the lamb or stag. There is such a figure again upon the Fishing-stone at Gosforth. It is the emblem of Christ, especially the emblem of His resurrection, and therefore fitly set upon monuments of the dead.

In the oldest symbolism of the Christian churches we see our Lord trampling on a lion, adder, or serpent ; this occurs here on one of the side stones ; on the pillar the lamb stands above the bound Loki ; and over the lamb is the sacred sign of the true faith.

All over the large cross is one and the same pattern, rings and bands, chains interminable, nothing but chains : the hell-gyves of which Cædmon sings.

On the north side at the top is the stag, quite plain to see ; and down the edge these same chains.

The Thumb is a circular-headed cross ; the two designs on the edges are reproduced on the new step, so that this re-erection will preserve the cross and its sculpture, and maintain it in the prominent and honoured position which it rightly should command.

It may be of as early a date as the coped stones, to which we will now proceed. These two have been raised out

RE-ERECTED ON NEW BASE
CARVED DESIGNS REPRODUCED
FROM THE CROSS.
1887

THE GIANT'S THUMB.

PENRITH.

(TO FACE P. 248.)

PENRITH,   249

of the ground and set upon bases for their better preservation.

The Rev. T. Lees, vicar of Wreay, has shown me a
drawing from one of them by Mr. Atkinson, which represents
the great serpent with a figure standing on the serpent's
head. This detail comes out in my rubbing, and in a
photograph; as also in Dugdale's drawing, sent me by Mr.
Bellasis. In Mr. Atkinson's sketch a long row of figures
stands underneath, apparently chained together (or joining
hands). These are not now visible, but the faithfulness of
the sketch in other details makes it appear that he may be
also as true as regards the figures below.

*   *   *   *

THE GIANT'S GRAVE.

This hogback, the one seen nearest in the upper view of our plate,
has been much broken, and is patched with cement and iron clamps.
It has large tegulæ on the roof, and the left-hand part of its wall
bears a snake on whose head a small figure is standing. A similar
design, more or less symmetrical with the snake and figure, seems to
have occupied the right-hand side, recalling the Gosforth hogback
(the Priest's Tomb). The back has been defaced. It measures 80
inches in length, 24 in height and 9 in thickness.

The next in the same view is 56 inches long, 26 high, and 8 thick.
Nothing of the ornament remains, except some weathered indications
of tegulæ.

That seen to the right hand and nearest in the lower view in our
plate measures 70 inches in length, 27 in height and 8 in thickness.
It bears a scroll without flowers or leaves, above which is a ring-
plait; and the roof is covered with small tegulæ. The white line
along its edge represents the cement with which the crack in the
stone has been filled. Its back has been cut flat.

The next, to the left hand in the lower view, is seen again in the
upper view behind the nearest on the right hand. It measures 75
inches in length, 30 in height and 11 in thickness. It is ornamented
with a broad band of plait-work with six strands, and has larger
tegulæ on the roof.

The hogbacks are all of red sandstone.

The two standing crosses, of which only the lower parts are seen
in our photographs, are both of light coloured sandstone. The
western cross is 135 inches in height from the ground in which it is
sunk, and measures a little over 5 feet in girth at about 3 feet from

the bottom. The lower part of the stone is decayed, giving it an appearance of *entasis*, which is perhaps accidental. For the height of 81½ inches the shaft is cylindrical; above that, it is cut away into four flat panels, like the shafts at St. Bridget's, Beckermet, and the Gosforth cross. The panels have round bottoms; two of them are 13 inches broad, tapering to 10 inches at the neck, under the cross-head; and the other two are 10 inches broad, tapering to 7. All bear similar ring-plait patterns, and there is a band of similar pattern round the shaft at the junction of round and square, in the same position as the cable moulding round the inscribed cross of St. Bridget's, Beckermet. The head of the cross is much smaller in proportion to the shaft than is usual.

The eastern cross measures 126 inches in height; the cylindrical part of the shaft is 61 inches high, and 4 feet in girth at 3 feet above the ground. The panels of the upper part are 28 inches in height; the two broader panels 12 inches in width; the edges 8 inches broad. Three of the panels are filled with sharply cut ring-plaits; the fourth, which faces the west, has the figures described above by Mr. Calverley. The general shape of the head is larger in proportion than that of the western cross, but it is of the same type, not a ring-cross, but with free arms and round " armpits " like Irton.

In a paper dated January, 1897, Mr. George Watson says that the western cross stands in what is evidently its original socket stone, a regularly shaped circular stone of Blencowe or Lamonby flesh-coloured rock, the same as the crosses themselves. The eastern cross is clumsily fixed into an unwrought square block of local red freestone, now sunk a foot below the surface of the soil.

From examination of the place when the Giant's Grave was re-erected, Mr. Watson thinks that when the church was re-built in 1720-22 the hogbacks and eastern cross were moved to their present place; while the present western cross, originally the eastern one of the two, still retains its old position. Formerly, he thinks, there were two graves, each with a cross and two hogbacks; and the arrangement of the stones as we now see them is comparatively modern.

The Bishop of Bristol (the Rev. G. F. Browne) writing on the early sculptured stones of Cheshire (*Arch. Journal*, vol. XLIV., No. 174, 1887, p. 151) says: " The eastern part of Cheshire is particularly rich in circular pillars, cut at the top into four flat faces." After describing the smaller Ilam pillar he says: " There is one pillar of this kind dated to a certain extent . . . the pillar of Eliseg, bearing an inscription which no one is able to put later than the ninth century. . . The two tall stones in the churchyard at Penrith are, when they are carefully examined, examples of pillars of this description, only more elaborately sculptured. They are usually engraved as covered with an unintelligible mass of holes, but a careful investigation makes out almost all the patterns upon them, and some of the patterns are very curious and unusual."

THE GIANT'S THUMB.

In a paper on the "Giant's Grave; Giant's Thumb; Penrith Churchyard," Mr. George Watson says :—

" The cross in Penrith churchyard, as we have been accustomed to see it (before re-erection in 1887), is by no means an imposing relic. It has been mutilated by knocking off the upper part of the cross. It has been broken off from its base-stone or pedestal, and re-set in comparatively modern times by inserting it two feet and a half in the ground. Time and weather have all but obliterated its sculptured ornamentation.

" When it was ignobly placed in this position is not recorded; but from the fact now ascertained that it was set upon a portion of a seventeenth or early eighteenth century headstone, and wedged up with blue slates, I should conjecture that it originally stood near the old church, the ' pretty and handsome church ' Camden tells us about, and was removed to make room for Dr. Todd's great Georgian church in 1721 or 1722.

" The original form of the cross has been a Greek cross and circle, i.e., the emblem of the redemption surrounded by a nimbus or glory, familiarly styled a ' four-holed cross.' The holes, however, are too large and too shapeless to come within any proper geometrical delineation, and, in my opinion, have been tampered with, by widening out in an irregular manner.

" I have heard a tradition that may possibly account for this. The late Mr. William Grisenthwaite, of this town, who had quite a store of local traditions, told me that the Giant's Thumb was at one time used as a pillory, the universal mediæval corrective of all social delinquencies; and as if stamping the tradition as an his-torical fact, he said the last time it was so used the unfortunate offender was a young woman, who died of a broken heart in consequence of her shameful exposure.

" If this alleged tradition has a foundation in fact, it may account for the holes having been enlarged to accommodate the culprit's wrists."

The present position of the thumb and the hog-backs of the grave is chiefly owing to Mr. George Watson's interest and influence. The photograph of the thumb here reproduced was taken for him by Mr. Huff, formerly of Penrith, and is copied by Mr. Watson's permission ; with some interfering detail in the background effaced by stippling, to show the form of the cross more distinctly.

The Giant's Thumb of white freestone, measuring 17 by 8 inches at the base, and tapering at a height of 60 inches to 10 by 5½ inches. The head is 19 inches broad across the arms. The whole "thumb" of one stone is 77½ inches in height.

The northern edge, facing the road, has a scroll of distinctly Anglian type, with flowers in some of the whorls, and spiral twigs in others. Though it is much decayed one can see that it is close design, not leaving spaces of ground between the twigs and flowers of the pattern.

The north edge of the cross-head has a kind of a rosette, with a common plait beneath.

The west face, here seen, bears a double scroll, starting rather curiously and clumsily from one root, making a sort of boat-shaped line at the bottom.

The south edge had a ring-plait; and the east face seems to have resembled the west.

THE PLAGUE STONE.

The Plague-stone at Penrith is a block weighing about a ton, of stone, so Mr. George Watson says, from the Lazonby district; roughly squared, and with a large hollow in the upper surface. In times of plague the hole was filled with vinegar, into which people from infected houses put their money, and retired to a distance, while the tradesfolk came and laid their goods beside the stone, taking the money out of the vinegar, which was thought to clear it of infection. But the hole was not made for this purpose, and the stone seems to have been the base of a cross.

The Hogbback.

PLUMBLAND.

(TO FACE P. 253.)

PLUMBLAND.

The Hogback.

A AND C are the two parts of one red sandstone shrine-shaped tomb, now lying under the ancient yew tree in Plumbland churchyard. It has been broken in two, one part (A) was cut by an early English mason into a very beautiful impost or springer for an arch, with honeysuckle moulded ornament beneath (a). The sides were roughly scabbled to make a firm and good bed, and the carved block built face downwards into the wall, and the new arch sprung from this impost. ·Hundreds of years afterwards this new part of the church was pulled down and the tell-tale sculpture once more exposed to view.

Place the circular end—the early English impost—(a) next the broken end of C, and it will seem that both sides of the original have been carved in a similar manner, and that both ends or gables were ornamented with a similar design. B is the end in view of A, and shows the gable which was opposite to the one seen in C before the stone was broken.

We have here enough of the original work to give us a clear idea of the intention. The whole is a solid miniature stone house with carved sides or upright wall, a tiled roof, and ornamented gable ends. I saw Roman tiles, the exact shape of the two rows distinctly seen on both sides of this roof, taken out of the excavations at the Roman baths in the city of Bath in 1887. The ridge has been knocked off by the early English wallers to suit their work. It was not hog-backed or curved, but a straight ridge.

The reader must remember that A and C give views of the *two* sides of the stone. The back of C has been scabbled away until there is scarcely any of the original work left, but the other half of the stone has been scabbled on the *opposite* side, and thus we can see what was originally carved on *both* sides. I thank the mediæval mason for sparing to us, though unwittingly, the whole design, as well as for his own very perfect and beautiful work.

The side walls of this grave-house were both covered with serpent forms plaited or intertwined. In Λ the head, mouth and eyes of the creature are seen. The body is divided lengthwise, into one central broad band and two outer narrow bands by lines apparently drilled or picked out or worked with a pointed tool.

Here is the Vala's description taken from the Völuspá (Strophe 42) of the habitation of Helia, the goddess of death, born of Loki and Angrboda, she who dwells "beneath the gratings of the dead."

> " She saw a hall standing
> far from the sun,
> in The Strand of corpses,
> its doors are *northward* turned,
> venom-drops fall
> in through its apertures :
> entwined is that hall
> with serpent's backs."

But the dead man here has hope of deliverance by the power of the Holy Trinity, and his shrine-like tomb has its gable ends signed with the Holy symbol, the triquetra. There was no cross set up at the head or foot here. The stone was intended to be complete in itself, and the sign of the Holy Trinity takes the place of the cross. This symbol is here formed of a single broad flat band, with lines marking a triple composition, and having the lower ends in one case (B) prolonged and ornamented in peculiar manner. This form of knot reminds one of the knots by which in one of the illustrations to the Cædmon MS. Satan is bound hands and feet over the flames of hell.

※   ※   ※   ※

The fragment shown in figs. A and B. measures 23 by 16 by 12 inches; that represented by fig. C is 32 by 18 by 10 inches. They are both in soft red sandstone, hacked or picked, not chiselled.

LATE COPED STONE.

Placed upon the churchyard wall, there is also a coped stone, measuring 56 inches in length, 10 high and 7 broad, ornamented merely with incised semicircles, which seem to represent the edges of ridge-tiles, and under them alternate large and small triangles, as if decadent survivals of the ordinary tegulæ on hogbacks. This may be a case of hogback in transition to grave-slab, and date from the 12th or 13th century.

FRAGMENT OF WHITE SPIRAL CROSS.

Figured in the plate opposite *Gilcrux* is a fragment of a " spiral" cross, resembling the remains of the type at St. Bees, St. John's (Beckermet) and elsewhere. Of this Mr. Calverley said :—

Triskele fragment of shaft from Plumbland. White sandstone, 17 inches by 14 inches. Built into tower wall within. The Plumbland triskele fragment was walled into the church tower at the time of the rebuilding and has remained unnoticed. It bears a rude spiral running scroll between pieces of plaitwork of divided strands, having triskele signs, 8-shaped figure, bosses, and svastika-like raised surface between the strands, and points, I think, to a Teutonic settlement at a very early time.

* * * *

Reginald of Durham, in the 12th century, calls this place " Plumbelund," and derives it from *lund*, " nemus paci donatum," because it was in the midst of a forest (chap. cxxix). Now *Lund* is a Scandinavian word, not Anglo-Saxon in this sense. *Plóma* is used in the Edda for " plum," the A.S. *plum*. The word " plump" (*i.e.*, " clump,") does not seem to be Norse or Anglo-Saxon, though *plum-fether* (from Latin *pluma*) is " down" in Anglo-Saxon.

A religious house on the site seems to have existed as early as 880, being a temporary refuge for the Anglian bearers of the body of St. Cuthbert ; to whom the church was dedicated at the time of the invasion of William the Lion, 1173-4. It may then have been newly built, that is to say, the Norman structure pulled down in 1870-71 ; and before that time there may have been an Anglo-Saxon building which has totally vanished, except for this hogback and cross-fragment.

RHEDA.

The Cross Lacon.

THIS is what Whellan describes (*History of Cumberland*, p. 372) as "An ancient cross of rude workmanship, about 3½ feet high. It is connected with the .ceremonies of the Catholic church by a tradition which says that, in olden times, when a corpse was being brought to St. Bees for interment, it was set down here for a short time while a portion of the burial service was read by one of the monks ; the indentation on the top of the cross having been made for the purpose of supporting the book used on those occasions."

Our view shows that the indentation means simply the loss of the upper arm of a wheel-cross head. After the missing part had been broken, it was refixed with a metal tenon, for which the socket-hole is still to be found. Subsequently this was broken again, and the piece lost. Finally the cross was brought farther up the road, and placed on the garden wall of Rheda Lodge, supported on large blocks of stone and well fenced. But from the number of recent wounds on the side towards the road, it would seem that local stone-throwers consider it intended for a target.

It is of red sandstone ; 44 ins. high from the modern base. The head is 19 inches across the arms, by 10 thick ; the shaft measures 13½ by 12 inches at the base, tapering to 12 by 10 at the neck, The edges of the shaft are chamfered, but there is no ornament.

The head is a wheel-cross, with arms outside the wheel, and a Maltese cross in relief, set as a St. Andrew's cross, in the centre.

This is, of course, one of the later high crosses, ranking with the Resting cross at St. Bees, which it most nearly resembles ; though we take leave to doubt the part played in the tradition by the monks.

CROSS LACON.

RHEDA.

(TO FACE P. 256.)

Rockliffe. S. Mary.

(TO FACE P. 257.)

ROCKCLIFF.

THE STANDING CROSS.

A T Rockcliff, St. Mary's, we come upon the type of the smaller Bromfield cross. The conception is that of a rectangular cross built up of wickerwork, having two broad sides and two narrow edges ; around the upright cross-shaft are two horizontal strengthening bands; around the cross arms is the plaited circle, wheel, or glory, through which the ends of the arms pass. A boss surrounded by a raised ring appears in the centre of the cross-head. The stone between the arms of the cross and the circle has not been perforated as at Dearham.

The main body of the cross is covered with interlacings, the design of which cannot be traced with certainty. The edges have a design which is in some parts traceable, and which is given approximately in outline in the accompanying sketch ; it agrees with one of the designs on the Bromfield cross, and is also an adaptation of some of the work on the great cross at Gosforth.

The horizontal bands which are worked round the main body of the interlaced or wickerwork cross (done in stone) have upon them beasts with huge open jaws, eyes, ears, and teeth. The bodies of these beasts are bound with bands and terminate in the same manner as those seen on the Gosforth cross. They are, in fact, the same progeny of the evil one, combining the serpent and the wolfish nature, which appears on that cross.

At Aspatria, at the bottom of the standing cross, is figured one of these creatures in a somewhat different form.

At Cross-Canonby the wolf, the serpent, and the human form are all three combined and bound with a fetter.

✻   ✻

This fine effective monument is well placed in the churchyard, at the corner of a grass-plot with a dark yew-tree for background. It is of light-coloured sandstone; 74 inches in height, 26½ inches across the arms of the head, 17 across the neck. The thickest part of the shaft is 9 inches thick; the head is 6 inches thick. The red sandstone base measures 44 by 32 inches, and stands 6 inches above the soil.

The pattern is rudely picked, not chiselled; the back, as far as its defaced condition allows it to be seen, resembles the front.

'Rockcliff' on the Ordnance Map; 'Rocliff' as spelt by Bishop Nicolson, 1703; 'Rothcliff' in Denton's *Cumberland*, about 1610; 'Routhclive' in *Pedes Finium*, 1204, are a few of the variations of the name, as collected by Chancellor Ferguson (*Trans.* C. & W. A. & A. S., vol. XV., p. 189). Commenting on the list, Professor A. S. Napier thinks that the *Routh* or *Roth* is the Old Norse *raudr* 'red,' and that the name means 'Redcliff.'

Mr. Calverley inclined to believe that it might signify the Rood-cliff, from this cross; but perhaps the possible old Norse *Ródhu-klif* (Rood-Cliff) is not so near the name as Old Norse *Raudh-klif* (red cliff). In any case the place-name seems to be Scandinavian, and the cross resembles some of those which we refer to the Scandinavian period.

THE DRAGON LINTEL.

ST. BEES.

(TO FACE P. 259.)

ST. BEES.

IN the *Transactions of the Cumberland and Westmorland Antiquarian and Archæological Society*, vol. ii. p. 27, and vol. iii. p. 95 (the last published in 1877), Canon Knowles gave figures and brief descriptions of a number of pre-Norman fragments. These have been re-drawn from the originals, with the exception of two early fragments which Canon Knowles says are underneath the south aisle floor, and "an early stoup, shaped in front like the bow of a barge," which may be seen on a window-sill in the church. We have omitted a number of other early stoups as doubtful in date, and hardly illustrating the art of our period.

THE DRAGON LINTEL.

This relief is sculptured on what seems to have been a pedimental lintel—hardly to be called a tympanum—of the Irish form, now set up opposite the west door. It is of red sandstone, 67 inches in length, 18 inches high in the middle and 12½ at each side; 9¼ inches in thickness. It is carved only in front, chiselled cleanly and deeply, and in high relief. St. George (or St. Michael), with helmet, shield, and sword, is seen standing behind the dragon, whose scales and convolutions are given with much spirit, and in a style suggesting 12th century work rather than what we have of pre-Norman art. But the elaborate interlacings finely illustrate the development of the old Anglo-Irish motive; and with them might be compared, by a visitor to St. Bees, the interlaced capitals of the grand Norman doorway opposite.

ST. BEES.

THE STANDING CROSS.

In the churchyard to the north side of the church is the shaft of a pre-Norman cross, of white sandstone, 38 inches high, 13 broad and 4½ thick. It stands in a red-sandstone socket-base, measuring 26 inches square, and rising 6 inches above a platform of smaller stones.

The northern side, seen to the left hand in our plate, shows a debased plait of a double strap with rings, and a dragon. The western edge is much worn, but must have been like the eastern edge, with a figure-of-eight plait. The south side has a large double-strand plait, with triquetræ inserted to fill the interstices; and in the middle of the design there seem to have been two dragons face to face, as terminations of the interlaced bands. The carving is done with the pick.

THE NORSE CROSS

(" *Spiral*" *White Shaft*).

Another fragment, described by Canon Knowles as of " Norse design " is of white sandstone; 26 inches in height, 12 in breadth at the base, tapering to 10 inches at the neck, from which the broken arms of the cross-head spring ; and 7 inches in thickness at the base, tapering to 6 inches at the head. The pattern is picked, like the standing cross.

One side bears the "Norse" chain pattern which Mr. Calverley connected, in the case of the Dearham, Gosforth and Muncaster crosses, with the tree of Yggdrasil: and above this one are the abortive spirals or degraded scroll-work which characterize many of these white crosses. The opposite side has spirals like the example at St. John's, Beckermet, and pseudo-interlacing, in which the original naturalistic imitation of a knotted strap has become a mere series of curved ridges. One edge has a debased plait, and the other a simple key-pattern, incised. The whole, though we call the ornament debased and degraded, is of a very interesting and unusual type; and its Norse motive suggests that it is the monument of a Viking settler in the tenth or eleventh century.

THE STANDING CROSS.

THE NORSE CROSS.

ST. BEES.

"Spiral" Fragment.

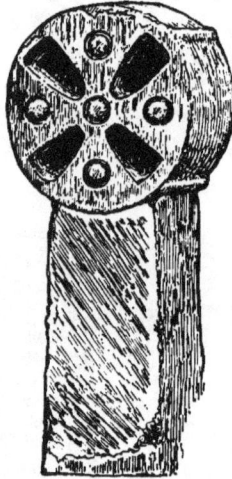

The Resting Cross.

ST. BEES.

ST. BEES.

"Spiral" Fragment.

On a window-sill in the church is preserved a fragment of a cross of white sandstone, measuring 7 by 5½ by 4 inches ; picked work; of which part of the pattern has been defaced with a chisel, or by sharpening a tool on the stone. Though somewhat similar to the two above mentioned, it seems to be part of a different cross.

The Resting Cross.

Beneath the dragon lintel is now set up a mediæval cross, originally brought from somewhere at a distance; the site unknown.

It is of red sandstone, 38 inches high ; the shaft 11 inches broad at the base, tapering to 10 at the neck; and 9 inches tapering to 8½ in thickness ; the diameter of the wheel-head is 16 inches. It is chiselled, and, though different in design, resembles Cross Lacon in character.

This belongs to our series of later crosses, of which we have had examples in various stages of demolition at Arthuret, Cliburn, Cumwhitton, Dovenby, Kirkland, Lazonby, Milburn, Newbiggin, (and perhaps the Plague stone at Penrith and the lost corpse-crosses at Castle Sowerby), showing the development of the ancient high crosses in the hands of mediæval workmen.

Canon Knowles mentions also a fragment of which he says, " part, I suppose, of an ante-Norman dial "; which may possibly be a bit of a mediæval grave-slab, such as abound at St. Bees. We may perhaps note that, up in the belfry, there is built into the wall, upside down, part of a finely carved shield in high relief, bearing three fish (Luces of the Lucy family) and a lion ; also the cross of of a grave-slab.

In the churchyard there is a sun-dial standing on what looks like the base of a cross of earlier date ; having three (Calvary) steps, and a socket-hole which would have held a shaft measuring 12 by 6½ inches, if not more, for the stone has been cut and clamped together. This base might possibly have held the " Norse " cross.

STAINMOOR.

The Reycross.

A LIST of the crosses in Cumberland and Westmorland would be incomplete without some notice of the Reycross; for though it is now just over the border and in Yorkshire, it was always regarded in former days as being itself the boundary-mark; and therefore as much ours as our neighbours'.

It is of yellowish-white gritstone, very rough in quality, with large pebbles in it; a kind of stone which we have noticed as used for several monuments of the Scandinavian age with the hacked, sketchy work of that period.

The base or socket-stone measure 26 inches by 27, and stands 14 inches out of the ground. The height of the shaft above the base is 27½ inches; it is 11½ by 10 inches thick. This may be only a fragment; if so, it is the upper part of a somewhat longer shaft. The neck and lower part of a wheel-cross head seem to be visible.

There is no carving to be seen at first sight, except the two ordnance crow-feet on the base, and the initials of some Vandals on the head of the stone. But at the bottom of the western side, in a favourable light, the surface, now thickly crusted with lichen, shows forms too regular for mere weathered roughness, and suggests a rudely hacked pattern of diverging straps with pellets, something like the shafts at Burton and St. John's, Beckermet.

That there were formerly carvings on the stone is clear from the description given by Speed (1623) :—

" A stone crosse, on the one side of whose shaft stood the picture, and armes, of the King of England, and on the other the image and armes of the king and kingdome of Scotland."

Mr. Hylton Longstaffe in his *Richmondshire* (1852) quoted by the late Rev. Thomas Lees, F.S.A., in a paper read here July 8, 1887, says that near the cross "is a weather-worn slab, about 4 feet long, having traces of a human figure, apparently once inlaid with some precious metal. A conical aperture in the top perhaps contained a metal cross." Of these no vestige now remains. But Speed's

THE REYCROSS ON
STAINMOOR.

(TO FACE P. 264.)

account, and what we can now see of the shape and the stone, incline us to believe that the Reycross was one of the usual pre-Norman monuments, more than usually defaced by weather and wanton injury.

Until lately " the shaft of the cross," as Chancellor Ferguson says (*History of Westmorland*, p. 52) " was loose in its socket, and was frequently displaced by idle persons. In the year of the Queen's Jubilee, 1887, it was secured and railed in, at the joint expense of the Yorkshire Archæological and Topographical Society and the Cumberland and Westmorland Antiquarian and Archæological Society."

Our photograph was taken on the occasion of a meeting of the last named society to view the cross after its re-erection. On this occasion Mr. Lees read the paper already mentioned, in which he quoted General Roy's opinion, accepted by Dr. Guest and himself, that the cross had been a Roman milestone. He referred to the myth of King Marius (supposed to flourish in A.D. 75), who killed Roderic the Pict and set up this stone as a trophy; and to another error of early historians by which the battle of Fethan-leag (A.D. 584) was located at Stainmoor; also mentioning the claim of John de Cheham, Bishop of Glasgow (1258) to a diocese extending " usque ad Rer Cros in Staynmor."

We may add the notice in the Scalacronica, a MS. at Corpus Christi College, Cambridge, which contains a Norman French chronicle of the Picts and Scots, quoted at length by Skene, and dated by him 1280 (*Chron. P. and S.*, p. lix). In this it is said " Edmound, freir Athelstan, duna a cesti Donald, roy Descoce, tout Combirland, pur quoi lez Escoces ount fait clayme, tanque al Reir croiz de Staynmore." This does not say that Edmund (died 946) fixed the Reycross as the boundary; but that in more recent times the Scotch had claimed up to Reycross. There is no evidence that the cross existed in Edmund's time.

In the next century an event happened which Speed, Camden, Holinshead, and Boece, locate at Reycross—the meeting of William the Conqueror and Malcolm of Scotland. This actually took place at Abernethy in 1072 (see Freeman's *Norman Conquest*, vol. iv. p. 516), but the chroniclers fancied that it must have been at the old border-mark of the two races and kingdoms—the spot where the ancient British, and then Roman, road passed out of the old country of the Angles, over the otherwise hardly passable hills, into the land of the Cymru, Cumberland. They thought that the cross was the memorial of the kings' meeting; that the carving on it had meant their arms, and that its name was a corruption of Roi-crosse—a belief in which they have been followed by some good modern historians.

Whatever the cross was meant for, the place was a natural and important boundary; and the cross, once there, must have been looked upon as a boundary-mark.

Now Rá is an early Norse and Swedish word for " land-mark," and *rá-merki* is " boundary-mark " in old Norse law, though the word became obsolete in all the Scandinavian languages; and is not Anglo-Saxon in this sense (unless akin to *ræw*, *raw*, a "row," or hedge-row). But the old Norse is preserved in our dialect; for example, in the Bounds of the Manor of Coniston we find "the Rear or Ray Cragg," obviously the crag that is the *rá*, "land-mark." There can be no doubt that Reycross, Recross, Rie cross, Rer cross, Rere cross, are like Rear or Ray Crag, only variants of some ancient Norse word *Rá-kross*, " boundary cross."

The fact that it is known by a name which is no earlier than the Scandinavian period points to that period as the age of its erection. As to its purpose—we have no instance, in our district, of pre-Norman crosses, such as we take this to be, set up for any other purpose than as tombstones; unless it be the mediæval Jocelin's statement that Kentigern set up a cross from which to preach. (See *Crosthwaite*.) A tombstone might well be *used* as a boundary mark; as this certainly was used in the thirteenth century and later; but we have no evidence to show that it was *set up* as a boundary mark.

Now this is not likely to have been a preaching cross, and if a tombstone, why not in a churchyard?

Mr. Lees in his paper already referred to, recurred to a previous paper in which he had tried to explain a local tradition of a great battle on Stainmoor. He found an explanation in the fourteenth century romance of *Child Horn*. The story is that in the fifth century Hatheolf, a king of Yorkshire, was attacked on Stainmoor by three kings from Ireland, Ferwell, Winwald, and Malkan. The only survivors of vast slaughter were Malkan and thirteen of his men; but he was afterwards slain by Horn, son of Hatheolf. Mr. Lees thought that Melkinthorpe might contain the name of Malkan; and that this battle might be the traditional battle of Stainmoor.

The tale of Child Horn is practically the same with that of King Horn (*Early English Text Society*, No. 14. ed., J. R. Lumby, 1866), which says nothing about Stainmoor; but if in any respect historical, is founded on traditions—not of the fifth century but of the Viking age, the tenth century; as indeed Mr. Baring-Gould suggests by his version for children in *Old English Fairy Tales* (1896). It is a mediæval reminiscence of the Viking age, like the stories of Beorn Buzecarl and, as Mr. Gollancz has shown, of Havelock (Olaf Cuaran): we may add, perhaps, the legend of the " Roi Guillaume d' Engleterre " versified by Chrestien of Troyes.

Now, though Mr. Lees did not suggest it, the slaughter of a

Christian king in battle on Stainmoor would be the occasion for his burial there and commemoration by a cross; which would after-wards become known rather as a boundary-mark than as the tomb-stone of a forgotten personage. We English forget the persons of our earlier history, because they are not, in many cases, our own ancestors; they are often alien to the dwellers on the soil. In Ireland or Iceland, Scotland or Wales, the peasantry claim descent from the heroes of a thousand years ago, and hold them in remem-brance. This is why a tomb of a person famous in his own day might, 300 years later, when his dynasty and kindred had passed away, be named only as a boundary-mark. We have seen already that events of the tenth century were retold in the fourteenth as a cycle of wild romances.

We can find battles more historical than that of Child Horn to locate at Stainmoor; and the fact of its being a noted battlefield, on the confines of two races and two kingdoms, was the reason why the romancer made use of the name.

The Pictish Chronicle (facsimile in Skene's *Chronicles of the Picts and Scots*) records that about 971 Kenneth MacMalcolm ravaged the Sassenach as far as *Stanmoir*. But twenty years earlier there was a battle on the spot of great importance at the time, though subsequent history wiped it out of general recollection.

Roger of Wendover, under A.D. 950, says that King Eilric was overcome *a Macone consule* through the treachery of Earl Osulf of Bernicia, and slain, together with his son Henry and brother Reginald, "in a lonely spot called *Steinmore*."

A quite independent story of the battle is told by Snorri Sturluson, the Icelander, in the *Heimskringla* (*Hákon*, chap. IV). Eric Bloodaxe, son of Harald Fairhair, invited to reign at York by King Athelstan, and converted to Christianity, was driven from his throne. He went into Viking, with headquarters in the South Isles (Isle of Man and Hebrides); but once, venturing far inland, was slain by a King Olaf, who had been set up as sub-king by Edmund, and with him fell his son Harek (Henry) and Rögnvald (Reginald) and others.

Eric at York is mentioned also by such diverse witnesses as the *Anglo-Saxon Chronicle* (A.D. 948); Symeon of Durham, *Hist. Regum*, 948; Florence of Worcester, 949; Egil's Saga, and the *Life of St. Cadroë* (quoted in Skene's *Chronicles of the Picts and Scots*, p. 116).

Symeon of Durham in another book (*Historiæ Continuatio;* ed. Hodgson Hinde, vol. i. p. 90) says that Eric was killed by Maccus, son of Anlaf (Olaf); which links together Wendover's Maco with the Olaf of Heimskringla. Olaf, who was made king of York by Edmund in place of Eric, the protégé of Athelstan, was the famous Olaf Cuaran; who, indeed, had been once ejected from York, but still claimed the throne, as representing the Danish line, while Eric was the leader of the Norwegian Vikings—the Fingall as opposed to the Dubhgall, Among Olaf Cuaran's family we hear no more of Maccus, for as Roger of Hoveden tells us, Amancus, son of Anlaf, was killed by the Northumbrians, as the final act of expulsion of the Viking rulers from York. The name afterwards was borne by other North-men, variously spelt until it settled down to Magnus, erroneously said by Sighvat the Skald, in the christening of St. Olaf's son, to be equivalent to Karl Magnus, Charlemagne.

We can see, then, how Eric, raiding England and Bretland (Wales and Cumbria) from Man and the isles, ventured for once along the great road towards York, invited by Oswulf of Bamborough, under whose protection his wife Gunnhild was living; and how Olaf Cuaran, warned by Oswulf, sent Magnus to meet him at the natural point for offering battle. This, perhaps, is the event dimly recorded in the romance of Child Horn, just as the life of Olaf himself becomes a romance in the tale of Havelock the Dane; and this is the historical battle of Stainmoor.

We have then an occasion upon which a cross might have been erected, and a cross that might have been erected upon such an occasion. But to go farther, and suggest that Reycross was Eric's monument, would be mere romance.

TEBAY.

THE BRANDRETH STONE.

BISHOP GIBSON'S *Camden* mentions the "Red Stone" (Brandreth Stone) in a field called Gallaber "about an ell high, with two crosses cut deep on one side. The tradition among the inhabitants is that formerly it was the Mere-stone between the English and Scots."

Whellan, who calls it the Brandery Stone, says "there was formerly an inscription" upon it.

" Brandreth " (Icelandic *brandreith*, also Anglo-Saxon *brandræd*, a fire-dog, grate,) means, in the dialect of the north, an iron *tripod* to support the girdle-plate in baking oat-bread. A Brandreth Stone is the mere-stone which marks the junction of *three* counties or parishes. At Tebay, where three streams and valleys meet, may have been the three-fold boundary of Appleby, Kendal, and Yorkshire.

The stone is an unhewn boulder measuring 47½ by 33 by 18 inches and stands as the lowest step to a stile in a field of the Castle Howe farm, a little south of the farmhouse, to north of which is the fine *burh* close to the watersmeet.

Mr. Jackson, the tenant, says that formerly the stone was built into a wall about 20 yards south of the present position. About 1887 the whole wall was moved, and the Brandreth Stone placed as we now see it. When it was moved, no carving was found upon it; and nothing is now visible.

TORPENHOW.

The Dial.

THIS dial was discovered by me after the restoration of
Torpenhow church by Mr. Cory, the Rev. C. H. Gem
being vicar. Both vicar and architect have spared the holy
relics, and treasured them carefully, or this strange witness
of old times could never have been seen. Here has stood an
old church before the days of Norman conquerors. The walls
of this old church have been partially removed, and a south
aisle added ; and the building stuff of the original wall has
been again used for the new south wall of what is now a very
ancient aisle ; and so it has come to pass, that *inside* the
church, between the two square windows of the south aisle,
and 2½ feet west of the top of the more eastern one of the
two, you may see the traces of a dial which was once cut
on the *outside* of the church, and served to guide, perhaps,
our earliest Christian *fore-gangers* in the matter of the hours
of divine service. At the restoration of this church, the
workmen left the stone bare of plaster and whitewash, and
peeled it off so tenderly that the rays of this tell-tale dial have
not been chiselled out of recognition.

※　　※　　※　　※

Mr. Calverley's original sketch of the dial showed only three rays,
which would stand for tierce, sext, and one o'clock. There seems, however, to be another ray for three p.m., which is accordingly marked
in our sketch, in the plate opposite *Bolton*. The hole for the
gnomon is ⅞ of an inch deep, and the diameter of the circle about 6
inches. It seems to have been cut upon one of the Roman stones
which were freely used in the original building.

THE FONT.
TORPENHOW.

(TO FACE P. 271.)

THE FONT.

An interesting development of interlacing is seen in the font; of which the basin is no doubt contemporary with the church. The interwoven arches resemble Ingleton font, but here we have no grotesque Herod below, nor wandering line of plait-work above; but a broad band of cleanly cut interlacing of the Norman open kind (compare Dearham font), with trefoiled twigs set crosswise in the intersections of the bands (like patterns on the Adam stone at Dearham).

The stem of the font is much later, and bears heraldic ornament. It is of yellow sandstone, 17 inches in diameter, 11 in height. The basin measures 24 inches in diameter, and is 14 in height. It is made of a silvery sparkling white sandstone, of which a quarry exists hard by. This is a softer material than the yellow stone of the stem, and crops out along the edge of the high ground above the red sandstone of the valley.

On the south side of the chancel is a Norman piscina, decorated with a large wheel-rosette like the orb on Bridekirk font, and a cable moulding. The great chancel-arch has grotesque capitals; that on the north bears four figures with their legs and arms interlocked in a kind of impossible dance, spirited and ludicrous.

On the abacus of the capital opposite, there are, to the left hand, very small chequers, as if in imitation of rush-matting, the raised squares overlapping the sunk ones a little. On the right-hand side of the abacus is a pattern like spiral scrolls of Anglian work, but here becoming almost the pure Greek *kymation*. Underneath, the bulk of the capital is covered with a row of absurd people whose bodies are mere swaddled cylinders. Can these represent souls,—"vapour done up like a newborn babe?" The soul-baby is usually naked, however, in mediæval art.

Here, on another capital at the west end of the church, four similar figures (souls?) are seen again, standing on the tail of a lizard-like creature, which, rising up at the edge of the capital, clasps in its four legs some great bundle, or figure, too worn to distinguish. A similar reptile repeats the action on the right-hand edge of the stone, but its tail is curled into one great spiral, and carries no souls, only one little face peeps over its great whorl. This curious stone is 8½ inches in height and 19 in length.

In this parish is Blennerhasset, where an old market-cross has been re-erected on a new base.

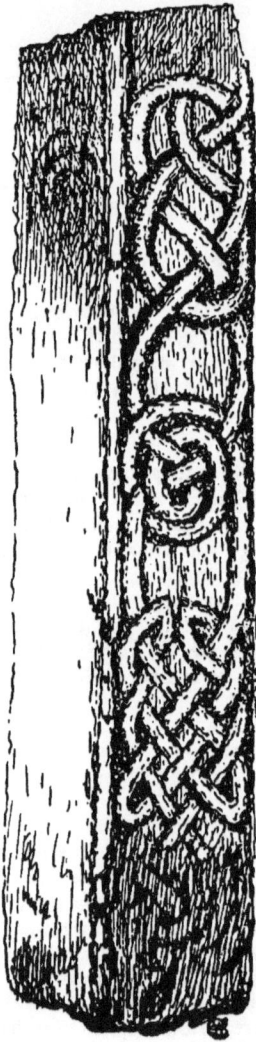

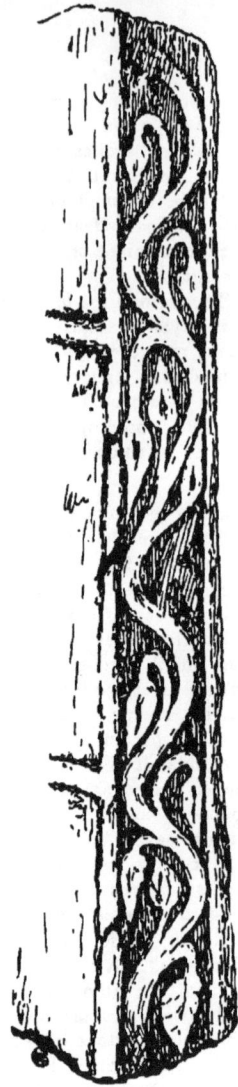

THE ANGLIAN SHAFT.

WABERTHWAITE.

WABERTHWAITE.

Fragments of Anglian Cross and Standing Cross.

IN vol. III., p. 95, of *Trans.* C. & W. A. & A. S., the Rev. Canon Knowles gives drawings of one face and edge of the large cross at Waberthwaite, which at that time was doing duty as a lintel over the church porch, and he mentions "another (cross) of the same school and date laid down on the threshold of the church door," the recovery of which, from its state of degradation, was then promised. This recovery has been accomplished.

The fragment lies in the vestry. One of the faces, as will be seen from my sketch, was divided into panels by horizontal bands, but the passage of many feet has worn away almost all traces of the designs, and one part is now quite smooth. One edge shows interlacing, the other has a freely drawn foliated vine scroll. The material is red sandstone, measuring 43½ inches long by 12½ inches wide at the bottom, and 11½ inches at the top by 7 inches thick at the bottom, tapering to less than 6 inches at the top.

The large cross also has, by the kindly aid of Lord Muncaster, been removed from the porch, and fixed in its own socket-stone, which we found lying unbroken in the church-yard. A damaged corner towards the bottom of the cross has been made up with cement, and with the exception of the head and a corner which has been broken away near the top, the monument is pretty much as it was when first set up. The material is red sandstone, measuring 6 feet 8 inches in height, 1 foot 7 inches bottom width, and 1 foot 3 inches top width, and 10⅜ at bottom, at the top 8 inches in thickness. The socket-stone stands 1 foot 3½ inches high, and is 2 feet 9½ inches long, and 2 feet 2 ins. wide. One face and both

edges of the cross are covered with interlacings of flat bands.
The other and chief face (formerly hidden as the upper side
of the lintel of the church porch) is decorated with symbolic
devices. The lower portion exhibits two circles in contact,
each within a square space, whose four corners are filled by
the points of the sacred triquetra (symbol of the Holy
Trinity), into which form the flat band of the ornament
is worked. In working out this device it will be further seen
that the four triquetræ which gather round the point of
contact of the two circles take the form of a third circle,
proceeding from the other two. Immediately over this, and
at a convenient height for the purpose, the surface has been
worn smooth and grooved by the sharpening of iron tools
before the stone was seized as handy building-material for
the porch. Whether an inscription once filled this space we
may not now tell.

The principal panel contains the figure of an animal (? a
horse) moving amidst an apparently inextricable tangle, and
in the uppermost panel appear two creatures facing each
other, and having their lower extremities intertwined and
knotted together. These two panels deserve much attention.
The upper one is very much like the lower panel of the cross
at Collingham, Yorks., which was taken out of the foundations of the church in 1841, and on which is a Runic
inscription which gives the name ONSWINI, and which
Professor Stephens, F.S.A., dates A.D. 651, saying that it
was, in all probability, raised to the memory of that amiable
sovereign ONSWINI (OSWINE), son of King OSRIC, and ruler
of Deira (the lands between the Humber and the Tyne), who
was defeated at Wilfaræsdun (Wilbarston in Northampton-
shire) by King Oswiu, and murdered by his order or
instigation at Ingetlingum (now Collingham), August 20th,
651.*

The Waberthwaite work is not so elaborate as that at
Collingham, judging from the engravings, but the idea
appears to be the same in these two panels, and is again
found on the Ilkley cross. It may be noted that the two

---

* *Old Northern Runic Monuments,* part II., p. 390, Prof. George Stephens.

THE STANDING CROSS.

WABERTHWAITE.

(TO FACE P. 274.)

THE STANDING CROSS.
WABERTHWAITE.

(TO FACE P. 275.)

edges of the Collingham stone are ornamented with interlacing and scroll work, as are the edges of the fragment of
the cross now lying in the vestry.

If the figure in the central panel, which has in some places
crumbled away, was intended to represent the horse, we may
well remember the part which this noble creature played in
some of our early religious rites, and in the mythology of our
northern ancestors. At Halton (Lancashire) Grani, Sigurd's
famous horse, is figured on what may be the funeral stone of
Tosti, earl of Northumbria, and brother of Harold Godwinson,
who made common cause with Harold Sigurdson against his
brother the English King, and fell at Stamford Bridge A.D.
1066.

The cross itself is the horse upon which the devoted one
" the hanged man," the Crucified, rides to his great victory.
At Dearham the horse appears on a very early cross. At Gosforth and at Penrith, the Lamb and the Hart appear as the
symbols of the *devoted One*, and walk nobly on in spite of the
" tangle of tragic events " and the presence of the old enemy—
the serpent. At Brigham, in the head and arms of the cross,
the God Man Himself wrestles victoriously with the *Evil One*,
which has entwined itself around His body and knotted
itself beneath His left hand.

Waberthwaite has been spelt Wyberghthwaite and Way-
bergthwaite, and was the old home of the Wybergh family.

I desire to seize this opportunity of acknowledging with
gratitude the kindness and hospitality shown by Mr. and
Mrs. Postlethwaite on more than one occasion to myself, and
Mr. Fletcher, whose admirable photographs form the basis of
my illustrations.

※ ※ ※

The fragment in the vestry is too worn to allow the technique of
the carving to be seen; but the design connects it with Irton and
Heversham. The standing cross is chipped or hacked work, not
chiselled; the natural smooth surface of the stone contrasting with
the pitted or dotted background, as we often see it in wood carvings
on kists, etc., of the seventeenth century. The stone must have
come from St. Bees or Gosforth.

WARCOP.

CROSS.

WHELLAN'S *History of Westmorland* (p. 770) mentions that " An ancient Cross, which stood on the common, was removed after the enclosure, and placed in the village."

This seems to be the same as the remains of the churchyard cross mentioned in a note by Mr. Calverley as possibly of Norman date. It adds another to our list of later high crosses.

WORKINGTON.

The " Tower " Fragment.

ON January 24th, 1887, Mr. W. L. Fletcher of Stoneleigh, Workington, went down to the parish church of St. Michael to examine the walls and débris after the havoc made by the fire which had destroyed all the church, save the tower. On the north side of the arched eastern entrance, leading from the nave into the tower, and 3½ feet above the ground, Mr. Fletcher discovered a sculptured stone which he rightly judged to be a portion of an old cross shaft. On February 8th, in company with Mr. Fletcher, I visited the relic ; we removed the plaster from the face of the stone and took a rubbing and a photograph of the precious treasure.

The type of cross is not the very earliest, but suggests its erection between the seventh and the end of the ninth centuries, and before the Norsemen and Danes had greatly devastatated these coasts or firmly planted themselves here.

The fragment is 17 inches long by 9 inches broad at the broadest part, rudely worked with a broad chisel into *triple* bands forming most graceful curves and reminding one very forcibly of delicate basket work ; a *single* band appears in two places to hold back the triple wythes.

The part of the tower in which this carved sandstone block is built is, I believe, of late Norman date, and the stone itself had become damaged by long (centuries) exposure before it was built into the tower wall and thenceforward sheltered from the weather. A crumbling away, the work of ages, may be noticed beneath the lime when removed.

I should assign this cross to the period of the Cuthbert pilgrimage, and take it as a witness to the presence of the later Lindisfarne brethren, who would be welcome at Brigham, Bridekirk, Plumbland, Aspatria, Dearham, Crosscanonby, &c., where the old Christian inhabitants remained. They had traditions then of more than two hundred years concerning Bishop Kentigern, and still older traditions of St. Ninian and St. Patrick; for each of these places had at that date been an old mission centre, and at each place there still remain fragments of the very earliest type of white sandstone cross.

In the year 883 the bearers of the body of St. Cuthbert arrived at Chester-le-street, and St. Cuthbert's body rested there 113 years. At the last restoration of the chancel of the church at Chester-le-street a portion of a sculptured cross, bearing work of a similar character with this now found at Workington, was taken out of the wall; the Chester-le-street cross, like the one erected at Derwent mouth, having been used by the masons of later age as merely building stone.

I find that Professor Stephens assigns this Chester-le-street cross to the eighth century.

[Two years later Mr. Calverley wrote:—]

The fragment which was formerly built into the tower has been taken out, and proves to be worked on all sides with plait-work of wythes.

The ornamentation on the face here shown consists of a series of double rings placed down the centre, two double bands cross each other in the centre of each ring and pass

Workington. St. Michael. 3.

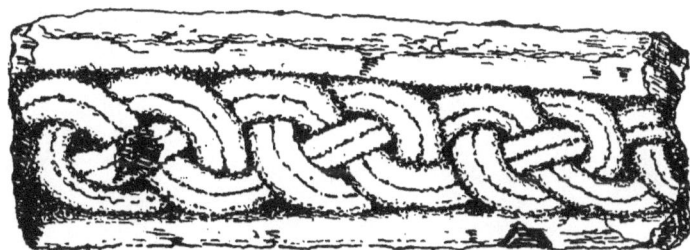

(TO FACE P. 278.)

the one over the other and under the ring on either side, and proceed to each alternate ring, passing over and under each other alternately as they come in contact. These double bands, when they near the edges of the cross, are kept in place by a narrow fillet, as the wythes in basket-work are held together.

The same basket-work feature is to be noticed on the opposite face of the stone which was figured before removal from the tower wall.

*   *   *   *

The fragment of which the three late-found sides are given in the plate lettered " Workington, St. Michael, 3," and the first found side in the block from Mr. Calverley's sketch is of yellowish-white sand-stone, measuring 16½ by 9 by 5 inches. It is chiselled carefully and skilfully, but not over smoothly; the touches of the chisel are seen. The background is not cleared out, but the whole surface is filled up with close design. There are no drill-holes, but here and there deep cutting with the chisel, to contrast with the general shallow and delicate modelling. The rise and fall of the strands is subtly indicated; and the whole must have been a very dainty bit of sculpture. The "ear-shaped guilloche," as Canon Knowles called it in discussing the lost fragments at Haile, is that pattern seen on the edge to the left-hand in the plate.

WORKINGTON.

THE FIRST CURWEN VAULT FRAGMENT.

During the work done at the parish church of Workington, St. Michael's, since the fire, two fragments have been taken from the vault of the Curwen family, where they had been used as building material.

One is represented by the two upper figures of the plate opposite ; giving two sides and one edge of a white sandstone fragment, 19 inches by 13, and 5½ inches thick. A plait with bosses in the spaces is seen on one side, whilst on the edge is the key pattern ending in a curve ; and on the other side, part of an uncommon design of spirals.

✳

This is unlike the Tower fragment in having the background cleared out flat, and in being much more smoothly chiselled. The design is ugly ; the interlacing does not fit quite so neatly as drawn in the plate, being like the pseudo-interlacing of the late white shafts at St. John's, Beckermet, and St. Bees. The side seen in perspective has diverging spirals of Irish character.

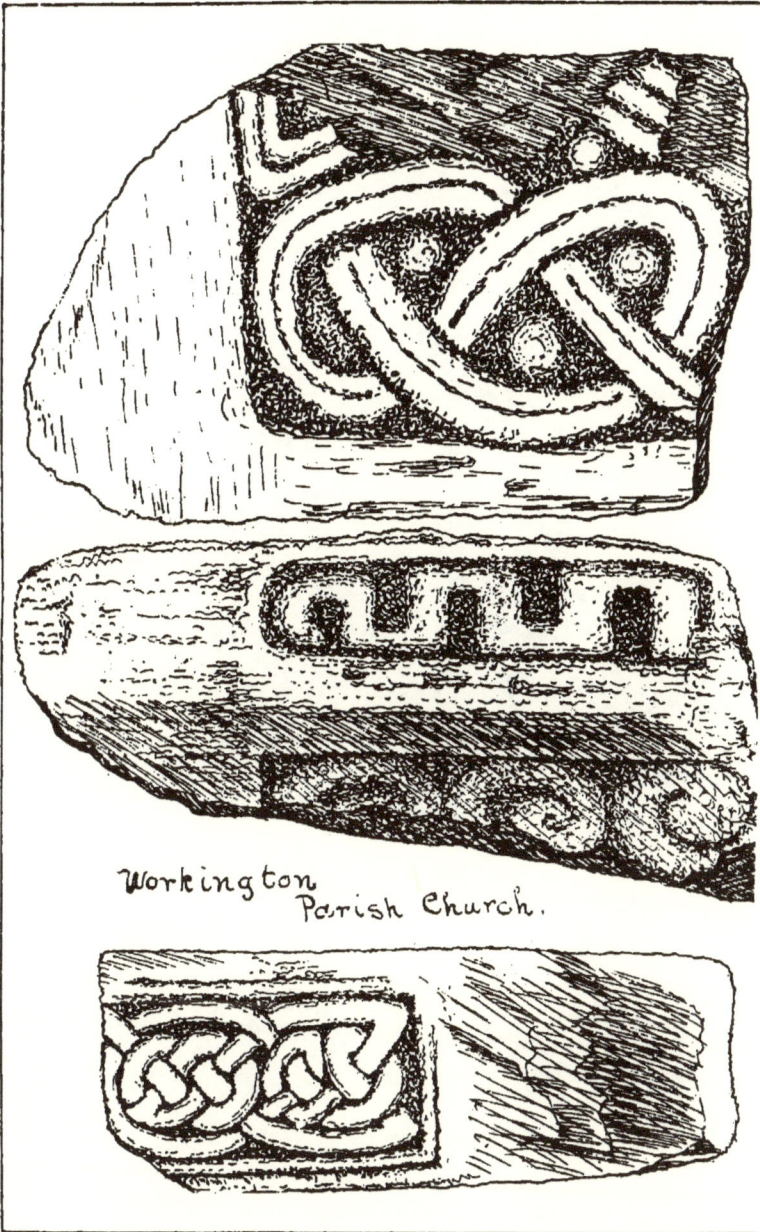

Workington
Parish Church.

PARISH CHURCH WORKINGTON. S. MICKAEL.

(TO FACE P. 281.)

WORKINGTON.

The Second Curwen Vault Fragment.

The lower figure in the preceding plate and the two figures opposite represent the second fragment recovered from the Curwen vault. It is of white sandstone, 14 inches long, 7½ broad, and 5½ thick at the lower sculptured end, tapering to 5 inches thick at the narrower end. It is the upper part of a cross-shaft from which the arms and top have been broken off. The (Paradise) tree would be the centre of the cross-head ; beneath it is a finely worked geometrical pattern such as seen in the *Book of Kells* and other early MSS., formed of H-shaped lines, set diagonally. On either side of the tree, the arms of the cross formerly extended ; these have been cut away, most likely by the workmen who built up the vault. The two edges have knotwork, finishing off square beneath the cross arms—see the horizontal drawings, where the uncarved portion shows the position of the cross arms.

*　　*　　*　　*

This is finer work than the preceding, though not such good art as the Tower fragment. It is carefully chiselled, with some ground cut away; the Irish box-pattern very flatly treated; the plaits of that ear-shaped character noticed at Haile and elsewhere on this coast.

WORKINGTON.

The "Fretty" Fragment.

The lithographic plates lettered "Workington St. Michael, 1," and "Workington St. Michael, 2," shew the sides and edges of the upper part of a cross which has had a circular head something like the Rockcliff crosshead, or perforated between the arms. The lower part of the circle is seen in No. 2. This fragment is 18 inches long, 5½ inches thick, and tapers from 9½ inches wide at the bottom to 8 inches at the top. The two faces are ornamented with plait-work. On one side there are three two-stranded bands doubled over at the top and plaited together, forming a six-plait. On the other face there are four bands divided down the middle (two-stranded), doubled over at the top and plaited together, making an eight-plait.*

These designs correspond with the "fretty" of heraldry, a "frett" being simply a small portion of the whole plaited design.

The Salkelds of Little Salkeld, Corby, Whitehall, &c., Thornborowe of Selsheyd, Thwaytes of Thwaites, and afterwards of Ewanrigg Hall, Morton of Morton, and Stavely of Renwick, bore arms fretty in some form. Harrington Lord Harrington, whose family took their name from the village of Harrington, Curwen of Workington, Hudlestons of Millom and of Hutton-John, all bore "a frett" upon their shields.

The particular stone here figured was found on the floor level at the bottom of the old tower wall near the foot of the belfry staircase. The tower is said to be Norman from the presence of a window and an arch which appear to be of that period.

---

* This stone is chiselled and neatly cut, with a little background which is not made too smooth for effect.—(ED.)

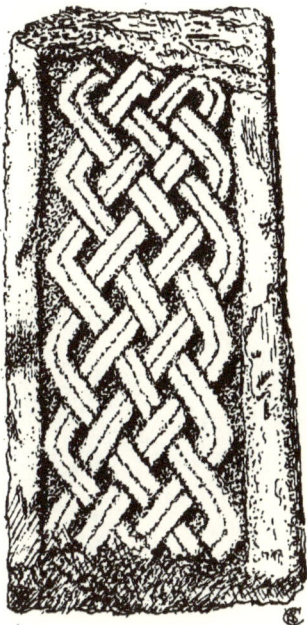

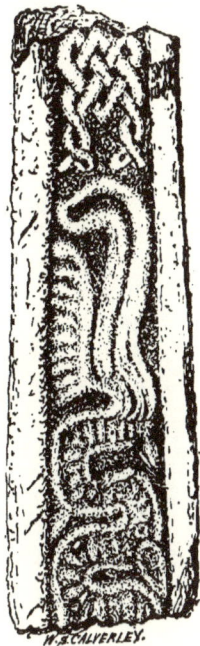

WORKINGTON   S.ᵗ Michael. 1.

WORKINGTON   S.ᵗ Michael. 1.

WORKINGTON   S.ᵗ Michael. 1.

WORKINGTON   S.ᵗ Michael. 1.

W.S.CALVERLEY.

WORKINGTON   S.ᵗ Michael. 1.

'(TO FACE P. 282.')

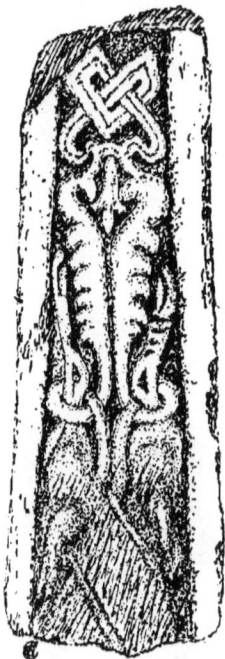

WORKINGTON. St Michael. 2.

(TO FACE P. 283.)

The edges of this little cross are very interesting. One edge shews beneath a prettily formed knot the tail part of some water leech or reptile. The other edge shews, beneath a very beautifully formed knot, bearing an inverted trefoil within two ornamented bands, two birds, their long necks and beaks stretching upwards, the ornamented bands entwining their necks and holding them up. The eyes of the bird are like swan's eyes, and one can hardly fail to suppose that the powers of light and motion heavenwards are contrasted with the lower powers of darkness and grovelling, and that the idea of the swan-maidens who having put on their " swan-shifts " can travel through air and water, who " love to linger on the sea shore," was in the mind of him who designed this cross and was by him being used for the illustration of the highest Christian doctrines teaching of the soul's flight to the bright home where God dwells, in grand contrast to the hopeless creed of darkness and the serpent's den.* The Celts seem to have known about swan-metamorphosis in very early times.

These remains, together with the remains of other crosses found about the same time, are now fixed with copper dowells upon a large Norman respond built into the south wall of the tower, inside the baptistry. An old font and some mediæval incised slabs are placed near, and the whole forms an interesting historical corner for which the curate in charge, the Rev. T. Hackworth, and the building contractor may be thanked, as they very readily acquiesced in the suggestions made to them as to the desirability of preserving such treasures worthily.

Outside the church, on the south side of the east window of the south aisle, there is a fragment of purple sandstone, 14 inches by 3½ inches, showing interlaced work.† Thus we have, at this church, remains of five crosses of varied character, all of a date earlier than the time of the Normans.

---

* Grimm's *Teutonic Mythology*, vol. I. p. 427. (tr. Stallybrass).
† This is about 10 feet above the ground; hardly recognizable as interlaced sculpture, and looking like the mere dressing of a stone. [ED.]

WORKINGTON.

LATE CROSS.

"In a niche in an old building erected in 1703, at Cross Hill, Workington, is a small equilateral cross, said to have been taken out of a chapel erected there in the reign of King Richard I. by some one who went out with the king. Parties formerly, when bringing their dead to bury from the country, used to rest the bier, etc., at this spot, and a homily was read over the corpse before proceeding into the town." (Whellan, p. 464.)

It has free arms, about 1 foot across; without ornament; now painted, but apparently of freestone; set on a small square base of which the top edges are chamfered and the front is inscribed, with a date that looks like 1103, but stands for 1703, when it was built into the Cross House named from it. Earlier, the relic may have served as boundary-mark and resting cross; but originally it must have been a finial on the gable-end of a chapel.

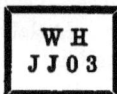

W H
J J 0 3

EDITOR'S AFTERWORD.

REVIEW OF EARLY CUMBRIAN ART.

WESTMORLAND RUSHLIGHT-HOLDER.

VIKING KNIFE.

KIST-PANEL, CUNSEY, 1692.

REVIEW OF EARLY CUMBRIAN ART.

I.—POST-NORMAN DEVELOPMENTS OF PRE-NORMAN FORMS.

WE have now given all known pre-Norman remains in Cumberland and Westmorland, that is, in the present diocese of Carlisle, for there seem to be none in Furness and Cartmel at present discovered. Beside these, we have noticed a few later monuments as necessary examples to show what difference there is between Norman and pre-Norman treatment of identical motives, and to explain why we cannot regard certain works as post-Conquest, although they have cable-mouldings or chequers upon them.

We learn something more from these. We learn how deep-rooted and living a thing was the art of the people ; how it survived what schoolbooks have usually taught us to look upon as the Deluge. We see that the Conquest was at first a political fact rather than a social overturn,—at least in this corner of the country. To the masses it meant new lords, but not new habits of life and thought ; and so the native artists and their pupils went on carving the same notions on the graves of their dead or the walls of their churches, until at last, after a century, the monks, and the new culture they introduced, brought folk to admire new fashions and despise the old.

But even then the old art-notions did not entirely die out. It is a commonplace of art-history that motives of ornament survive as long as the race that evolved them, though sometimes latent for a while. Interlacing lingered, and showed itself occasionally. It had a fine revival in the Jacobean woodcarving, and does not seem quite dead now. The old Anglo-Irish key-patterns lived again in the knitting sticks of last century, and flourish now under the name of "chip-carving." The use of high crosses lingered. In the west of Scotland they were made, with interlaced ornament, right down to the Reformation; in Southern England they were elaborated by Gothic architects down to the days when the Commonwealth men smashed them. But here they developed quietly—no doubt from defect of wealth and taste—into the plain shafts and uninteresting heads we have sketched.

We have omitted the market-crosses which exist even in Furness, as at Broughton and Ulverston; in Cumberland, as at Bootle and

Ireby; in Westmorland, as at Ambleside and Burton; of various dates from the thirteenth century.

We have also omitted mediæval grave-slabs, of which Mr. Calverley gave some examples; they are a large and separate class; but perhaps among them should be reckoned the Haile ring-cross and the zigzagged circle at Kirk-Oswald.

But of churchyard or boundary-crosses, later than Norman and yet obviously descended from pre-Norman types, we have quite a large number. Some indeed we know only by repute, but we may include Warcop, the two Castle-Sowerby Corpse-crosses, the Lamplugh cross and the Stone Cross between Ulverston and Dalton. Some we can only guess from the sockets,—Cliburn, Milburn, Penrith Plague-stone; and of others we have the socket and shaft,—Cartmel Headless Cross, Dovenby, Lanercost, Lazonby, Newbiggin. Five trunkless heads are known—two at Bromfield (in the vicarage toolhouse wall), one at Cumwhitton, that marked B at Kirkby Stephen, and a single arm of one at Kirk-Oswald. Of the later cross at Gosforth we have both head and socket; and four are complete—three with wheel-heads, Arthuret, Cross Lacon and St. Bees resting-cross; and one with a free head, Kirkland.

The tendency in these late crosses towards plainness is perhaps also the reason for two stones that seem to be belated and unadorned hogbacks. There is the coped stone on the churchyard wall at Plumbland, with semicircles and triangles hinting the tegulæ of the older shrine; and there is the quite undecorated coffin-stone of Bridekirk. In all these the ancient impulses have nearly died away; but in the twelfth century it was not so.

II.—THE NORMAN PERIOD.

The Normans arrived late here in the north-west. The date 1066 to us means Stamford Bridge; Hastings is foreign history. East Cumberland and Westmorland hardly began to feel the influence of the invaders before the twelfth century; the sea coasts not until much later; the mountains, never—until after the Normans had given place to the new English of the thirteenth century.

Now this makes it difficult to settle the age of some remains on the border-line between Norman and pre-Norman: for instance, the Dials.

There is abundant evidence that our dials are of a "Saxon" type; but they occur in masonry which, at earliest, is Norman, at latest, as late as the Newbiggin dial, given for its likeness to Bewcastle. Some are obviously re-set, as the two at Milburn, and one at Torpenhow; one (possibly moved) at Bolton. But others, at Caldbeck, Cliburn, two at Dearham, one at Isel, and one each at Great Salkeld, Kirk-Oswald and Newton Arlosh, are carved on the jambs of doors, exactly where they would be first placed and always wanted. It is difficult to believe that so many villages should have had stone churches before the twelfth century. St. Michael's (Bongate) is thought to contain pre-Norman masonry, and perhaps others do ; but the pre-Norman church at Triermain was of wood ; and probably most of our Anglian country churches—of which there certainly were many—were *Stav-kirke* such as one sees in the Bayeux tapestry, or were even humbler cells of wattle-and-daub.

Now supposing that the dials were pre-Norman, every bit of the stone churches on which they were carved must have perished— except the dials; and these must have been treasured and re-inserted. But when we find some evidently re-inserted they have evidently not been treasured ; at Milburn one is upside down, and at Torpenhow one is built *inside* the church. The conclusion is that these dials, though of " Saxon " type, were cut on Norman (and later) buildings by twelfth century (and later) people, who still, however, kept up the pre-Norman manner of marking time.

Of real Norman work we have some definite remains.

The Bridekirk font, second half of twelfth century, is a fair starting-point, though exceptional as being the masterpiece of a genius, not mere pot-boiling, trade work. It shows freshly-felt Italian influence, but the old Northern motives are there in the figures and grotesques, and the interlacing of tree-boughs and dragons'-tails.

In figures, we find nothing equal to this (nor are likely to) ; but serious attempts in the Bolton knights, the Dearham 'Adam' and his companions, the Kirk-Bampton figure with a crook—three degrees of rustic incompetency. A step farther, and we get the swaddled souls of Torpenhow, really very puzzling in their inade- quacy; and yet perhaps not without intention, for the opposite capital is rather clever with its interlocked dancers—like late viking fibulæ of arms intertwined, in the "bandy-chair" style.

At Great Salkeld the sculptor of Norman age was not without some skill of drawing animals, though he had caught the infection of ugliness, which cuts him off from earlier Anglo-classic art. The monsters of Long Marton and Dearham font are not inferior to twelfth century monsters anywhere else ; they are decorative, pure in line, free from the rotting, decomposing taint of low-class mediæval grotesques ; but they do not fall into place as part of a tight and piquant design, like earlier monsters of the interlaced dragonesque school.

There is the wild *motive* of the Viking Age, but the *treatment* has been modified, the fierce energy has degenerated by the softening influence of civilisation into dulness; without as yet being replaced by fresh imaginative growths.

At the same time, given the genius, and there is always a chance for any style and any age. Who would anticipate the existence of the Bridekirk Font, from the materials and models which Richard had before him?—the dainty "Tower Fragment" at Workington, the drilled shaft at Beckermet, and one or two other bright particular stars in the mass of mediocrities? The men who did these bits must have been like Herrick in Jacobean Devonshire, or Kormak among the Vikings, or Gainsborough among the Squires.

Now the average craftsman of Norman days had the ideas of interlacing, chequers and scrolls among his stock-in-trade; but he did not know what to do with them. Interlacing became perfunctory, loose, uninteresting. There is a bit of really bad interlacing on the Ingleton font over the monstrous Herod; less bad, but dull, on Torpenhow font; a little better and perhaps earlier on the Adam stone at Dearham; but its character stamps the design as twelfth century, however the runes may read. Much better, and of earlier style, is the St. Bees lintel, which links Norman with pre-Norman work, and seems to be of the transition, before the new influence was fully felt in a neighbourhood full of Irish-Viking traditions. It takes us back to the debateable border between the two epochs.

In the same way, perhaps, the Bridekirk tympanum may show some survival of pre-Norman feeling in figures—rude but dignified; and in another way it is possible that the "Lawrence" slab at Cross-Canonby may be a work of the transition time. This and its companion "Thunderbolt" stone, and the zigzag shaft at Burton, seem to be rude and dull attempts by workmen of an earlier school to adapt themselves to new fashions. When work is ugly and not at all funny, it generally means that the artist has been trying to reach something he does not understand; and when it is done cheaply it is always decadent. Brain power starts a style; hand-skill ruins it.

III.—The Viking Age.

Before the Normans came, our district was Scandinavian. The Danes burnt Carlisle in 876 and settled in the eastern parts of Yorkshire. There is reason to believe—but this is not the place to discuss the whole subject—that Norse began to settle the western parts not much later, coming in from the Isle of Man and Ireland. They behaved here as they behaved elsewhere at this period; not as raiders, but as colonists. They wanted homes, and settled quietly down. In the course of 200 years their descendants became leading landowners, as we see from Norse names in twelfth century records. The map (over leaf) sketches the probable distribution of races.

Naturally, the art of the district must have been influenced by such people; especially by the Scandinavians who had lived in Ireland, till then a very artistic country. Partizan historians dispute whether Irish taught Norse, or *vice versa*. We see that there was at any rate a quantity of artistic work produced, especially along the sea-board, with Irish-Norse characteristics; and we are lucky in having analogies not far to seek.

In the Isle of Man the earliest series of crosses are some which have eleventh century runes, and figure-subjects from the Edda and the Sigurd story. One of these crosses bears the legend "Gaut carved this and all in Man;" another, "Gaut carved it, son of Björn, from Cooiley." He was a genius in his way; not of the laborious kind, but a bold sketcher with the chisel, careless of finish but full of subjects for illustration, and ready with adaptations of a few favourite patterns. His series of Sigurd crosses were thought by Mr. Calverley to be tombstones of Godred Crovan's family, and therefore late eleventh century. Mr. P. M. C. Kermode, F.S.A. Scot., dates them 1050-1150 (*Saga-book of the Viking Club*, vol. i. p. 369.)

We have then remains in Man of a kindred race to ours in the age before the Normans came; and we find resemblances between these Manx crosses and some of ours both in subject and in style. (*a.*) In subject the eleventh century Sigurd crosses of Kirk Andreas, Jurby and Malew find a parallel at Halton, which Mr. Calverley places late eleventh century, and attributes to people under strong Scandinavian influence—but Danish, as it happens, rather than Norse. The Halton crosses are not Norse in style. They are like late pre-Norman work in Yorkshire, where the Danes lived. With Halton go the shafts and head at Burton, as similar in workmanship.

Another set of subjects on the Manx crosses—the myths of Loki, etc.,—we refer to the Edda rather than to older Anglian folklore; and these we find, not on monuments of undoubted Anglian age, but on stones of which the work suggests Viking influence, at Gosforth, Penrith and Kirkby Stephen. On the great Gosforth cross and the Fishing stone, on the Giant's Grave and on the Bound Devil shaft there are no scrolls like those of Bewcastle, Irton, Heversham; but worm-twists and decorative monsters such as are common in Irish and Norse work; and the stories illustrated seem to be comparatively late myths. Dr. Gudbrand Vigfússon shows reason why the Edda may be regarded as a tenth century development of the Viking settlements in the isles, that is, in Man and the coasts of the Irish sea. He thought *Hávamál* pre-Viking; but the hanged Odin of that

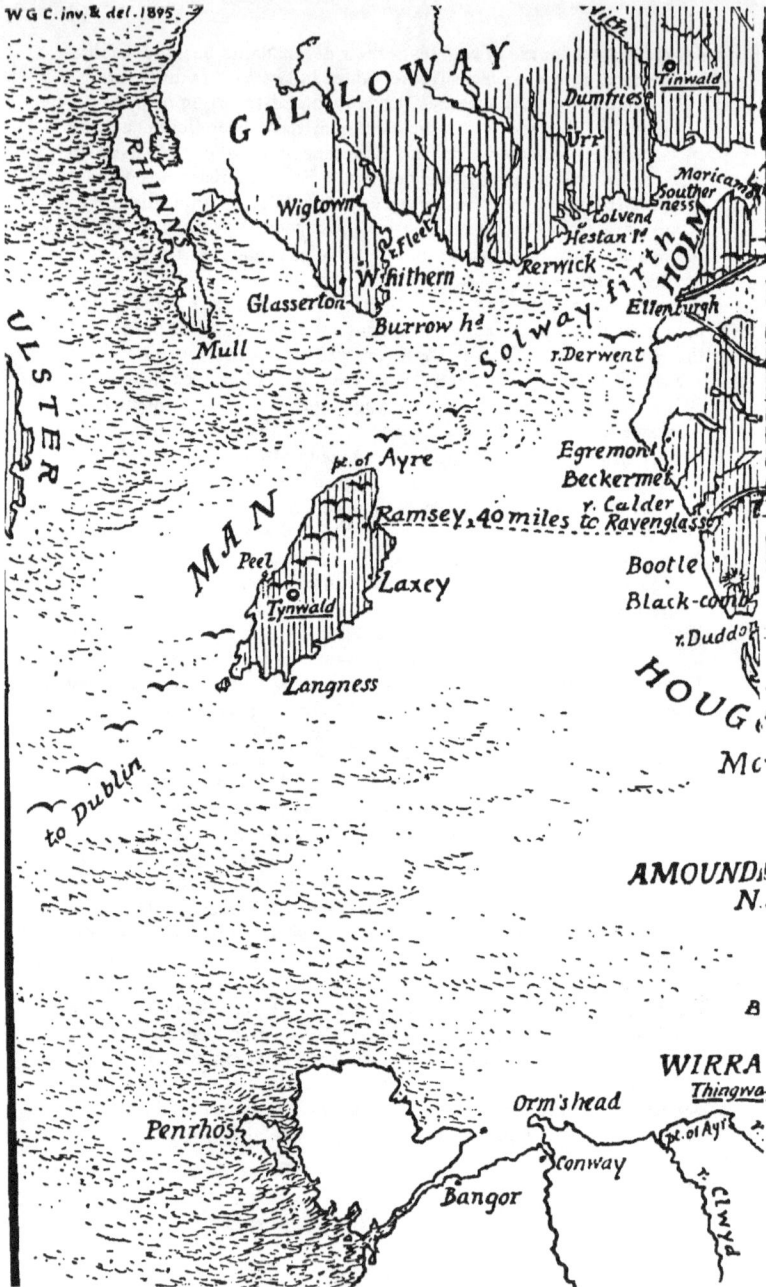

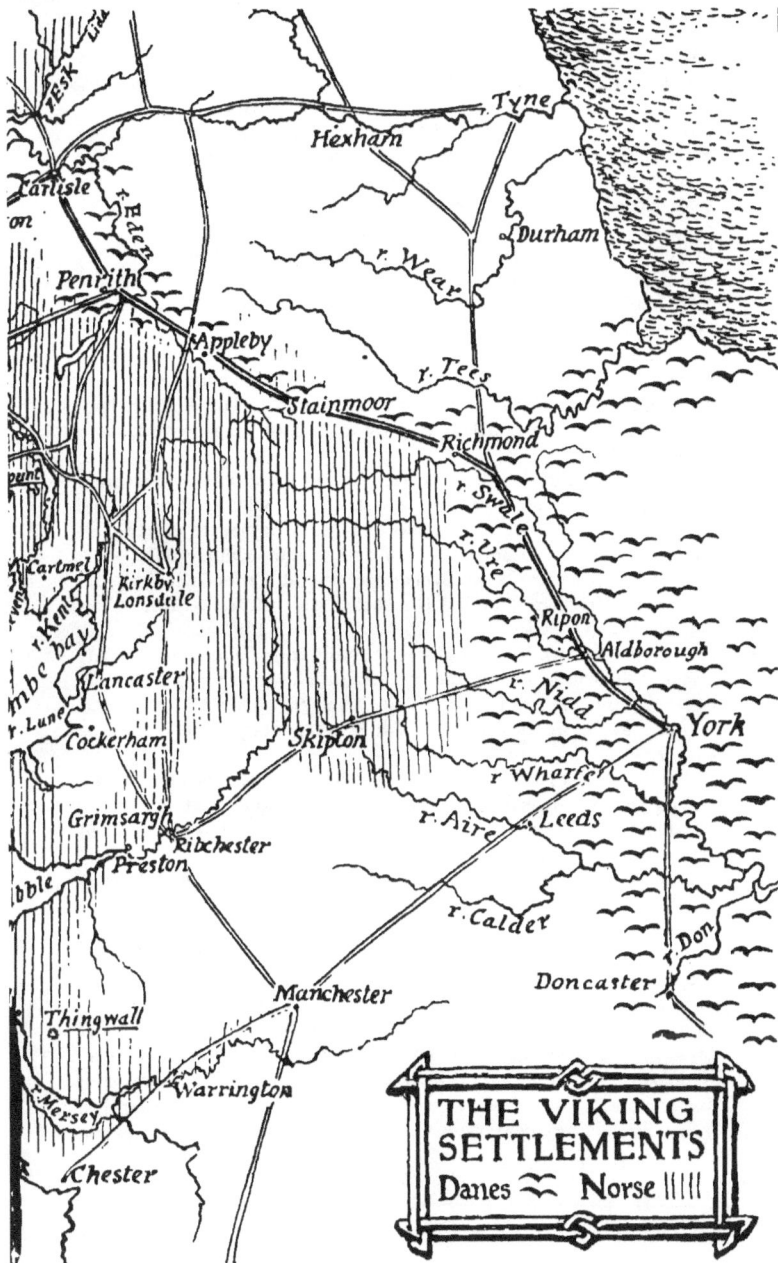

THE VIKING
SETTLEMENTS
Danes ≈ Norse ‖‖‖‖‖

poem is considered by Mr. Eiríkr Magnússon to be not earlier than
the end of the tenth century.   Again, the Fishing stone evidently
illustrates *Hymiskvida*, one of the Greenland series of poems, and
Greenland was not discovered until A.D. 982-3.   This does not "prove
too much," for the poems travelled fast as any reader of Saga knows;
this coast was a great resort of the race; nothing is more likely than
that Edda songs were known here before they were known in
Iceland or Norway, and even that our very Gosforth cross may have
helped to spread the new notion of Odin hanged in a tree.

But these are guesses; it is hardly a guess to conclude that the
Loki sculptures and all that are akin to them were works of the
eleventh century.   Later than that they could not be; for by the
next century's end they were superseded.   The crosses were spared
as sacred, but the grave-stones—the Gosforth hogbacks—were used
as building stuff in the new Norman Church.   The Penrith hogbacks, which similarly belong in style to the two high crosses, were
also spared.

(*b.*) The style of the Manx crosses in some points resembles ours.
There is a sort of dragonesque interlacing which, whatever its
origin, is characteristic of Norse and Irish rather than Anglian
work, and seems to suggest tenth or eleventh century date.   We
have it on three shafts at Beckermet, one at Cross-Canonby; the
socket at Brigham (carving the socket was an Irish rather than
Anglian habit); also in the Rockcliff cross; Plumbland hogback
and High Aketon head.   More finished and elaborated dragons
appear at Gosforth and on the St. Bees lintel, which we have already
dated as in the transition.   The "fretty fragment" at Workington may be another case of Viking dragonesque, or it may be
earlier.

Another Manx pattern (Cornish also) is the "ear-shaped guilloche"
at St. John's, Beckermet, with dragonesque work; at Haile and
Workington (Tower fragment) without dragons.   The ear-shaped
plait is only a condition of angular interlacing, not always, but often,
connected with Irish work, and running to extremes in the late fragment at St. John's, Beckermet.

Again, the use of rings in plaits is common to this group; characteristic of the Penrith Giant's Grave and the neighbouring Hutton
fragment.   Still more marked is the "snake-sling"—not mere woven
strap, but almost zoomorphic interlacing with bands of varying
thickness.   St. Bees standing cross and Aspatria standing cross
both show this device, in different treatment: we may call them
perhaps earlier than the 11th century, or than the development of
Edda subjects, but of the same series.   With these may be classed
a few bits, too fragmentary or too defaced to analyze:—The Aspatria

scrap of red-sandstone wheel-head: the uninscribed shaft at Beckermet, St. Bridget's; two shafts and a head at Brigham; the Gilcrux head; the Glassonby key-pattern shaft; a late fragment at Halton; head C at Kirkby Stephen; Reycross. The Waber-thwaite standing cross may be 10th century or earlier; we have no analogy near at hand.

Then, the hogbacks have to be placed. We have fixed the Gosforth and Plumbland examples by their dragonesque work as of the Viking settlement. Those at Aspatria, Bongate, Bromfield, and Lowther have so many points in common that they must be of that age. That at Kirkby Stephen seems later, with less carefully wrought tegulæ. That at Cross Canonby is distinctly Scandinavian for the same reason that marks Bromfield and Rockcliff, Dearham and Muncaster crosses. All these have, like Gosforth, the chain-pattern which we find in Man and Cornwall; also in the font of which a cast is in the South Kensington Museum from Gällstad in Sweden. This is what Mr Calverley called the Tree of Yggdrasil; whatever it means, it shows that these monuments are of Viking origin.

One more cross has it, but in very different treatment; that one which Canon Knowles called the " Norse " cross at St. Bees. This is the link with another set; the most puzzling of all.

IV.—THE " SPIRAL " SCHOOL.

This "Norse" cross at St. Bees has the Scandinavian chain-pattern, together with a combination of patterns which Mr. Calverley, following Canon Knowles, called British; and referred to native Cymric Christian art. Most of the crosses on which these spiral devices are seen are of white sandstone, but not all. Adding-ham spiral cross is red, while this "Norse" cross is white, and many others are white or light-coloured, from Bewcastle to Kirkby Stephen Devil and the early masonry of Carlisle cathedral. We must perhaps put the colour of the stone out of count in reckoning period in general, though it undoubtedly goes for much in the consideration of local details of grouping.

There are two kinds of work illustrated by the St. Bees "Norse" cross, and seen in the "spiral" series.

(a) Debased plait-work or sham interlacing is when the pattern is not considered as really meant for a woven strap or snake, but for a rough imitation in stone of similar work in metal. Interlaced work in metal is often made, not by repoussé, nor by weaving a long wire and applying it, but by cutting curved strips and sticking them on the ground. Often these strips are not accurately in the line that would fit on with the curve supposed to correspond with them; the inter-lacing gets out of joint. Often, also, each segment is treated

separately with ornament of its own, and so the original idea is lost.
Now when the stone-carvers imitated fibulæ, etc., instead of making
their own designs with proper knowledge of the laws of their art,
they would produce this bastard interlaced work. It is sometimes
said that they imitated MSS., assuming that MSS. were pretty
common, and placed in stone-carvers' hands. This is far less likely
than that sculptors, at a distance from good models in stone, copied
patterns from metal-work, which were the most portable and most
accessible of all forms of art in the days before printing was invented.

Suppose, to make it plainer, the sorrowing survivor bids the
British workman carve a cross for the dead. "What like shall I
work it?" says the mason. "Like the fair crosses of England, or
Ireland; a knot above, and a know below, and so forth." "But,"
says the mason, and he might say it at St. Bees in the tenth century,
"I have never been in England or Ireland, nor seen your fair
crosses." "Then," answers the patron, "make it like this brooch, or
sword hilt;" and the British workman's copy is pretty sure to be
like the Chinese tailor's trousers, with indiscriminate reproduction of
the patches and rents of the original article.

In the Brayton Fibula we seem to have the very article at whose
existence we have been guessing. It was described in Pennant's
Tour, vol ii. p. 44 (published 1790). "In the same plate with these
druidical remains (Keswick) is engraven a species of fibula cut out
of a flat piece of silver, of a form better to be expressed by the figure
than words. Its breadth is, from one exterior side to the other, four
inches. This was discovered lodged in the mud, on deepening a fish
pond in Brayton Park in Cumberland, the seat of Sir Wilfrid
Lawson, and communicated to me by Dr. Brownrigg."

In this we find the interlaced triquetra ornamenting a penannular
brooch of the regular form, though one lobe is missing. It is like
the brooch found in a Viking grave in Shetland (Anderson's *Scotland
in Early Christian Times*, ii. p. 29), connecting this Christian Celtic
form, as Dr. Anderson calls it, with Viking robbery (or perhaps
trade).

A golden armlet was found in 1828 in the parish of Aspatria; in
1789 the barrow at Beacon Hill was excavated yielding a sword, a
bit, and other pieces of metal work of the Viking age. The Ormside
sword has no ornament, but the Hesket Newmarket sword, also at
Tullie House, Carlisle, has interlacing on the guard.

A still more remarkable instance of metal work brought into the
district is the Ormside Cup, which is early Anglian, but " imported "
by some rapacious Dane, perhaps. In this we have not only another
instance of a model from which native artists might copy, far more
likely than MSS., but an object lesson in the source of their peculiar

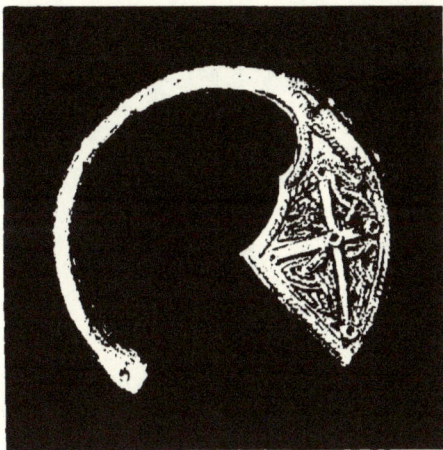

THE BRAYTON FIBULA.

(TO FACE P. 206.)

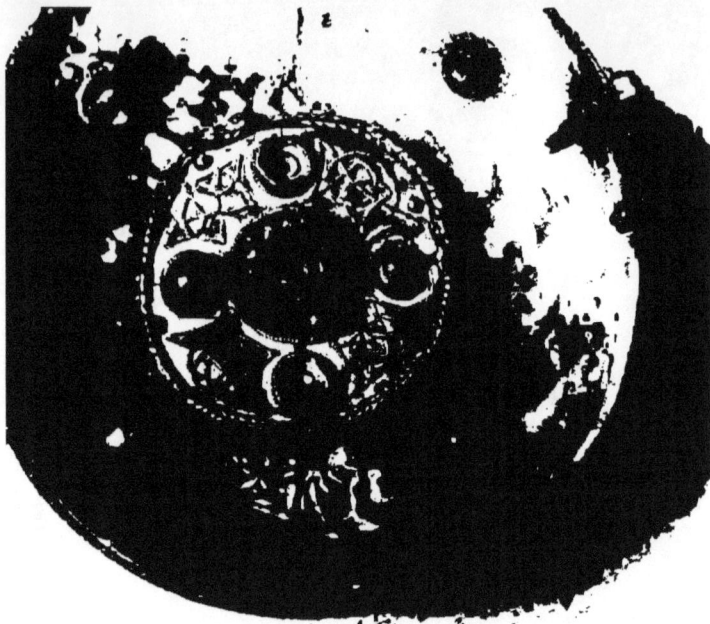

THE ORMSIDE CUP.

(TO FACE P. 297.)

fault. The want of sequence in the plaits of the "Norse" cross is stupid in stone work, but it is quite explained in the filigree of the cup (view of the inside in the coloured plate). The same bastard interlacing is seen in one of the Aspatria white shafts; in the white cross at Beckermet, St. John's; the Plumbland *Triskele* fragment, and the first Curwen Vault fragment, Workington.

(*b*.) The *Triskele*, "three legs" (—— of Man) is also typical of a motive often found in connection with the sham interlacing. On the four above-mentioned pieces we find spirals which never become real whirls or volutes, nor even flower-scrolls, though continually on the point of blossoming or whirling. They are as it were abortive. They are generally divergent, not in long lines of leafage, but broken, as if to fill little cells or panels. On the Isel white shafts they are quite rude, and on the smallest fragment at St. Bees; on the second white shaft at Aspatria, and on the Priest's Lonning fragment, and at Haile, they have a tendency to bud and blossom. On the Beckermet inscribed shaft they are very nearly flower-scrolls, and rather prettily arranged, but still unintelligent, and not for a moment to be compared with early Anglian work like Bewcastle and the Hexham school of crosses. They are imitations of inferior models, either of metal, or wood, or sketches of some sort; and they occur where the native Cumbrian artist would have great difficulty in seeing and copying really good stone-carving. At Distington, on the *Triskele* fragments, they are associated with rather better interlacing; at Dearham, on the Kenneth cross, better interlacing still, though still not good; while at Dacre, at the Anglo-Cymric monastery, the plaits down the edges are fairly good, along with bits suggesting spiral work.

The general arrangement of these spiral designs recalls the patch-work style of some (later) Anglian and Welsh crosses; for example, Winwick, and the Llantwit Samson cross (9th century). This spiral style is confined to Cumbria as far as we know; and the only parallel to it, though with the slight difference that place and perhaps time would create, is in the Rowler cross (Maughold, (I.O.M.), which Mr. P. M. C. Kermode assigns to the memory of Bishop Hrólfr, who died about 1050 (*Sagabook of the Viking Club*, vol. i. p. 364.) What Gaut Bjarnarson meant by his statement that he had carved all the crosses (then) in Man, if this be earlier, we need not enquire. He may have been the first, and this perhaps later; but in any case it looks as though Bishop Hrólfr had come from Cumbria, as a later Manx bishop came from Furness, and as most Norse missionaries from England; and with him the Cumbrian style was for the nonce imported.

With these we must connect a group of white cross-heads with bosses and spines and sometimes bits of spirals. This is fixed by the Beckermet St. John's white head, which has the shaft, and the Dearham " Kenneth " cross. In this group are the Cross-Canonby head, with bosses and spines and free arms; the Bromfield, nearly plain, with slightly " hammer-head" shape; the Bridekirk, with bosses and spines; the Brigham limestone head, with little incised cross, and two at Distington. All these are in West Cumberland, and they seem to be imitations of the old Anglian head at Carlisle. The hammer-head is Anglian, or a development, among neigh-bours, of Anglian originals; at Kirkholm, Wigtownshire, is a slab with very pronounced hammer-head cross (figured by Mr. Romilly Allen, *Christian Symbolism*, p. 149) which may be of the Anglian church at Candida Casa. But the oddest of the series is the Addingham standing cross; red sandstone, spirals, and hammer-head with an attempt at a wheel ; a mixture of all the three elements which must have co-existed at the site—Anglian, Cymric, and perhaps Irish.

Some of these spiral crosses betray Viking influence by their geographical situation, as well as by their art; and it is curious to find the nearest analogy to these bosses and spirals in a bit of metal-work of Anglo-Danish origin. The Kirkoswald fibula is one of the trefoil shaped brooches of characteristically Scandinavian origin and late Iron (Viking) age; and it was found with coins of Ethelred in what must have been an eleventh century hoard.

It is rather curious to observe this tendency to spirals among the Cumbrian folk, whose ancestors wrought the wavy volutes of " late Celtic" art, perhaps not so long before. These motives survived in all the seventh and eighth century work, both British and Irish; yet "late Celtic" metal work has been found with Roman remains on the wall; and close to Addingham, on Long Meg and on the Parks Tumulus, the spirals are seen, dating from prehistoric times. Art ideas are among the most indestructible of human attributes. Atavism shows itself in the most unexpected ways. The Anglian floral scroll revived again in the thirteenth century, interlacing in the sixteenth and seventeenth; and here we seem to find our Cumbrian Britons, even when imitating the more advanced work of their new neighbours, selecting from it what they found most to their inborn taste.

But this is wandering from strict criticism ; we can at least group our Cumbrian spiral crosses together ; suggest their place as a group; and while agreeing with our author as to their British character, venture to assign the earliest a date not earlier than about 700—since their art seems to be derived from, and subsequent to, the Anglo-classic epoch ; though they may have been in vogue among native Cumbrians down to the twelfth century.

We can now get upon firmer ground.

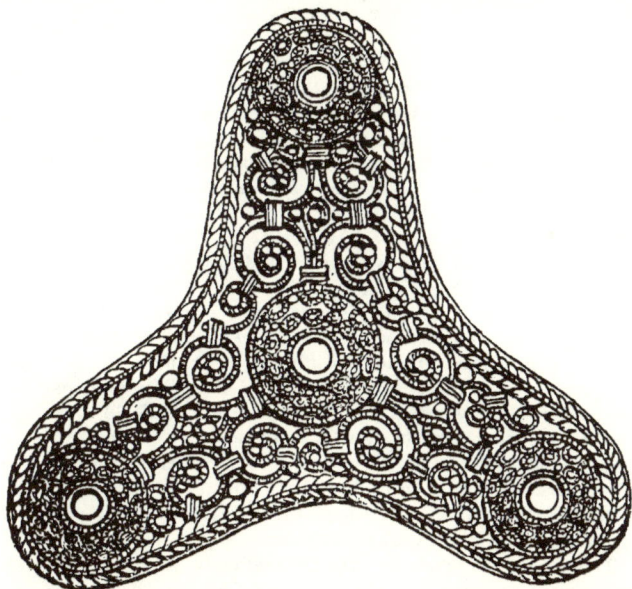

THE KIRKOSWALD FIBULA.

V.—THE ANGLO-CLASSIC SCHOOL.

Earlier in type than the spirals, though not all necessarily in age, are the scroll-work crosses of which we have so many examples in Northumbria and the rest of England, assigned to Anglo-Saxon workmanship, and ranging from the Bewcastle cross, seventh century, to the Halton cross late in the eleventh,—a gradual degeneration.

That the earliest are the best is no great wonder, when we remember what a stirring age was that of Wilfrith; how Italian artists and art were then accessible, and how the wealth and wit of a singularly noble nation were directed and stimulated into a passionate energy of religious expression. (For an appreciation of the Angles, read Ruskin's lectures on *The Pleasures of England*, and for examples of their art see the illustrated *Catalogue of the Sculptured and Inscribed Stones in the Cathedral Library, Durham*, part ii., by the Rev. W. Greenwell, M.A., D.C.L., F.R.S., F.S.A.)

One fine monument of this age, though not in stone, is the Ormside cup, now in the museum at York, to which it was given in 1823 after discovery at Ormside (Westmorland), a place which has yielded the farther discoveries of the sword and other pieces of metal work now in the Carlisle museum.

The cup is remarkable for the combination in one design of interlacing work, apparently Anglian, with exquisite floral design, animals and birds, most delicately wrought, in the spirit and with the finish of the finest Greek-Italian craftsmanship. Our sketch of the English base (the patch around it is some later tinker's work) shows fairly well what native art could do, and did in heathen fibulæ; but the drawing of the side is too coarse to give the effect of dainty leafage and graceful plumage, repoussé and chased by a master's hand such as can hardly have been formed in Northumbria. The coloured plate gives the inside of the cup (if it was a cup) with one jewel still inset, and tiny filigree interlacing, and sheath of beaten metal gilt, broken in one place and showing the reverse side of the repoussé plate which forms the outer covering of the whole.

It is impossible to study the Bewcastle cross without seeing that it is the transcript in stone of the art of this cup. Neither of them can be assigned to any age but the age of Wilfrith, or his immediate successors.

In the style of the Hexham School are the shafts at Heversham and Addingham; a fragment in the tower of Halton may be later, but good Anglian work; its ring-plaits alone cannot make it Scandinavian, for the feeling and treatment are classic. The Giant's Thumb, a ring-cross with scrolls of which some are floral, seems to be a late Anglian monument; and the shaft in the vestry at Waberthwaite is a somewhat ruder work of the same class.

BASE AND SIDE OF
THE ORMSIDE CUP.

Irton cross is Anglian, by the runes; and by the beautiful floral scrolls of the edges, and the free armed head ; like those of Carlisle, which must be Anglian between the dates of Ecgfrith and Halfdan. The key-patterns and other details of Irton are also not Irish but Anglian, if the Lindisfarne Gospels are—as the names of their artists indicate ; and may be as early—dating from the beginning of the eighth century, to judge from the style. Anglian colonists evidently seized the harbour of Ravenglass; hence their monuments at Irton and Waberthwaite.

It is true that in this early Anglian age we have pretty distinct traces of Irish missionary work in our district. Before and perhaps after the synod of Whitby (664) Scottish monks and nuns had their *Kils* and *Lanns* and *Tighs* up and down the country; we learn as much from place-names, and from some hints in tradition and record. St. Bega is said to have founded her nunnery at St. Bees about 650, the time when Irish teachers were welcomed by the English. St. Molaga and St. Becan Ruminni, as well as the bishops Finan and Colman may have visited Cumbria about the same time. Kirk-Santon and Kirk-Cambeck must be early dedications to Sanctan and (Finian) Camog or Cambach, the diminutive of *Cam* in Irish or Welsh, making the old forms *Camboc* and *Cambak*. We have Gilcrux (the *kil* of the cross), Gilcambon (of Caman or Colman), Gilgarron (of Gerain or Carthan), Gilgooden (of Codan), Gil-shaughlin (of Seachlan), Gilthroton (of Rodan), like Kilridding (also of Rodan), and Killerwick (in Domesday Chil-vestrewic, whatever that may be). We have also Tebay (Tigh-Begha), Tymperon ('Tigh m' Barron), Lamplugh (Lann mo-Loch), to show how the memory of Irish missionaries yet lingers in a disguised form; while the dedications to Patrick, Bridget, Columba and Ninian are in some cases no doubt pre-Norman. (*Trans.* C. & W. A. & A. S., vol. XV., Art. 28).

Of these Irish churches a certain number may have been founded by Irish-Viking Christians; especially the Ninian dedications, which can hardly reach back to the year 400 A.D., but may well have been introduced by Galloway Vikings from Ninian's country. Where the Irish influence was of Viking date, the art must have been such as we have described under the Viking age. But where it was of the seventh century, what remains do we expect? What Irish art was there before the great Anglian outburst of Wilfrith's time? There was plenty in the period following the Bewcastle cross and Lindisfarne Gospels; but any Irish MSS. or metal-work or grave-stones that can be certainly and safely dated earlier than 700 A.D. are not elaborately ornamented, if ornamented at all. The earlier Irish Christians were highly intellectual and literary, but not at first artistic. Literature in all races precedes art; it would be contrary to all historical analogy if Patrick and Columba had lived in the artistic atmosphere of eighth and ninth century Ireland. Patrick's bell is no great credit to Assicus, his coppersmith; his crosier was a a plain stick; and there is no indication in our remains that the Irish missionaries of the seventh century brought a single art-idea into the country. It was the Irish-Viking Christians of the twelfth century who did.

VI.—THE BRITISH PERIOD.

Before the seventh century we had Christian teachers in St. Kentigern (sixth century), St. Patrick (fifth century), and St. Ninian (end of fourth century). All these were Britons of the North-West by birth; and by traditions, by dedications, and by history they are certainly connected with the early religious life of our district.

In any part of our islands the monuments of that distant age are few and far between. They are usually rough stones with incised patterns of a simple nature, things that in populous and cultivated parts would be soon lost and destroyed, and for that reason are found more easily in the least frequented neighbourhoods. But unlike some parts of Wales, Scotland and Ireland, the more ancient sites in Cumberland and Westmorland are now thickly inhabited, and the many successions of races and industries have left the less interesting remains very little chance of survival. Our Lake District was certainly a wild place in the early times, when once the Romans had left it; and there are no sculptured monuments whatever from the pre-Norman age in the dales of the great mountains. If the Crosthwaite "Bolster Stone" be a pre-Norman antiquity it is an exception to this rule.

At Casterton, on the Maiden way, we have a very simple relief (the "Barbon" cross) which may be quite early. It is not entirely unlike crosses at Hawkhill (Alloa) and Ratho (Mid-Lothian), carved in relief on rough stones (and figured in Dr. J. Anderson's "*Scotland in Early Christian Times,*" ii. pp. 91, 92).

On the same line of road there is the Tebay Brandreth Stone, which is said to have borne two crosses incised. A monument of this type might belong to the pre-Anglian age; and then again it might be a mere rustic freak at any time. Still, we have a tradition of great antiquity attaching to the Brandreth. If Tebay means, as we believe, the house (church) of St. Bega, and if that foundation dates from the seventh century, a rude incised cross might mark the grave of the Irish votary of the saint, or it may have been the tomb of a still earlier Briton.

Mr. Calverley thought that some Roman stones built into Irthington church (a twelfth century dedication to St. Kentigern on a Roman site), and into the vicarage wall, might have the *Labarum* upon them now partly defaced. This is doubtful, but another monument seems to carry us back to pre-Anglian work, and to justify a claim for very high antiquity—the Aspatria *Svastika* slab which we have noticed as like one from Gillespie (Glenluce). It has features in common with a group that may be referred to Ninian's Romano-British church of Candida Casa.

About that church existing in Cumbria we know nothing, except by inference. In Roman times, State Christianity had not come into working here; but among various races and religions,—Syrian, Spanish, German, Roman and Celtic deities, Serapis, Mithras and the rest,—it would be strange if the Christians, who were certainly making way in the rest of Roman Britain, were unrepresented. So early as 314 the British bishop of York was at the council of Arles, and after that he or his successor is mentioned twice or thrice in the fourth century. Cumberland with its network of roads and forts was closely connected with York; and though the garrisons as a whole were far from being Christians, many individuals among them must have been. The church would be a missionary church; the members few and feeble folk: and yet if there is any truth in the "Confession" of St. Patrick, a very old and apparently genuine writing, he was born (about 386) either in Cumberland or Strathclyde, at Bowness or near Dumbarton, of a Christian family whose members held civic office; and there he lived in peace and in piety for sixteen years. There *must* have been a Romano-British church in Cumbria, if York on the one side, and Strathclyde (or the Solway shore) on the other, contained Christians. Or if one instance is not enough, there is Ninian, Patrick's countryman, born on the Solway some twenty years earlier, educated as a Christian in Rome; returning,—it must surely have been with Stilicho's legion which cleared the Picts and Scots from the intramural region in 396; for in 397 he built Candida Casa among the Attacotti, then being enrolled as Roman soldiers, and afterwards remaining peaceful neighbours. The 402 raid was "of the Scots" only. It this mission was Stilicho's work, it was a statesmanlike thing to do. As a mere adventure, it would have hardly been so well timed and so successful. Fifty years later, these Picts seem to have relapsed, for St. Patrick in the (genuine) Epistle to Coroticus—who must be identical with Ceretic Gwledig of Strathclyde—upbraids the Christian Britons for joining "Apostate Picts" in raiding the poor Irish-Scots of Ulster.

But note here how the tables were turned. The Britons are now (middle of fifth century) raiding the Scots, capturing women and children for slaves, behaving like tyrants. And this, just at the time when some think they were enervated, effeminate and impotent

to the last degree.   To call a second witness:—the same Gildas who
scolds his countrymen for cowardice, complains that no sooner were
the Picts repelled, than the Britons became so rich and luxurious
that they indulged in licence.   Any words of his describing the
horrors of war must be referred to special occasions—the era of
Pictish raids, and subsequently of Anglo-Saxon invasion; the
normal state of things was not starvation and savagery, but
indolence and ease.

These post-Roman Britons of the north-west no doubt reverted to
ancestral habits in many things.   They had never been stone-
masons; and when the Picts and Scots burnt the Roman border
camps, the Britons let the ruins lie.   But they were not exterminated
nor enslaved.

On the map of Cumberland and Westmorland there are about a
dozen Caers,—places beginning with *Car*, and a dozen more Blens,
Duns and Pens, and other names indicating Cymric strongholds—
the fortified places of petty kings or chiefs.   They can only be
referred to Britons of the post-Roman period.   There are also a
number of such strongholds remaining, some with these Cymric
names attaching, and some with no tradition.

Some history it is possible to gather from sources which are not
to be set aside as mere romance. This is worth our while, in order to
understand the archæology.   It was in Mr. Calverley's plan, also,
to say a few words on Cumbrian Christianity, and the misty
personalities of Rhydderch Hael and Urien of Reged.

VII.—The Story of Cumbrian Independence.

Our sources are, first, the additions to the *Historia Britonum*—
not Nennius himself, the compiler of legends, but subsequent entries
in MSS. of his book, business-like notes of events connected with
Cumbria.   These are confirmed by Gildas, whose story is regarded
by Mr. Elton (*Origins*, chapter xii) as dealing with Cumbria ; by
Bede and the Anglo-Saxon chroniclers, different Irish annals,
Adamnan's *Life of Columba*, Jocelin's *Life of Kentigern* (late, but
compiled from Irish MSS.), and, for what they are worth, Welsh
poems.

The first events after the leaving of the Romans are also recorded
by Prosper of Aquitaine, Constantius in his *Life of Germanus*, Sidonius,
and Pope Gregory in his *Commentary on Job*.   These all agree with
our British chronicle that twenty years after the Romans had gone,
the British church was strong enough to have bred a heresy, which
it was worth the trouble of two Gaelic dignitaries to repress, at the
cost of a journey to Britain.   How SS. Germanus and Lupus came

over, and beside putting down Pelagius or Morgan, put down the last Picts and Scots at Mold, by the Alleluia victory, is well known. But it must be noted that in consequence of this united action of the scattered groups of Christian Britons they got the name of " Comrades "—in the language of their time *Combroges*, in later form *Cumbri*, in modern Welsh *Cymru*.

The union, even as a temporary arrangement, was possible only when it could be enforced by one king able to lead the rest; for by now many masters had started up, chiefs of tribes and district rulers reasserting themselves. The one king who was man enough to lead was a Northern Briton, from Strathclyde, Cunedda or Cunedag. We are told that he came from beyond the Solway and fixed himself first at Carlisle; then, as more central, at Chester, where about 550 we find his descendant Maglocunos (Maelgwn) still overlord of the kinglets of the Combroges, and roundly abused by his contemporary Gildas. A little later Maelgwn's son Rhun led the chiefs against the Picts of Lothian, showing that the overlord (Gwledig) could carry on operations at some distance from his base.

This Gwledig at Chester was, until about Rhun's time (560), chief king of the Combroges or Cumbri. There was no "kingdom of Cumbria;" all were Cumbri, from Dumbarton to St. Michael's Mount. But in our district there were kinglets in Carlisle, Penrith, Ravenglass perhaps, etc., and about Rhun's time the North Cumbri began to be separated from the South Cumbri, who afterwards were called Cambri or Cymru. And this is how the gradual separation arose :—

Ida, reigning in Bamborough, 547, was successor to a long line of Angles who had already for 100 years lived on the East Coast, and fought, not always successfully, for a footing. In 507 they had reached York, and the British bishop, Samson, had fled to Brittany; but they were driven out of York, for in 522 Piran was bishop there, and Thadioc up to 587. It was a very long and very tedious business, the Anglian conquest of Deira and Bernicia; it took, we shall see, nearly 250 years. And all that time the Cumbri were independent, uninvaded; inhabiting our district as a free Christian people.

In 553 Ida died, and one after another six sons followed him,— Hussa in 567, and Theodoric the Flame-bearer in 574, these being the most ambitious and active in fighting the neighbouring Cumbri. About 550 the chief British kinglet in the North was Dutigern; he must have been lord of Carlisle or some fort to the east of it; for he is recorded as fighting bravely against Ida. In 560-580 Ida's sons had four famous opponents; *contra illos quatuor reges Urbgen et Riderch hen et Guallauc et Morcant dimicaverunt.*

Urbgen, Urien, "city born," claiming Roman descent and father of Romanus, Rum, was king of Reged or Murief, which means the country of the Wall. The Welsh poems say that Urien was leader of thirteen kings; the sober entries of the *Historia Britonum*, after naming Theodoric the Flame-bringer, say "Against him Urbgen with his sons used to fight, *dimicabant*, bravely. During that period sometimes the enemy, sometimes our *cives* used to conquer, and (Urbgen) himself once shut them up for three days and three nights in the island of Metcaud (Lindisfarne); and while he was in this (?) campaign he was assassinated on the instigation of Morcant, through envy, because *in ipso pre omnibus regibus virtus maxima erat instauratione belli*," in a word, because Urbgen was the best general of the Britons. This Kingdom can hardly have been the district of Loch Lomond on the *Northern* Wall; all these evidences point to the neighbourhood of the *South* Wall, Hexhamshire.

There is a very curious puzzle about his son Romanus, who is said to have baptized the first Anglian converts when Eadwine was converted. Some have thought that Paulinus was this son of Urien; chronology hardly allows us to identify him with a Romanus at the Council of Whitby, in 664. Another son of Urien's was the Owain, already mentioned (p. 244) as, like Arthur, partly historical, partly a solar myth ; or rather, around real memories of the hero of a lost cause, folk-lore accumulated until he became the almost comic " Mr. Cæsarius " of a lingering tradition.

The other three kings are connected with St. Kentigern. Morcant, who assassinated Urbgen, was a Strathclyde king. He was the villain of the period, in spite of his carrying on war with Bamborough. He opposed Kentigern, did not keep up Christian traditions, and finally was dispossessed or slain by Kentigern's friend, Rhydderch Hael.

This no doubt the Riderch *Hen* ("the elder") of *Historia Britonum*; *Hael* being the "Magnificent" or "Free-handed." Adamnan in the *Life of Columba* called him *Rodercus*. He rose by the battle of Armterid or Ardderyd (pronounced, as now written, Arthuret, but not connected with King Arthur). This battle is often mentioned, and, in spite of some romance attached to it, seems to be historical, and dated 573. In it Rhydderch, with a number of Christian "Combroges," including Aidan the Scot, fought Gwenddoleu, of Caer-Gwenddoleu, Carwinelow on the Liddel; obviously pushing his boundaries northward from Carlisle; for next he attacked Strathclyde. Some have identified Gwenddoleu with Gwallauc, but this is doubtful, for the pedigrees of the two do not tally, not to say the names. But we have simultaneous British (Cymric) kingdoms of Urien on the wall, north or south ; Morcant in Strathclyde,

Gwenddoleu in Dumfriesshire, Rhydderch in Cumberland, and Guallauc, as well as Elmet in Yorkshire, whose king was Certic or Ceretic (a form of Caradoc, Caractacus, Coroticus), named very little later; and a number of less noteworthy royalties. No "kingdom of Cumbria," however, existed until Rhydderch, having eaten up Gwenddoleu and Morcant, reigned at Alclyde (Dumbarton) over Strathclyde and Cumberland, at last united in his person.

After Arthuret he recalled Kentigern and placed him at Hoddam; after gaining Strathclyde he brought him to Glasgow (582 ?). He died 597, in the same year with St. Columba; St. David in Wales, and St. Kentigern following in 601 and 603.

With the date 600 A.D. we may roughly round off a golden age of Cymric power. In 586 Theodoric the Flame-bringer had taken York, and in 594 a new Angle king had succeeded, whom the Welsh called Eadfered Flesaurs, Æthelfrith the Destroyer. At the battle of Dægsastan (Dawston in Liddesdale) he beat Aidan, the Christian king of Scots, and brought the borders of English Northumbria up to what is now Cumberland. But there is still no account of any invasion of Cumberland or Westmorland; the "buffer" state of Elmet, Western Yorkshire, was not reduced until about 620. Æthelfrith's great raid ending in the battle of Chester left Elmet for many years intact; and in 627 or 8 the throne of Rhydderch was held by Owain (Eugenius), one of his descendants. In 633 there was the great British re-action, when York was taken from the Angles; Cadwallon, the descendant of Cunedda, now king of North Wales, being *Gwledig* or hereditary leader of the Combroges, and, after his death, his son Cadwaladr, who, in alliance with Penda, kept up the war until 655. Then, at the battle of Winwæd or Gaisfield (near Leeds), Cadwaladr deserted Penda, Oswiu and Alchfrith overcame him, and English Northumbria had British Cumbria at her feet.

It had been a struggle of 200 years. The Britons had been independent in our district for two centuries and a half; and it was always as Christians that their leaders were described.

By our map shewing the distribution of early monuments the subsequent settlements are indicated. We see the Angles coming in along the Wall to Bewcastle, Carlisle, and Ruthwell; over Stainmoor to Kirkby Stephen and Addingham; up the Maiden Way to Lancaster, Halton, Heversham; and over the fells or round the coast to hold the important harbour of Ravenglass with settlements on both sides of it at Irton and Waberthwaite. These places have monuments of the earliest Anglian period.

Then in the lowland of North-West Cumbria they seem to have settled and mixed with the native Welsh, producing the group of "spiral" crosses, with outliers at Addingham and perhaps Dacre.

These seem to be of a secondary age and derivative art, lasting into the period of Scandinavian settlement.

After 876 the Danes began to flock in from the East, over Stainmoor ; and a few years later the Norse came from Man and the Isles and Ireland. Their art is seen at Gosforth and along the West Coast; that of the Anglo-Danes (connecting with types more common in Yorkshire) at Halton, Burton, Kirkby Stephen, and generally along the eastern side of our district ; and both styles gradually and gently slide into the Normanized through still appreciably English ornament of the twelfth century, such as we have seen in Bridekirk Font.

＊　　＊　　＊　　＊

So far we have sketched the story of Cumbria, to redeem Mr. Calverley's promise, and to justify his favourite statement,—that there has been a continuous Church here ever since the days of the Romans, in spite of all vicissitudes, and that we have monuments of every period bearing witness to the fact.

Is it not wonderful that they still survive—some of them a thousand years and more of weathering and warfare, neglect or insult ? And now as education and an interest in antiquities yearly increase the respect with which they are viewed, surely they will be safe for the future on the sites that belong to them, where alone they can be properly seen and understood.　They are not merely scientific specimens, or examples of ancient art : ruined as they have been, they are still churchyard crosses, or tombs of Christian dead.

In this diocese, happily, the clergy and Church authorities have taken keen interest in the matter.　It is entirely through their initiative that so many fragments have been found and preserved. In their hands we may leave the keeping of the monuments which are credentials of the inheritance they claim, and reminders of the duties they owe.

SKETCH-MAP OF CROSS-PLACES.
Fell, forest, fordable sands and deep water are
variously shaded Anglian sites in capitals,
Cumbrian (spiral crosses, etc) in Roman type,
Viking in Italics, post-Conquest in Gothic.
Roman roads known //, - supposed ..

INDEX.

(Authorities in *Italics* ; Localities in SMALL CAPITALS.)

Adam and Eve, in sculpture, 69, 70, 113, 115.

Adam grave slab, 120-123, 289.

Adam's Cross, 112.

ADDINGHAM, remains, 3, 4, 295, 298, 300.

Addison, Rev. F., 29.

Æthelwold's Benedictional, 63.

Agnus Dei, in sculpture, 39, 42, and see *Lamb*.

AKETON cross-head, 86, 294.

Alabastron on Gosforth Cross, 162.

Alchfrith, King, 40, 46.

Allen, Mr. J. Romilly, F.S.A., 70, 183, 186, 193, 214, 230, 298.

Anderson, Dr. Joseph, 25, 98, 296, 302.

Andrews, Mr. W., 54.

Angles, 3, 14, 47, 217, 218, 300-308.

Anglian Crosses, 4, 39, 42 (*plate*), 114, 197, 202, 206, 252, 273, 278, 281.

Anglian cross-heads, 95, 223, 250, 298.

Anglian inscriptions, 27, 28, 44-47, 68, 95 (*plate*), 122, 206.

Anglian metal-work, 14, 226.

Anglian time division, 92, 226.

Anglo-classic art, 43, 196, 203, 207, 300.

Anglo-Cymric art, 26, 115, 296-298.

Anglo-Danish art, 196, 221, 291.

Anglo-Irish art, 44, 259, 301.

Anglo-Saxon chronicle, 267.

Animals in sculpture, see *Birds, Cetus, Dragon, Fish, Hart, Horse, Lamb, Lion, Mermaid, Monsters, Serpent, Wolf*.

ANTHORN Cross, 7.*

APPLEBY, see *Bongate*.

Archer in sculpture, 189.

Archy Armstrong's grave, 8.

Armstrong, Mr. John, of Melmerby, 236.

ARTHURET, 8, 13.

Arthur, King, 244, 247, 306.

Art of the Crosses, etc., 287-303, and see *Anglian, Anglo-classic*, etc. *Byzantine, Celtic, Cumbrian, Irish Influence, Manx, Norman, Norse, Spiral Crosses ;* also, *Animals in Sculpture, Basket Work, Cable Moulding, Chequers, Drill, Figures, Fret, Hammerhead, Interlacing, Key Patterns, Manuscript, Metal Work, Portraiture, Quarries, Rustication, Scroll Work, Svastika, Thor's Hammer, Trees in Sculpture, Triple Pellets, Triquetra, Triskele, Vesica Piscis*.

Askulf Thorkelsson and his Berserk, 30.

ASPATRIA, 11-25. 81, 176, 294-297.

Aspatrick, 12, 20.

Athelstan, King, 114, 115, 192, 240.

Bailey, Mr. George (on Elstow), 63.

Baldr, 149, 155-162, 164.

BARBON Cross, 97, 302.

Baring-Gould, Rev. S., 129, 266.

BARNSPIKE, Baronspike Runes, 48-53.

Basket Work and interlaced ornament, 17, 257, 279.

BEACON HILL hoard, 14.

BECKERMET Remains, 13, 25-38, 294, 297.

Bede quoted, 27, 46, 111, 177, 240.

Bega, St., 13, 301, 302.

Bellasis, Mr. E., 240.

Bell, "papped," 129.

Benedict Biscop, 202.

Beowulf, 74.

BEWCASTLE Cross, etc., 23, 24, 39-55, 300

Birch, Dr. (Ancient Pottery), 15.

Bird and Bantling, 130.

Birds in sculpture, 128, 178, 189, 202, 283.

Blair, Mr. Robert, F.S.A., 25.

* Greenwood's Map of Cumberland (1823) marks two crosses at Anthorn as "Taylor's Crosses."

BLENNERHASSET Cross, 271.
Bolster stone, 111.
BOLTON remains, 57, 58.
BONGATE hogback, 59, 295.
Borran, boireann, barn, burn, 48.
Boundary Crosses, 112.
Bower, Canon, 100, 109.
Brandreth, 269.
BRAYSTONES Jubilee Tower, 38.
BRAYTON fibula, 14, 296.
BRIDEKIRK remains, 43, 60-71, 289, 298.
Bridget, St., 13.
BRIGHAM remains, 72-79, 141, 294, 298.
British, see *Cumbrian*.
Britton and Brayley, 244.
BROMFIELD remains, 12, 25, 80-87, 223, 298.
Browne, Rev. G. F. (Bishop of Bristol), 17, 33, 44, 46, 139, 183, 186, 250.
Buddha's Symbol, 20.
BURTON remains, 88-91, 290, 291.
Byzantine influence, 38, 43, 44, 61, 115, 300.

Cable moulding, 33, 72, 106 (plate), 155, 156 (plate), 196, 229.
Cædmon, 41, 165, 218, 247.
Cædmon MS., 74, 194, 254.
CALDBECK remains, 92.
Calvary Steps, 4, 81, 117, 141, 185, 224, 263.
Camden's Britannia, 42, 44, 240, 265, 269.
Carbo, in *Gentleman's Mag.*, 169, 170.
CARLISLE Cathedral, cross-head, 95, 301.
CARLISLE Cathedral runes, 93.
CARLISLE Cathedral window, 75.
CARLISLE Fratry, cross-head, 96, 301.
Carnarvon, Caer-n ar-mhon, 30.
Carr-Ellison, R., 29.
Casts of Crosses, 42, 127, 136, 165, 206
CASTERTON Cross, 97, 302.
Castle Ewain, Hewen or Lewen, 240, 244.
CASTLE SOWERBY Crosses, 98.
Celtic Art, 12, 17, 44, 175, 296, 301, and see *Cumbrian, Irish*.

Cenn and Cromm Cruaich, 3.
Cetus, 70, 131.
Chad, tomb of St., 177.
Chalmers, Mr. (of Burton), 88.
Charlton, Dr. (of Newcastle), 49, 93.
Chequers, in sculpture, 43, 44, 85, 131, 214, 229, 271, 290.
Chester-le-Street Cross, 278.
Christ in sculpture; baptism, 69; crucifixion, 161, 176; resurrection, 89, 176; blessing, 39, 41; overcoming the serpent, 76, 121, 249; glorified, 63 (186?).
Christian Symbols, see *Cross, Griffin, Hart, Holy Breads, Lamb, Mermaid, Paradise Tree, Saints, Serpent, Svastika, Symbols, Triple Pellets, Triquetra, Triskele, Vesica*.
Circles, Megalithic, near crosses, 3.
CLIBURN remains, 99.
COLLINGHAM Cross, 274.
Constantine, King of Scots, 115, 240.
Cooper, Canon and Mr. Edward, 203.
Coped Tombs, see *Hogbacks*.
Copies of Crosses, 11, 24, 47, 136, 165.
Corpse Crosses, 98.
Cory, Mr. J. A., 229, 270.
Cospatrick, Earl, 65, 89.
CROGLIN, remains, 99.
Crookdake Chapel, 87.
Crosfield (Crosthwaite), 111.
CROSSCANONBY remains, 60, 100-110, 290, 294, 295, 298.
Cross, forms of: Anglian, 42, 95, 206 (plate), 223, 298.
——boss and ring, 34 (plate), 60, 80, 95, 109, 128, 133, 223, 297.
——florée, 99, and see *Grave Slabs*.
——free armed, 76, 85, 97, 170, 224, 250, 284.
——Greek, 4, 226, 229.
——Hammerhead, 4, 78, 80 (plate), 128, 298.
——Latin, 89, 109, 111, 186, and see *Grave Slabs*.
——Maltese, 8, 19, 85, 110
——Ring, 180, and see *wheel* (below).
——St. Andrew's, 119, 207, 256.

Cross, Wheel, with arms inside the ring, 86, 124, 238, 257, 263; with arms overlapping the ring, 4, 8, 78, 85, 88, 112, 136, 139 (plate), 170, 221, 248, 256.

Crosses, their purpose ; as grave monuments, 246, 266 and *passim*.

——as grave slabs, 38, 81, 82, 99, 109, 117, 169, 180, 205, 214, 263, 283, 288.

——as market crosses, 91, 205, 271, 287.

——as mere stones, boundary marks, 112, 265, 288.

——as preaching crosses, 13, 111.

——as resting or corpse crosses, 98, 256, 263, 284.

——as terminal ornaments, finials, 112, 236, 284.

Crosses set up in pairs, 26, 43, 91, 98, 171, 250.

——with hogbacks, see *Gosforth, Penrith*.

Crosses (or other monuments) used or misused—for building material, 20, 59, 80, 83, 86, 103, 107, 120, 127, 134, 136, 137, 172, 177, 189, 204, 211, 253, 273, 277, 280.

——for ordnance mark, 97, 135, 264.

——for ornament to porch, 76; to house, 284.

——for pillory, 251.

——for plague stone, 252.

——for public notices, 80.

——for sharpening tools, 19, 38, 83, 175, 214, 274.

——for sundials, 169, 170, 183, 202, 235.

——for target, 256.

——for tethering post, 11.

——for threshold, 273.

Crosses lost, 47, 98, 181, 227, 236-239. See also, *Casts, Copies*.

Cross Lacon, 256.

CROSTHWAITE (Keswick), 3, 13, 111, 302.

Crucifix, 155, 162.

Cumbrians, Cymru, Britons, Welsh, 3, 13, 298, 303-307.

Cumbrians, their Christianity, 12-14, 129, 295, 302-304.

CUMWHITTON Cross, 112.

Cuthbert, St., 111, 255, 278.

——pectoral cross, 223.

Cutts' Sepulchral Slabs, 81.

DACRE Cross, 113-115, 240, 297.

Dante (on the Griffin) 70.

David, in sculpture, 189, 214.

DEARHAM remains, 18, 72, 73, 86, 101, 117-132, 141, 289, 297.

Denton, John, (*Hist. Cumb.*), 49, 52.

Devil Bound, at Kirkby Stephen, 145, 218.

Dials of Anglo-Saxon Type, 40, 54, 57, 92, 98, 99, 132, 178, 208, 225, 237, 239, 263, 270, 288.

——cube, 205, 227.

——shafts and bases, 169, 170, 183, 202, 205, 235, 239, 263.

Didron's Iconographie, 61, 70.

DISTINGTON remains, 133, 297, 298.

Dixon, Mr. John (gave casts of Beckermet inscription), 29.

Dolfin Runes, 48, 93.

Domesday book, 27, 199.

DOVENBY Cross, 135.

Dragons, see *Cetus, Fafnir, Fenrir, Griffin, Interlacing, Midgard's Worm, Nidhögg*.

Drill, used in sculpture, 38, 69, 92, 167.

Du Chaillu's Viking Age, 191.

Dugdale's drawing of Giant's Grave, 240, 249.

Dunstan, St., 193.

Dykes, Mrs. (on the Crookdake Chapel) 86; (re-erected Dovenby Cross) 135.

Easter Controversy (Synod o Whitby, 664), 46.

Ecgfrith, King, 40, 46, 47, 95.

Edda subjects in sculpture, 74, 102, 107, 125, 142-165, 168, 191, 254, 291, 294.

Edith (supposed at Beckermet), 29.

Edmund, King, 265, 267.

Edward the Confessor reads Norse, 195.

Eliseg, pillar of, 26, 33, 250.
Elstow tympanum, 63-65.
Eric Bloodaxe, 267, 268.
Eweine, Hugh, or Owen Cæsarius, 240-245.

Fafnir, dragon, 190.
Fenrir and Fenris-wolf, 11, 73, 107, 108, 142, 147.
Ferguson, Chancellor, 17, 27, 42, 122-124, 265.
Ferguson, Mr. C. J., F.S.A., 174, 208.
Fibulæ, 296, 298.
Figures in sculpture :—
    Abbot (?), 214.
    Adam and Eve, 69, 113.
    Adam, Christ, and Mary (?), 121.
    Alchfrith (?), 40.
    Archer, 189.
    Athelstan and Constantine, or Owain (?), 115.
    Christ, see *Christ in Sculpture*.
    Dancers, 271.
    David (?), 189, 214.
    Devil, 218.
    Horseman with Sword, 130.
    Kings and their Arms, 264.
    Knights tilting, 58.
    Lady unknown, 190, 194.
    Man with Sword, 18.
    Mitred Head, 121.
    Norse gods, see *Baldr, Heimdal, Hymir, Loki, Odin,Regin,Sigun, Sigurd, Surt, Thor, Vidar*.
    Pope, 194.
    Saints, see *George, John, John Baptist, Kenneth, Lawrence, Longias, Mary, Magdalen, Michael*.
    Souls in Limbo (?), 231, 249, 271.
    Unknown, 90, 110.
Fish, in sculpture, 168, 178, 263.
Fishing stone at Gosforth, 168-171
Fletcher, Mr. Isaac, M.P., F.R.S., 79.
Fletcher, Mr. W. L., 39, 107, 172, 275, 277.
Fonts, 68-71, 113, 131, 270, 283.
Freeman's Norman Conquest, 66, 192-194.

Frett, 282, and see *Interlacing*.
Fylfot, 23, and see *Svastika*.

GALLOWAY Crosses, 25, 298.
Gammadion, 23, and see *Svastika*.
Gaut Bjarnarson, Manx sculptor, 291, 297.
Gem, Rev. C. H. 170.
George, St., in sculpture, 191, 259.
GILCRUX cross-head, 136, 295; font, 113.
Gildas, 304.
Gillebueth legend, 49-52.
GLASSONBY, 3, 137, 295.
Glastonbury wattled walls, 17.
Godred Crovan, 194, 291.
Gollancz, Mr. (on Havelock), 266.
Goodchild, Mr. J. G., 57.
GOSFORTH remains, 24, 26, 38, 43, 139-177, 291, 294.
Gough, Mr. (on Penrith), 243, 244.
Grave Slabs, see under *Crosses*.
GREAT SALKELD remains, 178, 289.
Greenwell, Rev. W., 300.
Griffin, 69, 70, 130.
Grimm's Teutonic Mythology, 73-75, 283.
Guest, Dr. (on Reycross), 265.

Hackworth, Rev. T., 283.
Hagen, legend of, 130.
Haigh, Rev. (Father) D. H., 27, 54, 68, 206, 208, 225.
HAILE remains, 180-182, 294, 297.
HALTON remains, 43, 183-197, 291, 295, 300.
Hammer-head Crosses, 4, 78, 80 (plate) 95, 128, 223 (plate), 298.
Harald Godwinson, 192-196.
Harald Hardrada, 192, 194.
Hart or Stag (symbol in sculpture), 16, 113, 115, 142, 150-153, 168, 248.
Havelock, Saga, see Olaf Cuaran.
Hastings, Rev. S., 183, 189.
HAZELGILL, or Hessilgill Runes, 49-53.
Hazel wands in graves, 118, 119, 122, 123.
Heimdal, 148, 157, 165.
Heimskringla, 195, 267.

Hel, Helia, 11, 73-75, 100-104, 142, 150, 173, 233, 254.
Herbst, Archivary C.F., 29.
Herebert St., 111.
HEVERSHAM Cross, 198-203, 300.
Hexham School, 203, 300.
HEYSHAM remains, 104, 177.
Hinde, Mr. Hodgson, *On the Early History of Cumberland*, 49.
Hoddam, Hodelm, 13.
Hodgetts, Prof. J. F., 160.
Hodgson, Rev. J. F., 217, 218, 223.
Hödr, 155-161, 164, 190.
Hogbacks, coped or shrine tombs, 12, 15-17, 59, 60, 83, 100-104, 167, 172-177, 221, 231-235, 253, 255, 294, 295.
Holy Breads, 23.
Horn, Child or King, 266.
Horse of Odin, 125, 149, 163, 275; of Sigurd, 190, 196, 275; unknown, 274.
Howard, Mr. Henry, 44, 68.
Hutchinson's Cumberland, 80; *Excursion*, 244.
HUTTON-IN-THE-FOREST remains, 204, 294.
Hut-urns, 15.
Hymir the giant, 168.
Hymiskvida, 294.

Inflected rod, symbol, 3, 122.
INGLETON Font, 271, 290.
Inscriptions :—
——Barnspike and Hazelgill, 48-53.
——Beckermet, 27-31.
——Bewcastle, 39-47.
——Bolton, 58.
——Bridekirk, 68.
——Carlisle, 93, 96.
——Dearham, 122, 123.
——Irton, 206.
——Lanercost, 316.
——Workington, 284.
Interlacing (A), Anglian, geometrical, 4, 40, 167, 206, 207, 273; not Irish in origin, 44, 207; seen in heathen fibulæ, 300; and classical vine scrolls, 40, 43, 202, 203.

Interlacing, frett, 107, 282.
——regular plaits and knots, 33, 37, 38 (plate), 59 (plate), 84, 86, 113, 127, 186, 260, 281.
(B) Cumbrian (derivative and bastard), 19, 34 (plate), 130, 221, 260, 280; originates in copying metal work, 295-297.
——debased and irregular, 77, 178, 196, 221, 290.
(C) Irish Viking Types; dragonesque and zoomorphic, 37, 73, 76, 86, 147, 150, 153, 158-163, 168, 169, 173, 175, 259, 260, 274, 294.
——ear-shaped guilloche, 78 (fig. *e*), 181, 279, 294.
——freehand, 14, 35-38, 72.
——ring-plaits, 11, 35, 78, 108, 173, 248-250, 277-279, 294.
——Yggdrasil or chain-pattern; the close variety, 103, 124, 142, 238, 295; the loose variety, 84 (plate), 89, 257, 260.
(D) Twelfth Century, 69, 123, 131, 271.
IREBY Crosses, 205.
Irish influences in Cumbria, 3, 13, 14, 30, 46, 48, 156, 163, 167, 259, 301.
IRTHINGTON remains, 13, 302.
IRTON Cross, 24, 206, 207, 301.
ISEL remains, 20, 92, 208-213, 297.
Italian influence, 43, 44, 300.
Iuan, John, 30.

Jackson, Mr., of Tebay, 269.
James, St., Emblems, 229.
Jefferson's Leath Ward, 226.
Jewitt, Llewellyn, 16.
Jocelin of Furness, 111.
John Baptist, St., in sculpture, 39, 42, 69.
John, St., in sculpture, 89, 186.
John, various early forms of the name, 30.
Jörmungandr, 74.
Judith, Countess, 65-67.

Keene, Rev. Rees, 169, 172.
Kells, Book of, 140, 163, 176, 281.
Kemble on the Anglo-Saxon mark, 201.

Kemp's grave, 246.
Kenneth, St., 12, 13, 83, 111, 119, 247, 302.
Kermode, Mr. P. M. C., 34, 291, 297.
KESWICK, 111.
Key-patterns, 128, 137, 207, 231, 260, 280, 281, 287, 301.
Kil, Cil, Gil, 98, 136, 301.
KIRKBAMPTON remains, 214, 289.
KIKRBY STEPHEN remains, 145, 217-223, 291, 295.
KIRKLAND Cross, 224.
KIRKOSWALD remains, 225, 226; fibula, 226, 298.
Knowles, Canon, 26, 34, 35, 109, 128, 132, 141, 181, 238, 259-263, 273.
Künnburug and Küneswitha, (SS. Cyneburga and Cyneswitha) 41, 46, 47, 177.

Lake District has no pre-Norman monuments, 302.
Lamb, in sculpture, 39, 42, 113, 178, 247.
LAMPLUGH lost cross, 227.
LANERCOST, 8, 10, 17, 49-52, 227.*
Lappenberg's History of England under the Anglo-Saxons, 46.
Lawrence, St., 109, 290.
LAZONBY Cross, 227.
LEEDS Cross, 43.
Lees, Rev. T., F.S.A., 80, 109, 128, 129, 161, 229, 231, 249, 264-266.
Leland's Itinerary, 240.
Lions in Sculpture, 214, 263.
LLANTWIT pillars, 26, 297.
Loki, 73-75, 108, 139, 141-148, 155-158, 218, 246, 247, 254, and see Fenrir.
Longias, or Longinus, 161.
LONG MARTON tympana, 229, 289.
Long Meg, 3, 298.
Longstaffe's Richmondshire, 264.
LOWTHER remains, 177, 231-235, 295.

Lubbock, Sir John (on Hut-urns), 14.
Lyell, Mr. A. H., F.S.A., 95.
Lysons' Cumberland, 8, 27, 29, 66, 68, 69, 206, 226, 238, 243.
Lyttleton, Bishop, 242, 243.
Maccus, Maco, Amancus, Magnus, 267,

Magdalen, St. Mary, 161, 162.
Magnússon, Mr. E., 125, 167, 291.
Mag Selce, 3.
Malcolm, King of Scots, 66, 193, 265.
Managarm, 107, 108.
Manuscript illuminations and sculptured ornament, 11, 40, 74, 96, 140, 150, 163, 175, 194, 207, 254, 281, 301.
Manx Crosses, 294.
——Andreas, Jurby, Malew, 192, 291.
——Kirkmichael and Ballaugh, 238.
——Maughold, 30, 34, 115, 178, 297.
Margaret, St., Emblems, 229.
Marius, mythic King, 265.
Market Crosses, see under Crosses.
Mary, the Virgin, in sculpture, 89, 121, 186.
Mason's marks like dials, 55, 226.
Matthews, Canon, 114.
Maughan, Rev. John, 29, 44, 45, 48-53, 55, 93.
Mediæval and late crosses, 8, 85, 91, 98, 99, 112, 135, 170, 180, 205, 221, 224, 226, 227, 235-239, 256, 263, 276, 284, 287-288.
——grave-slabs, 38, 81, 82, 99, 109, 117, 169, 180, 205, 214, 263, 283, 288.
MELMERBY remains, 236.
Mermaid or Siren, 229, 230.
Metal work influencing sculpture, 14, 89, 295-300.
Michael, St., in sculpture, 259.
Midgard's worm, 75, 142, 168.
MILBURN remains, 237.
Mithraic Symbols, 20.

---

* The fragment of shaft now in the Church, with inscription dating it 1214 (Lysons' Cumberland, p. ccii.), is thought to have been the original for the base on the green. The notches on the standing shaft are perhaps in rude imitation of the moulding which ornaments the edges of the original.

Monsters in sculpture, 229, 257, 271, and see *Dragon*.
Moore, Mr. A. W., 30, 31.
MUNCASTER Cross, 238.
Muncaster, Lord, 273.
Mungo, St., 12, 13, 85, 92, and see Kentigern.

Naworth Castle, oratory, 161.
NEWBIGGIN remains, 239.
NEWTON ARLOSH dial, 239.
Nicolson and Burn's Cumberland, 205.
Nicolson, Bishop, 44, 241, 245.
Nidhögg, 142, 152.
Ninian, St., 13, 239, 301-303.
Norman architecture, 57, 85, 95, 99, 101, 103, 118, 132, 237, 283.
—— art, 58, 68-71, 79, 91, 123, 131, 179, 214, 226, 271, 276, 289, 290; compared with pre-Norman art, 43, 44, 71, 169, 197, 221, 259.
—— Conquest of Cumbria, 66, 93, 265, 287, 288.
—— inscription, 58.
Norse art, 107, 124, 141-177, 212, 238, 260, 291-295.
—— mythology, see *Edda*.
—— settlement of Cumbria, 290.

Odin, 18, 104, 125, 148-167, 291, 294.
—— his horse, 125, 149, 163.
—— his symbol, 212, 213.
Œgisdrekka (Ægisdrekka), 143, 153, 158.
Olaf Cuaran, 266, 268.
Olaf Tryggvason's Saga, 192, 195, 217.
ORMSIDE Cup, 297, 300.
Oswiu King, 40, 46, 274.
Owain ab Urien of Reged, 244, 306.
Owain Cæsarius, 240-245.
Owain, King of Cumbria, 115, 240, 244.

Pægnaleth, 27.
PAPCASTLE, 66, 68.
Paradise tree, 41, 70, 281.
Parker, Dr., F.S.A. Scot, 139, 140, 167, 170.

Patrick, St., 3, 12, 20, 23, 302, 303.
Peel towers in churches, 117, 178, 239.
Penda, King, 46.
Pennant's Tour in Scotland, 241, 296.
PENRITH remains, 43, 240-252, 291, 294.
Peterborough, Anglo-Saxon art at, 46, 177.
Petersen, Prof. Magnus, 107, 127, 142, 162, 212.
Petriana, 52.
Pipe Rolls, 3.
Pigott, Rev. J. C., 136.
Place-names, 3, 4, 12, 20, 27, 30, 48, 52, 59, 66, 89, 98, 100, 134, 136, 199, 200, 217, 226, 245, 255, 258, 260, 301.
Plague stone, 252.
Platnauer, Mr. H. M., 15.
PLUMBLAND remains, 177, 233, 234, 253-255, 294, 295, 297.
Portraiture in sculpture, 40, 115, 173, 194.
Prescott, Archdeacon, 17.
Purday, Mr. C. H., 93, 95.

Quarries, and sources of the stones, 23-25, 43, 50, 206, 250, 252, 271, 275.
Queen Arlec (supposed at Beckermet), 29, 52.

Ragnarök, 143, 148, 152, 157, 165.
Rainbow in Edda myths, 104, 124, 148.
Rawnsley, Canon, 111; two sonnets, 166.
Reged, 304-306.
Reginald of Durham, 69, 255.
Regin the Smith, 190, 191.
Resting Crosses, 256, 263, 234.
Reycross. 78, 264-268, 295.
RHEDA, 256.
Rhydderch Hael, 13, 66, 304.
Rhys, Prof., 130.
Richard of Durham, 68-70.
Robert de Vaux, 49-52, 204.
ROCKCLIFF cross, 84, 257, 258, 294, 295.
Roger of Hoveden, 268.
Roger of Wendover, 267.
Rogers, Mr. John, 31.

Roman altars, 20, 110, 128, 180.
—— camps, 43, 48.
—— influence in Cumbria, 23, 303.
—— roads, 14, 110, 139, 198, 224.
—— stones used, 119, 214. 265, 270.
—— tiles, 253; tiled tombs, 15.
Rowler cross, 34, 115, 178, 297.
Roy, General, 265.
Runes, 39-53, 93, 122, 123, 206.
Ruskin, Mr. (on the Griffin) 70; (on the Angles), 300.
Rustication, 91.
RUTHWELL cross, 23, 24, 41-43, 165, 189.

Saga, Eyrbyggja, 195.
—— Gautrek's, 213.
—— Olaf Tryggvason's, 192, 195, 217.
—— Viking-age stories surviving in England and France, 266.
—— Völsunga, 191; and see *Heimskringla*.
ST. BEES remains, 13, 20, 34, 256, 259-263, 290, 294-297, 301.
Saints in sculpture, see *George, James, John, John Baptist, Kenneth, Lawrence, Longias, Magdalen, Margaret, Mary, Michael*.
Sandford's Cumberland, 241.
Säve, Prof. C., 191, 195.
Scandinavian influence in Cumbria, 3, 14, 30, 59, 68, 73, 89, 93, 104, 141-177, 191, 195, 217, 218, 238, 291-295.
Scroll-work, Anglian, 4, 40-43, 197, 202, 203, 207, 249, 252, 271, 273.
—— debased, 18, 27, 221; and see *Spiral*.
Senhouse, Mr., of Netherhall, 63.
Serpent in conflict with God-man, 121, 158, 162, 165, 176, 248.
—— in sculpture, 178; on hogbacks, 233, 237, 248, 254.
Sharpe, Rev, W. H., 208, 213.
Sigun, 143, 145, 247.
Sigurd in sculpture, 190-197.
Skene, Mr. W. F., 66, 265, 267.
Simpson, Canon, 49, 217.
Smith in sculpture, 186.

Snorri Sturluson, 194; and see *Heimskringla*.
Socket-stones, 4, 8, 10, 11, 35, 42, 72, 135, 141, 142, 169, 185, 206, 237, 238, 294.
Speed's Chronicle, 264, 265.
Spiral crosses, 4, 18-20, 23, 27, 34, 60, 95, 115, 128, 133, 182, 213, 255, 260, 263, 280, 295-298.
Spirals, pre-historic, 3, 298,
Stænanby, 100.
Stag, see *Hart*.
STAINMOOR, 264-268.
Standing stones, 3.
Steele, Rev. J., 37.
Stephens, Prof. G. (of Copenhagen), 29, 39, 40, 43, 44, 49, 55, 68, 69, 93, 108, 115, 122, 123, 139, 140, 145, 160, 206, 218, 245, 274, 278.
Stone-worship, 3.
Strathclyde, 12, 13, 23, 303.
Stoups, 80, 81, 132, 259.
Stukely, Dr., 241.
Sun and Moon, 20.
Sundials, see *Dials*.
Sun-snake, 211, 231.
Surt (Surtur) 164.
Svastika, 4, 18, 20, 23, 25, 69, 128, 134, 174, 211, 212.
Swan myths, 283.
Swedish art, 191.
Symbols, Christian, 3, 17, 40, 41, 70, 89, 113, 121, 134, 176, 185, 203, 248, 254, 274, 281.
—— Pagan, 3, 103, 108, 212, 213.
—— used by Christians though of Pagan origin, 11, 18, 20, 75, 86, 102, 104, 124, 131, 141-165, 213, 231, 254, 275, 283.
Symeon of Durham, 66, 244, 267.

Taylor, Rev. R., 12, 81, 84, 86, 87.
TEBAY, Brandreth, 269, 302.
Thor, 20, 143, 157, 164, 165, 168.
—— his hammer, 141, 143; thunderbolt, 212.
Thornley, Canon, 4, 137.
Thumb, Giant's, 251, 300.
Thunderbolt pattern, 38, 110, 212.

Todd, Dr. Hugh, 242.
Tolfinæ, Dolfin, 93.
TORPENHOW, remains, 270, 271, 289.
Tosti, Earl, 192-196, 199.
Townley mysteries, 161.
Tree in sculpture, 194 ; see Paradise, Yggdrasil.
Treverman, Triermain, wooden church, 17, 289.
Triple pellets or dots, 25, 115, 121.
Triquetra, 16, 40, 86, 108, 134, 140, 147, 158, 163, 176, 177, 238, 254, 274.
Triskele, 113, 133, 134, 211, 255, 297.
Troughs, stone, 38 ; and see Stoups.
Tuda, bishop, 27.
Tympana, 61-67, 85, 214, 229, 259.

Uchtred, Earl, 66,
Urien of Reged, 304.

Vala (Völva), 149, 150, 158.
Valhöll, Walhalla, 74, 142.
Venables, Precentor, 12.
Vesica piscis, 65.
Vidar, 158-160, 165.
Vigfusson, Dr. G., 291.
Vikings, see Scandinavian.
Völuspá, 107, 143-164, 254.

WABERTHWAITE crosses, 273-275, 295, 300.
Wægnaleth, Wagele, 27.

Wagner's Epics and Romances, 130.
Walker, Rev. E , 45, 47.
Walker's History of Penrith, 245.
Waltheof, Earl, 65, 66.
WARCOP cross, 276.
Watmore, Rev. A., 212.
Wattle, wicker, basketwork, 17, 257, 279.
Watson, Mr. G., 241, 243, 250-252.
Well of Mimir, 149.
Wells of Saints, 85, 92.
Westwood, Prof., 95, 96.
Whellan's History of Cumberland, 4, 8, 47, 97-99, 135, 205, 214, 224, 227, 236, 245, 256, 269, 276, 284.
Wigram, Rev. S. R., 64.
Wilfrith, St., 41, 44, 46, 203, 300.
Wilson, Mr. T., 88.
Wilson, Mr. W., 112.
Wolf on Monuments, 11, 107; with hart, 115, 150.
WORKINGTON remains, 277-284, 294, 295.
Wulfhere, King 46.

Yggdrasil, 74, 103, 104, 124, 125, 141, 213, 238, 260.
York Museum, 15,

Zoomorphic, see *Interlacing*.

www.ingramcontent.com/pod-product-compliance
Lightning Source LLC
Chambersburg PA
CBHW021842290326
41932CB00064B/351